Method, Theory and Policy in Keynes

Method, Theory and Policy in Keynes

Essays in Honour of Paul Davidson: Volume Three

Edited by

Philip Arestis

Professor of Economics and Head of Department of Economics, University of East London, UK

Edward Elgar
Cheltenham, UK • Northampton, MA, USA

© Philip Arestis 1998

Published by
Edward Elgar Publishing Limited
8 Lansdown Place
Cheltenham
Glos GL50 2HU
UK

Edward Elgar Publishing, Inc.
6 Market Street
Northampton
Massachusetts 01060
USA

A catalogue record for this book
is available from the British Library

Library of Congress Cataloguing in Publication Data
Method, theory, and policy in Keynes : essays in honour of Paul
    Davidson / edited by Philip Arestis.
    (Essays in honour of Paul Davidson : v. 3)
    Includes bibliographic references and index.
    1. Keynesian economics.   2. Economics—Methodology.   3. Economic
    policy.   4. Davidson, Paul.   I. Davidson, Paul.   II. Arestis,
    Philip, 1941–   .   III. Series.
    HB99.7.M47   1998
    330.15—dc21   97–25912
                                                                   CIP

ISBN 1 85898 626 5

Typeset by Manton Typesetters, 5–7 Eastfield Road, Louth, Lincolnshire LN11 7AJ, UK.
Printed and bound in Great Britain by Bookcraft (Bath) Ltd, Midsomer Norton, Somerset

Contents

Notes on the contributors

Philip Arestis is Professor of Economics and Head of Department of Economics, University of East London. He has also taught at the Universities of Surrey and Cambridge (Department of Extra-Mural Studies) and Greenwich University (where he was Head of Economics Division). He was editor of the *British Review of Economic Issues* and joint editor of the *Thames Papers in Political Economy*, and is joint editor of the recently launched *International Papers in Political Economy*. He has been on the editorial board of a number of journals and an elected member of the Council of the Royal Economic Society. His publications include: his co-authored *Introducing Macroeconomic Modelling: An Econometric Study of the United Kingdom* (Macmillan, 1982); his edited *Post-Keynesian Monetary Economics: New Approaches to Financial Modelling* (Edward Elgar, 1988); his co-edited *Post-Keynesian Economic Theory: A Challenge to Neo-Classical Economics* (Wheatsheaf, 1984), *The Biographical Dictionary of Dissenting Economists* (Edward Elgar, 1992), *The Elgar Companion to Radical Political Economy* (Edward Elgar, 1994), *Keynes, Money and the Open Economy: Essays in Honour of Paul Davidson, Volume One* (Edward Elgar, 1996), *Employment, Economic Growth and the Tyranny of the Market: Essays in Honour of Paul Davidson, Volume Two* (Edward Elgar, 1996), *Capital Controversy, Post-Keynesian Economics and the History of Economics: Essays in Honour of Geoff Harcourt, Volume One* (Edward Elgar, 1997), *Markets, Unemployment and Economic Policy* (Edward Elgar, 1997); also his two books *The Post-Keynesian Approach to Economics: An Alternative Analysis of Economic Theory and Policy* (Edward Elgar, 1992), and *Money, Pricing, Distribution and Economic Integration* (Macmillan, 1997). He has published widely in journals and books in post Keynesian economics, macroeconomics, monetary economics and applied econometrics.

Robert W. Clower is Professor of Economic Theory, University of South Carolina. He also taught at Northwestern University (where he chaired the Department of Economics for six years), University of Essex in the UK (where he was a Dean of the School of Social Studies), UCLA, Washington State University and at a number of other universities in the USA and Europe (where his most recent appointment is at The University of Sienna as a

Fulbright Professor). He was a member of the Executive Committee of the *American Economic Association* and Managing Editor of the *American Economic Review*, President of the *Western Economic Association* and Managing Editor of *Economic Inquiry*, and Vice-President and President of the *Southern Economic Association*. He has also been an active member of a number of other learned societies and professional associations. He has been on the editorial board of a number of journals in addition to the editorship responsibilities. His numerous publications include his co-authored *Introduction to Mathematical Economics* (Richard D. Irwin, 1957), *Intermediate Economic Analysis* (Richard D. Irwin, 5th edn, 1996) and *Intermediate Microeconomics* (Harcourt, Brace and Jovanovich, 1988), his edited *Monetary Theory* (Penguin Books, 1969; Italian translation, 1972), and his recent two important selections, *Money and Markets: Selected Essays of R.W. Clower* (Cambridge University Press, 1984) and *Economic Doctrine and Method: Selected Papers of R.W. Clower* (Edward Elgar, 1995). He has published widely in journals and books in monetary economics, macroeconomics and microeconomics, Keynesian economics and methodology.

John B. Davis is Associate Professor of Economics at Marquette University, Milwaukee, Wisconsin. He has been Editor of the *Review of Social Economy* since 1987, is an editorial board member of the *Journal of Economic Methodology* and *Research in the History of Economic Thought and Methodology*, and is editor or co-editor of book series in social economics with Routledge and Roman and Littlefield. He is author of *Keynes's Philosophical Development* (Cambridge, 1994) and co-author of *The Life and Thought of David Ricardo* (Kluwer, 1997). He has also edited or co-edited *The State of Interpretation of Keynes* (Kluwer, 1994), *The Economic Surplus in Advanced Economies* (Elgar, 1992), and *Keynes and Philosophy: Essays on the Origins of Keynes's Thought* (Elgar, 1991), and *The Handbook of Economic Methodology* (Elgar, forthcoming). Among the journals in which he has published are *Cambridge Journal of Economics, Journal of Post Keynesian Economics, Economics and Philosophy, Economic Journal, Journal of Economic Methodology, History of Political Economy*, and *European Journal of the History of Economic Thought*.

Panicos Demetriades is Professor of Financial Economics at South Bank University, London. He holds a PhD from Cambridge University and BA and MA degrees from the University of Essex. He was previously lecturer and Reader in Economics at Keele University (1990–95) and Research Officer at the Central Bank of Cyprus (1985-90). His general research interests are in the area of applied macroeconomics; his recent work focuses on the role of financial sector policies in the process of economic growth. He has published in leading academic journals such as *The Economic Journal, Oxford Bulletin of Economics and Statistics, Journal of Development Economics, Review of Economics and Statistics, World Development, Economics Letters*, and *Journal of Applied Econometrics*. He has been the general editor of *The Cyprus Journal of Economics* since its founding in 1988.

M.J. Gordon is Professor Emeritus of Finance, at the University of Toronto. He has published books and articles on accounting, finance, microeconomics, macroeconomics, and market socialism in China. The journals include *Accounting Review, Journal of Finance, American Economic Review, Journal of Post Keynesian Economics* and *Quarterly Journal of Economics*. Gordon's dividend growth model has become widely accepted as the best instrument for explaining how common shares are priced, and it has become generally used in rate-base rate-of-return regulation of public utilities. His recent *Finance Investment and Macroeconomics* presents a theory of investment that recognizes the problem of bankruptcy and what capitalists do to avoid it. The investment model is then used to arrive at a post Keynesian theory of the firm and both the short and long-run performance of capitalist systems. Gordon's contributions to knowledge have been recognized by honours that include President of the American Finance Association, Fellow of the Royal Society of Canada, and Doctor of Laws Degrees from the McMaster University.

Tony Lawson is Lecturer in Economics at the University of Cambridge. He is an editor of the *Cambridge Journal of Economics* and is on the Editorial Board of the *Journal of Economic Methodology*. He also edits the Routledge series *Economics as Social Theory*. He has published widely in books and journals and recently systematized his work in his book *Economics and Reality* (Routledge, 1997).

J.S.L. McCombie is Director of Studies in Economics and a Fellow of Downing College, Cambridge and is a member of the Department of Land Economy at the University of Cambridge. He was awarded his MA and PhD at the University of Cambridge and an MA at McMaster University. He began his lecturing career as a member of the Department of Economics and Commerce at the University of Hull and was later a member of the Department of Economics at the University of Melbourne. He has researched extensively on the reasons for economic growth disparities between the advanced countries, economic growth and the balance-of-payments constraint, Kaldorian growth models, the economics of Keynes, criticisms of the aggregate production function, and economic methodology. He has published in such journals as the *Journal of Post Keynesian Economics, The Economic Journal, Oxford Economic Papers, The Manchester School* and *Urban Studies*. He has recently published, with A.P. Thirlwall, *Economic Growth and the Balance-of-Payments Constraint* (Macmillan, 1994).

Basil Moore is Professor of Economics at Wesleyan University, Middletown. Conn., USA, and Stellenbosch University, Republic of South Africa. He studied for his BA degree at the University of Toronto, and for his PhD at The Johns Hopkins University. Since 1958 he has spent his professional career at Wesleyan, and from 1985 to 1988 served as Chairman of the Economics Department. Wesleyan has a liberal, sabbatical leave policy, and he has been Visiting Professor at Stanford University; Trinity College, Cambridge; University Sains Malaysia; Jawaharlal Nehru University; City of London Polytechnic (now London Guildhall University); University of British Columbia; Yale University; Simon Frazer University; University of Cape Town; National University of Singapore; and the University of Stellenbosch. He has also been a Visiting Scholar at the Bank of England in London, and the Korean Development Institute (KDI), in Seoul. He is on the Editorial Board of *The Journal of Post Keynesian Economics*. His publications include: *An Introduction to the Theory of Finance: Assetholder Behaviour Under Uncertainty* (1968); *An Introduction to Modern Economic Theory* (1972); and *Horizontalists and Verticalists: the Macroeconomics of Credit Money* (1988). He has published over one hundred articles, primarily in the areas of monetary economics and post Keynesian economics.

Wallace C. Peterson is the George Holmes Professor of Economics Emeritus, the University of Nebraska-Lincoln. His professional career has been at the University of Nebraska, where he served as Chairman of the Economics Department from 1965 through 1975. He had a Fulbright Research Fellowship in France in 1957–58, and a Fulbright Lecture Fellowship in Greece in 1964–65. He is a past President of the Midwest Economics Association, the Missouri Valley Economics Association, the Association for Evolutionary Economics, and the Association for Social Economics, the AAUP chapter, the University of Nebraska, and the Nebraska Conference of the AAUP. For a number of years he wrote a column on economics for newspapers in southeast Nebraska, for which he received the Champion Media Award for Economic Understanding in 1981. Also in 1981 he was awarded the University of Nebraska Award for Outstanding Research and Creative Activity, and in 1987 the Burlington Northern Faculty Achievement Award. He has been listed in *Who's Who in America* since 1977. During his academic career, he has written a number of books and articles. His books include: *Income, Employment, and Economic Growth* (8th edn, 1996); *Silent Depression: The Fate of the American Dream (1994); Transfer Spending, Taxes, and the American Welfare State* (1991); *Market Power and the Economy* (editor, 1989); *Our*

Overloading Economy: Inflation, Unemployment, and the Crisis in American Capitalism (1982); *Elements of Economics* (1973); and *The Welfare State in France* (1960).

Alessandro Roncaglia is Professor of Economics and Director of the Department of Economic Studies, University of Rome I. He has also taught at the University of Perugia and, as visiting professor, at Rutgers University, University of Nice, University of Paris XI. He is editor of *Moneta e Credito* and of *Banca Nazionale del Lavoro Quarterly Review*, and member of the editorial board of the *Journal of Post Keynesian Economics* and other journals. He is a member of the General Council and the Executive Committee and deputy chairman of ISCO (Istituto Studi sulla Congiuntura Economica), and has been a member of the Council of the Italian Economists Society. His publications include *Sraffa and the Theory of Prices* (John Wiley, 1978; Italian edition, 1975; Japanese and Spanish translations); *Petty: The Origins of Political Economy* (Sharpe 1985; Italian edition, 1983). He has published widely in journals and books (in Italian, English, French, German, Spanish, Catalan, Polish, Japanese, Russian) on the theory of value and distribution, on the history of economic thought and on energy economics. He contributes regularly to newspapers and weekly magazines.

Roy J. Rotheim is Professor of Economics at Skidmore College, Saratoga Springs, New York. He has published widely in the areas of uncertainty theory, post Keynesian models, and the history of economic thought. He is the editor of forthcoming *New Keynesian Economics and Post Keynesian Alternatives* (Routledge, 1997). He was formerly executive editor of *Challenge Magazine* and associate editor of the *Eastern Economic Journal*.

Kurt W. Rothschild is Professor Emeritus (Economics) at the University of Linz, Austria. He studied Law and Economics in Vienna and at the University in Glasgow where he was a member of the Economics Department before returning to Austria. After 19 years as a Senior Research Worker at the Austrian Institute of Economic Research in Vienna he became one of the founding professors of the new University in Linz in 1966 where he stayed until his retirement. He was visiting professor in several universities in Europe, the US and Australia and obtained honorary degrees from the Universities of Augsburg, Aachen, Bremen and Leicester. He is presently a member of the editorial board of several theoretical economic journals and acts as a consultant to the Austrian Institute of Economic Research. His publications include: *The Theory of Wages* (Blackwell 1957); *Economic Forecasting* (in German, Springer 1969); *Power in Economics* (editor, Penguin 1971); *An Introduction to Disequilibrium Theory* (in German, Springer 1981); *Theories* *of Unemployment* (in German, Oldenbourg 1988); and *Ethics and Economic Theory* (Edward Elgar, 1993). He has published widely in books and journals mainly on macroeconomics and questions of labour and income distribution. Collections of his articles are contained in *Employment, Wages and Income Distribution: Critical Essays in Economics* (Routledge 1993) and in *Economic Method, Theory and Policy: Selected Essays of Kurt W. Rothschild* (edited by J.E. King, Edward Elgar 1995).

S.P. Sethi is Professor of Operations Management and Director of the Laboratory for Manufacturing Research in the Faculty of Management, University of Toronto. He has published books and papers on operations management, economics and finance, marketing, operations research and optimal control. The books include: *Optimal Control Theory: Applications to Management Science* (with Gerald Thompson, 1981); *Hierarchical Decision Making in Stochastic Manufacturing Systems* (with Qing Zhang, 1994); *Optimal Consumption and Investment Problems with Bankruptcy* (1997). Other areas in which Professor Sethi has made fundamental contributions include decision and forecast horizons in dynamic optimization problems, scheduling in robotic cells, and flexibility in manufacturing. His contributions to knowledge have been recognised by honours that include Connaught Senior Research Fellow, Award of Merit of the Canadian Operational Research Society, Honorary Professor at Zhejiang University of Technology, and Fellow of the Royal Society of Canada.

Introduction

Philip Arestis

This is the third volume of essays published to celebrate Paul Davidson's work now spanning well over four decades, to pay tribute to his devotion to the discipline of economics and to record his pre-eminence as a proponent of post Keynesian economics in particular. Over this time, Paul Davidson has earned deep respect and enormous admiration from colleagues of varied persuasions, as the contributions to these volumes amply demonstrate. It is a measure of the demand to contribute to his *Festschrift*, that the editor has felt called upon to publish this third volume. Indeed, had it not been for his impatience, several further volumes might even now have been in prospect! The titles of the two volumes that have already appeared, *Employment, Economic Growth and the Tyranny of the Market* and *Keynes, Money and the Open Economy*, testify to the richness of the interest Paul Davidson's vast contribution has generated. This is just as true of the present volume.

Paul Davidson's contributions to our discipline are simply vast. They span such a wide range as natural resources, outdoor recreation, public finance, macroeconomic and monetary theory and policy (both domestic and international), income distribution, economic problems of developing economies, history of economic thought and methodology. With Sidney Weintraub he established the *Journal of Post Keynesian Economics (JPKE)* and has been its editor ever since its inception in 1978 (co-editor with Weintraub until Sidney's death in 1983). What is particularly interesting about the *JPKE* is that not only did it create a platform for 'dissenting economists' but also kept open the lines of communication with the mainstream. All of us who have had some association with the journal know very well and appreciate the enormous amount of time and energy the Davidsons – for we should never forget the heroic efforts of Louise too – have expended for our intellectual development and enjoyment. Paul Davidson has participated in practically every major conference involving post Keynesian economics, and many others, and has given lectures and seminars to students and colleagues throughout the world. And he has helped a great number of colleagues in their careers, especially the younger members of our profession at that crucial stage of their first published paper, and even before this stage, at the postgraduate level.

Paul Davidson was born on 23 October 1930 in New York and grew up in Brooklyn. His family put a great deal of emphasis on education and they wanted Paul to become a 'professional', a medical doctor preferably. However, Paul Davidson ultimately chose economics. He came to economics, however, after he had spent some time in the natural sciences. Upon graduating in chemistry and biology at Brooklyn College, he embarked upon postgraduate work in biochemistry at the University of Pennsylvania, and even undertook research for a dissertation on DNA. He also taught in the Medical and Dental Schools at the same time. He soon lost interest and changed gear radically by taking an MBA (his thesis was entitled 'The Statistical Analysis of Economic Time Series'), thereby preparing himself for the world of commerce. It must have been at that time when Paul, a trained biochemist used to experimental decision and statistical inference, realized he could do a better job as an economist. He thus returned to the University of Pennsylvania to do a PhD in Economics under the supervision of Sidney Weintraub. Weintraub's influence on Paul Davidson explains his early interests in Keynes's macroeconomics and in the distribution of income. His dissertation, therefore, focused on an historical exegesis of aggregate income distribution analysis, appropriately entitled 'Theories of Relative Shares', and in 1959 he was awarded the degree of PhD in Economics.

In June 1951 Paul met Louise, and in December 1952 they married. Ever since they have been inseparable – I cannot recall a time when I saw Paul without Louise, or Louise without Paul, at conferences or indeed anywhere else. After teaching economics at Pennsylvania and Rutgers for a short time, he joined the 'real' world as the Assistant Director of the Economics Division for the Continental Oil Company. A year in the corporate sector proved enough for Paul Davidson and he returned to the University of Pennsylvania. In 1966 he moved to Rutgers University, where he stayed for the next 20 years before joining the University of Tennessee in 1986 to take up the Holly Chair of Excellence in Political Economy.

In his critique of mainstream economics he identifies and rejects three axioms of orthodoxy, and uses them as a platform for his own contributions. These are the *axiom of substitutability* (which restores Say's Law and denies the possibility of involuntary unemployment); the *axiom of reals* (which affirms the neutrality of money which is a veil and does not matter; real decisions depend only on relative prices, and income effects are always outweighed by substitution effects); and the *axiom of ergodicity* (which views the future as probabilistic rather than fundamentally uncertain). Paul Davidson argues that it is vital that these axioms be abandoned in order to pave the way to a post Keynesian economics logically consistent with Keynes's analytical framework.

The object of his analysis is a monetary production economy, with money and money contracts being at the heart of the system. The money rate of interest is uniquely important in the system precisely because contracts are denominated in money terms; it is this property that can ultimately produce involuntary unemployment. It is, indeed, through the rate of interest that money exerts its impact on the demand for capital goods thereby controlling capital accumulation. A further crucial consequence of contracts being denominated in money terms is that a close integration of the real and monetary sectors is inevitable, which totally discredits the so-called 'classical dichotomy'. Another feature of Paul Davidson's analysis is that money is endogenously determined in a world of uncertainty, as opposed to risk, and in the modern credit-money banking system. Such a system, he claims, is precisely what Keynes had in mind, and indeed represents the real world. What Davidson terms the 'Keynes School of Political Economy' begins from the premise that monetary and real sectors are closely linked, where the money-wage rate is a fundamental magnitude but with income distribution being of lesser importance by comparison with post Keynesian analysis.

The Keynes school is at the centre of the political spectrum, and as such rejects both marginal productivity theories on the right and surplus approaches on the left. At the methodological level the economy is non-ergodic in real historical time, so that theories and policies based on logical time are disregarded. In this analysis the future is uncertain. It unfolds from decisions made in the present which, although embodying the results of past events, cannot provide probabilistic estimates of what the future might entail. This thesis, along with Sidney Weintraub's aggregate supply function (which involves productivity questions), and the finance motive (which implies a unique demand for money to finance business outlays before they materialize), are the main contributions which make Paul Davidson a Post Keynesian. The finance motive enabled him to show that the *IS/LM* framework did not yield a unique equilibrium, because the two relationships are interdependent. More importantly, though, it enabled him to integrate monetary analysis into Keynes's general theory in an original way. The ideas embedded in the developments described here led to his early book with Eugene Smolensky, *Aggregate Supply and Demand Analysis* (Harper and Row, 1964) and to his *magnum opus*, *Money and the Real World* (Macmillan, 1972).

One aspect of post Keynesian economics which still needs further development is international economics. Here, too, Paul Davidson's contributions have left their mark. In a series of articles and books, he has extended his ideas to the international economic landscape, drawing on his extensive knowledge of, and experience in, international economic relations. The proposal to revise the world's monetary system is his most important contribution in this area. Drawing on Keynes's writings, but substantially extending them, he suggests the creation of an international money clearing unit in a way that puts the onus of balance-of-payments imbalances onto surplus countries, in a global effective demand framework. These ideas are rooted in his *International Money and the Real World* (Macmillan, 1982) and further elaborated in recent academic articles. It is worth noting at this stage that a certain amount of his work has been put together in two volumes edited by Louise Davidson and published under the titles *Money and Employment, The Collected Writings of Paul Davidson*, Volume 1 (Macmillan, 1989), and *Inflation, Open Economies and Resources, The Collected Writings of Paul Davidson*, Volume 2 (Macmillan and New York University Press, 1991). His views on post Keynesian macroeconomics have been assembled recently in the book appropriately entitled *Post Keynesian Macroeconomic Theory: A Foundation for Successful Economic Policy in the Twenty-First Century* (Edward Elgar, 1994). In this book Paul Davidson shows how post Keynesian economics, which has evolved from Keynes's 'original logical framework', is the general case applicable to the real world.

In these three volumes friends of Paul Davidson elaborate upon a number of the issues emanating from his work, which have been briefly touched upon or mentioned above. In addition, there is a small number of entries which, although not directly related to Paul Davidson's work, fall, nonetheless, well within his interests as shown in the entries themselves. This third volume begins with three chapters devoted to methodology, before it turns, in the next two chapters, to theoretical issues which are directly related to the *General Theory*, and to another chapter which relates Marx's economics to Keynes's. The burning issue of 'rigidities' in New Keynesian economics – an aspect Paul Davidson has in fact written about – is discussed in the two chapters that follow. The rest of the volume, three chapters, deal with policy questions in three topical areas, the European Union, the international oil market and the financial liberalization thesis.

John Davis in 'Davidson, non-ergodicity and individuals' argues that Paul Davidson's emphasis on uncertainty and non-ergodicity needs to be understood specifically as an ontological, and less as an epistemological, thesis. Also that the relative stability in the economy is seen as depending upon conventions and institutions which influence, and are influenced by, the individual behaviour. Post-Keynesians interested in criticizing the atomistic individualism of neo-classicism, have done much to explain the impact of institutions on individuals. This chapter argues that complimentary analysis of how individuals impact on institutions is needed. Two problems with the atomistic conception of individuals are considered. First, neoclassical theory's implicit criterion for distinguishing individuals from one another is shown to be question-begging and circular. Second, this theory's individualistic-reductionism inherent in the microfoundations demand is argued to be inevitably unsuccessful on account of the socially embedded nature of individuals. These two problems signal the requirements of a post Keynesian account of individuals: that they be distinguishable as separate agents and yet also positioned within social frameworks. The chapter turns at this point to the ninth chapter of the *General Theory* on the subjective factors behind consumption for Keynes's view of what distinguishes individuals from one another. Keynes's account is shown to avoid the circularity of the neoclassical view of individuals. Then, Keynes's reasoning about bulls and bears is used to characterize individuals as embedded in institutions and conventions that position them with respect to one another. These foundations are thought to provide a Post-Keynesian conception of individuals as relatively autonomous, consistent with Davidson's non-ergodicity emphasis. The chapter concludes by addressing the question of whether the relationship between individuals and institutions can be understood in terms of the idea of organic connection.

Tony Lawson in 'Social relations, social reproductions and stylized facts', attempts to tackle three issues critics raised in relation to his thesis on critical realism:

1.   If there are no strict social event regularities 'out there', it is difficult to see how analysis is to be initiated or empirically checked.
2.   Few details of supposed explanatory *social relations* have been provided in previous contributions.
3.   If social explanation is to be couched in terms of human-agency-dependent social structures (such as social relations, rules, positions, and so on) – insufficient illustration of how such things come to endure when they do is normally provided.

In response to (1) Tony Lawson discusses the role of 'stylized facts' or, as he now prefers to refer to them, *demi-regs*. In response to (2) he discusses the paternalistic employer–employee relation – in the context of a specific case-study which focuses on the firm Pye of Cambridge. The phenomenon to be explained is that, counter to general experience at the time of the study, Pye combined a primary product market situation with secondary (poor) employment conditions (primary product and employment conditions were most frequently observed to correlate). The explanation of this phenomenon turns on the maintenance of the paternalistic relation at Pye, and the relatively peculiar local conditions which made this possible. Item (3) is investigated in terms of how this paternalistic relationship was continually reproduced in conditions where its demise might have been anticipated. This result turned on an active policy by management combined with a specific social context. He also discusses the nature of broad mechanisms acting in the economy more widely that may serve either to reinforce, or to undermine, this sort of paternalistic relation. Some fairly general methodological implications of the study are drawn in the conclusion.

John McCombie in 'Rhetoric, paradigms, and the relevance of the aggregate production function' contributes the third chapter on methodology. He begins with the observation that the neoclassical aggregate production function is one of the most widely used concepts in both microeconomics and macroeconomics, and certainly it is the heart of much macroeconomic modelling, including recent developments in endogenous growth theory and the recent revival of interest in the 'old' Solow–Swan growth model. However, it is noticeable that criticisms that have been levelled at the foundations of the aggregate production function are now almost totally ignored, both at the research level and in introductory textbooks. Such criticisms include aggregation problems and the implications of the Cambridge Capital Controversies. The standard defence of the use of the aggregate production function is normally along the lines of Friedman's instrumental argument, namely, that whatever these problems, the aggregate production function 'works'. That is to say, it produces good statistical fits with plausible estimates of the various parameters. However, this ignores the critique, which originated with Phelps Brown, that this is simply because the estimates are picking up the underlying accounting identity. Even though Joan Robinson considered this to be a more damaging criticism than the Cambridge Capital Controversies, it has also been widely ignored. This chapter considers these issues and provides a methodological explanation as to why this has occurred. It is argued that Kuhn's work (often mistakenly regarded as *passé*), when combined with McCloskey's rhetorical analysis, provides a useful insight into this failure of the scientific process. It is concluded that the aggregate production function is an example where influential rhetoric can, in McCloskey's words, 'block science for years'.

Robert Clower's is the first contribution on 'Keynesian economics'. In 'Keynes in Retrospect', he demonstrates how offending it is nowadays to see modern treatments of this school of thought pursue an *ad hoc* theorizing of macroeconomic theory. It is now recognized that the 1940s and 1950s 'Keynesian Revolution' was abortive. Early attempts converted the attack on orthodoxy of Keynes's *General Theory* into an aggregative variant of Marshallian short-period equilibrium analysis as Clower has shown elsewhere. Indeed Leijonhufvud also commented how the 'Keynesian Revolution' and the controversy that ensued was a waste of time and effort. Samuelson's Neoclassical Synthesis was also gratuitous in view of its thrust that the essentials of Keynes's *General Theory* entailed very little new material. Consequently, all those efforts of exegesis and debate could only manage to show that Keynes's *General Theory* was a 'revolution-making' but not a 'revolutionary' book. This chapter shows that textbook treatments of 'Keynesian economics' that emphasize output and employment adjustment, as opposed to (or in place of) price adjustment, as key elements governing the coordination of economic activities owe their origin not to Keynes and his *General Theory of Employment Interest and Money* (1936) but rather to Alvin Hansen and his *Full Employment of Stagnation* (1938). Moreover, it argues that textbook promulgation of Hansen's factitious (styled 'Bastard' by Joan Robinson) version of 'Keynesian economics' distorted Keynes's central message and seriously lessened the intellectual impact of Keynes's *General Theory*. Clower concludes by stating an important insight of the *General Theory:* that there exists *no* stationary point in the economic system, but only a *region of stability* within which all trajectories are 'neutral', 'uncontrollable', equilibria.

The second contribution to 'Keynesian Economics' is by Myron Gordon and Suresh Sethi in 'Consumption is not a fate worse than death'. In this chapter they ask the pertinent question of what happens to the allocation of a capitalist's net worth between risky productive assets and risk-free loans as net worth rises. A capitalist in this context is a proprietor, a portfolio investor or a corporation. These are important questions in the Keynesian theory of employment and output where employment and output are determined by aggregate demand, and aggregate demand is equal to the sum of consumption and investment in a closed system without government. The authors suggest that Keynes's demonstration that employment and output depended upon aggregate demand generated interest in the consumption and investment of a portfolio investor whose decisions in each period maximize the expected utility of future consumption. When bankruptcy is ignored, consumption and investment are both constant, rising or falling fractions of net worth, depending upon whether the investor has constant, decreasing or increasing relative risk aversion. However, as shown in this chapter, ignoring bankruptcy implicitly assumes that bankruptcy is a fate worse than death. In reality, the investor may take a job, go on the dole, or become a thief if necessary. When the investor expects some periodic income after bankruptcy, the authors find that the fraction of net worth consumed and invested in the risky asset both fall as net worth rises, regardless of the investor's attitude towards risk under all circumstances of practical economic relevance. This finding is shown to have considerable significance for the short and long-term behaviour of capitalist systems. A decision model is utilized within which the recognition of bankruptcy is demonstrated and its effects ascertained.

Wallace Peterson in 'Marx, Keynes and class war in America' brings Marx's and Keynes's writings closer together. He argues that class war is an idea that frightens Americans, evoking images of armed and angry workers rising up in a violent and bloody revolution to overthrow the existing social and economic order. It is an image that American conservatives invariably evoke; too much attention is directed and curiosity is aroused about the real distribution of income and wealth in America. Modern ideas about class war come primarily from Marx and his writings. Thus, his ideas provide the backdrop for the essential argument of this chapter, which is that in contemporary America conservatives have stood Marx on his head, waging a quiet and genteel version of class war against the poor and powerless. Much of their success stems from a 'blame the victim' strategy which deflects criticism over economic conditions to those who suffer most from the economy's poor performance of the last 20 years or so, plus pointing the finger at government as being at fault. The abandonment of Keynes, especially those aspects of Keynes championed by 'post Keynesians', is another reason for the fact that the counter-revolution and class war of the conservatives has taken place largely untouched by serious academic criticism. To reverse this development requires not just a 'return' to Keynes, but policy actions based upon key views of the Post Keynesians, especially those aspects concerned with distributional matters. The alternative is a continuation of the *status quo*, subnormal economic performance, high unemployment, a continued worsening of the distribution of income and wealth, a growing social and economic unrest that may lead to genuine Marxist class war.

The two chapters that follow are on 'rigidities' within New Keynesian economics. In the first of the two, entitled 'Why wage and price flexibility is destabilizing', Basil Moore shows that the simplification of the coordination problem to sticky wages and prices, due to the Walrasian General Equilibrium association of perfect price flexibility with perfect coordination, is at the root of the decline of new classical, new Keynesian, and much mainstream economics. The current literature argues that a lower wage and price level will operate to increase aggregate demand (the Pigou effect), while a falling wage and price level will reduce aggregate demand, due to the expectation of higher real returns on fixed price financial assets and liabilities. The total effect of downward wage flexibility on the homeostatic properties of the system then depends on the net effect of these two offsetting phenomena. These conventional accounts assume exogeneity of the money supply. However, with endogenous money, the money supply becomes credit-driven by the demand for bank loans, largely determined by business demand for working capital. As a result with endogenous money the Pigou effect disappears. There remains only the negative rate-of-change of prices effect of downward wage flexibility on aggregate demand. Given the level of interest rates, inflation will operate to lower real interest rates and so expand the level of aggregate demand, while deflation will raise real interest rates and so restrict the level of aggregate demand. Moreover, in a world of endogenous money, downward sticky or inflexible wages are not a market imperfection. They should rather be regarded as an adaptive institutional phenomenon that has evolved to increase price level stability, and so reduce the degree of uncertainty regarding future price levels and inflation rates.

In the second of the two chapters on 'rigidities', Roy Rotheim in 'On sticky prices: a post Keynesian perspective', demonstrates how Keynes thought of neoclassical economics as being founded on illogical structures. A post Keynesian perspective embraces the criticisms of Keynes's and proceeds to ask the more realistic question, not about price flexibility, but rather about the extent to which prices increase at slower or faster rates. Unlike the new Keynesian tradition which envisions price inflexibility at the level of the firm, whereas questions of rates of change in prices remain a question of the exogenous growth of the money stock, the post Keynesian questions such price changes also in terms of the price setting behaviour of the firms and industry as a whole. By not embracing the classical dichotomy between the real and monetary sectors, post Keynesian models consider all questions of prices to be situated at the place where they are set: being at the level of the firm, itself. Thinking about price setting in this fashion embraces questions of decisions to access finance externally, credit market conditions reflecting rational decision-making under uncertain conditions by financial institutions (including banks) and the role played by monetary policy in light of such pricing and credit market decision-making. It is shown that the extent to which prices increase at slower or faster rates, during an economic downturn, depends upon: firms' abilities to control the mark-ups over unit cost; the response of financial institutions to increases in the demand for money as means of payment by firms who find that they must continue to repay debts set in money terms despite unexpected shortfalls in sales revenue; and the extent to which central banks recognize their role as lender of last resort under such circumstances.

Kurt Rothschild in 'Some considerations on the economics and politics of the EU and the Maastricht Treaty', begins the first chapter on policy issues with an interesting observation. Namely that the social and economic environment is too complex and changeable with volatile human motives and actions to allow construction of an acceptable theoretical framework which would cover all possible situations and problems. Ideologies and interests complicate further an already complex situation, and it is not surprising to find that competing theories coexist, sometimes overlapping partly in contradiction to each other. The last quarter of this century is characterized by as sharp a reversal of conditions in the world economic situation and perspectives as one could imagine. While the third quarter, the 'golden' post-war period, was characterized by an optimistic stance, by a hopeful economic and social expansion with continuing growth and welfare (at least in the developed countries), the scene changed drastically during and after the 1970s to a disturbed and problematic picture with recessionary tendencies, unemployment, re-emerging poverty and an uncertain future. This dramatic change emerged from a multitude of deep-seated structural changes in the economic, social, and political environment, some elements of which can be indicated by such catchwords as: globalization, mergers and transnational firms, microelectronic and information 'revolution', financial innovation and liberalization, transformation of former 'socialist' countries, new industrialized states, and last, but not least, significant shifts in social power relations and the political and economic targets and ideologies accompanying them. It is against this background that the recent rapid developments in the European Union (EU) and the Maastricht Treaty are sketched and critically judged. It is believed that only such a wider political–economic perspective can reveal the 'logic' behind these developments.

In the penultimate chapter, Alessandro Roncaglia examines the international oil market relying on the idea of 'trilateral oligopoly', in the chapter entitled 'The international oil market: structural changes and stabilization policies'. The market structure depends on institutional and technological elements affecting the power structure within the sector, especially the pressure of internal and external competition (degree of collusion, size of the barriers to entry). The main stages through which the international oil market went over time are considered. First, in the stage up to the early 1970s, dominated by a few multinational vertically integrated oil companies, the market structure is mainly determined by four institutional pillars, the prorationing system and oil import quotas within the US, and two cartel agreements among major oil companies for operation outside the US, and by economies of scale and other technical and economic factors favouring major vertically integrated firms. The second stage is the golden period of OPEC, from the early 1970s until the 'countershock' of 1985–86; here the relevant factors are the unequal geographical distribution of giant low cost fields, the low cost of inventories for 'oil kept in the ground', and the elements favouring or hindering the collusion between OPEC countries (diverging socioeconomic, cultural and political conditions, and different long-term perspectives of crude availability). Thirdly, the present stage of highly volatile oil prices, determined on relatively small spot markets, is characterized by increased competitive pressure within the group of exporting countries and within the group of multinational oil companies, and by a greater role of consuming countries with their policies concerning taxation of oil products. Finally, since the instability of the oil market is a source of world-wide upheaval, the possibility of stabilization policies is discussed.

The final chapter is also on policy. Philip Arestis and Panicos Demetriades in 'Financial liberalization: myth or reality', deal with the theoretical developments that ascribe the poor performance of investment and growth in developing countries to interest rate ceilings, high reserve requirements and quantitative restrictions in the credit allocation mechanism. These restrictions, it is claimed by the proponents, were sources of 'financial repression', the main symptoms of which were low savings, credit rationing, and stagnation of the financial sector. In this framework, investment suffers not only in quantity but also in quality terms since the banking sector does not ration the available funds according to the marginal productivity of investment projects but according to their own discretion. The policy implications of this analysis are straightforward: remove interest rate ceilings, reduce reserve requirements and abolish directed credit programmes. The authors take issue with a number of theoretical foundations, focusing on the following aspects: (i) free banking leads to stability of the financial system, (ii) financial liberalization enhances economic growth, (iii) the relationship between savings and investment which implies that causation runs from the former to the latter, (iv) the absence of serious distributional effects and (v) the non-existent role for stock markets and speculation. The available evidence is also examined, and here too the authors find that it is not helpful to the thesis either. Two types of evidence are examined. The first concentrates on the experience of countries which implemented financial liberalization, to argue that the effect was destabilizing. The second is based on econometric evidence to demonstrate that this too is not complimentary to the thesis. It is concluded that the problems discussed in this chapter leave the thesis without serious theoretical and empirical foundations.

A number of colleagues and friends have suggested that a *Festschrift* for Paul Davidson is premature given that he is as productive as ever and no doubt will continue to be so for many years to come. There is a great deal in this reservation. On the other hand, though, while appreciating fully that Paul Davidson's intellectual capital is inexhaustible, celebrating his vast achievements and recognizing the enormous debt we owe him for his contributions, the enormous help to most of us and his continuous friendship, could take place anytime. Celebrating all these on his sixty-fifth birthday seems to be most appropriate. On behalf of all the contributors to this, and the other two volumes, I would also wish to express our gratitude to Louise Davidson for her great friendship to all of us and the enormous help she has been giving us not just on matters relating to the *JPKE* but on others as well, not least the most efficient and excellent organization of those extremely stimulating, generous, hugely successful and immensely enjoyable, conferences in Tennessee and elsewhere. At a more personal level, I would like to thank her for the help she gave me in preparing all three volumes.

Special thanks must go to the contributors for their willingness to respond to my comments and suggestions with forbearance and good humour. Thanks are also extended to June Daniels and Christine Nisbet of the Department of Economics, University of East London, for their secretarial assistance. Finally, Edward Elgar and his staff, especially Julie Leppard, Jo Perkins, Ian Garbutt and Dymphna Evans, who as always have provided excellent support throughout the period it took to prepare the three volumes.

1. Davidson, non-ergodicity and individuals

John B. Davis

The distinctiveness of post Keynesian economic theory from both neoclassical and neoRicardian economic theory rests in large degree on the former's emphasis on fundamental uncertainty. Paul Davidson has emphasized this difference time and again, arguing that Keynes's own thinking was most revolutionary in its attention to uncertainty, especially in regard to the analysis of liquidity and the properties of a monetary production economy. Partly in response to this insight, a 'fundamentalist Keynesianism' has developed in recent years that traces Keynes's understanding of uncertainty to his early *Treatise on Probability* account of probability in terms of degrees of belief (for example, Carabelli, 1988; O'Donnell, 1989). However, Davidson's treatment of uncertainty is explicitly rooted in a rejection of the idea that reality is an ergodic system, that is, an immutable, unchanging set of processes that eternally replicate past patterns of events. In his view, the world is non-ergodic, because important aspects of the future are created by human action. Thus though there is an epistemological dimension to his discussions of uncertainty that is not incompatible with an explanation of expectations in terms of degrees of belief, it is important to recognize that the idea that economic reality is non-ergodic is not an epistemological one, but rather an ontological one. Even more important for Davidson's understanding of uncertainty is the priority of this ontological claim over any epistemological claims regarding limitations on human information processing. Simon's bounded rationality conception, for example, looked at in purely epistemological terms involves what appears to be a rather fundamental sort of uncertainty. However, in Davidson's view, that Simon supposes the world is ergodic makes his conception close kin to Savage's expected utility analysis, and separates it off entirely from Keynes's more radical understanding of uncertainty (Davidson, 1995, p. 109). Uncertainty, then, cannot be understood solely in epistemological terms, and depends in the first instance on a correct understanding of the nature of reality itself.

To elaborate on this ontological theme, and to develop further the characteristically post Keynesian conception of uncertainty, this chapter sets forth an account of the functioning of a non-ergodic economic world in terms of the behaviour of individuals operating both within and upon conventions and institutions. In a non-ergodic world, according to Davidson, individual economic agents make choices on the assumption that the world is transmutable. They also, he emphasizes, rely upon conventions and institutions to stabilize and improve patterns of outcomes. Yet if the future is transformed in important respects as a result of human action, we must allow, first, that conventions and institutions may themselves be transformed – intentionally and unintentionally – by human action, and, second, that the transformation of conventions and institutions may in turn serve to transform the basis on which individuals themselves subsequently act as economic agents. In this non-ergodic picture of reciprocal influences of social structures and individual agency upon one another, post Keynesians have emphasized how conventions and institutions influence the behaviour of individuals, in part as a corrective to neoclassicism's atomistic individualism. Left largely unexamined, however, is how the theory of the individual economic agent needs to be re-developed, both to complete the picture of the economic process as non-ergodic, and to replace the static, ergodic view of individuals as atomistic agents in neoclassical economic theory.

Thus this chapter seeks to develop along Davidsonian lines Keynes's own *General Theory* account of the nature of individuals, linking it to Keynes's account of conventions, in order to better describe the nature of uncertainty in a non-ergodic world. The first section of the chapter begins with a brief summary of Davidson's recent thinking on non-ergodicity, in order to draw out the implications of his ontological view of uncertainty. An important aspect of this view is the idea that individuals operate both within and upon conventions and other institutional structures. The second section of the chapter then examines critically neoclassical thinking about the nature of individuals, in order to set the stage for discussion of the understanding of individuals to be found in Keynes's thinking. Though neoclassicism is methodologically individualist, ironically its account of the nature of the individual can be shown to be seriously flawed in two important respects. The third section of the chapter examines Keynes's views on the nature of individuals in two locations in *The General Theory*, and then turns to one post Keynesian interpretation of the nature of the relations between individuals. An important argument of the chapter that appears in this section is that Keynes did not reason in terms of organic connection. The fourth and final section of the chapter makes concluding remarks about Keynesian uncertainty in connection with individuals and conventions.

DAVIDSON ON NON-ERGODICITY

On an ergodic view of the world, reality is immutable and unchanging in the sense that the basic causal relations governing the world never change and always hold in all circumstances. Though we observe variation at the level of events, individuals, and particular practices, the principal cause-and-effect relationships underlying their variety and flux are themselves understood to be constant and unchanging. That is, just as in natural science the law of gravity always holds, so in economics and social science behaviour is always explained in terms of essentially the same causal relationships, irrespective of changing social conditions and historical development. Thus economics is the study of a single set of underlying relationships. And, as there can never be new relationships and new cause-and-effect patterns generated by changing historical circumstances, economists are able to continually refine and build upon earlier insights, so that economic knowledge may be represented as always involving cumulative advance and progress.

Davidson identifies one such purported advance as twentieth-century methods for modelling of economic agents' informational capacities (1995). Whereas nineteenth-century classical economists effectively assumed that individuals operated in a world of perfect certainty, contemporary orthodox economists assume that individuals predict future outcomes by estimating their probabilities based on past and present market data. There are a variety of such probabilistic approaches, ranging from new classical theories that postulate rational expectations in the short run to New Keynesian, expected utility, bounded rationality, and Austrian views that suppose that the future is not completely known in the short run due to limitations in human cognitive ability. However, all these views share what Davidson terms the 'Darwinian story' that economic agents who fail to adapt their subjective probabilities to the world's immutable objective probabilities do not survive (p. 107). Thus contemporary orthodox thinkers still share with the classical economists the idea that there is a single, determinate, unchanging economic reality. Their 'progress' on classical economics is merely to add that economic agents may fail in the pursuit of their objectives not only because they may make poor economic decisions (as the classicals allowed), but also because they may fail to forecast future conditions successfully however good their economic decision-making.

For Keynes, on the other hand, the world is transmutable or non-ergodic in the sense that the principles underlying the phenomena we observe are historically specific and may change with development in the economy's structure. The passing of the age of entrepreneurship and owner-led firms was an important change in the economy's structure of organization. Consequently, as he stressed in his critique of Tinbergen's econometric methodology, economic time series may often not be stationary, because the underlying economic environment can be 'non-homogeneous through time' (Keynes, XIV, p. 285). This is not, however, what all commentators emphasize when discussing Keynes on uncertainty. Rather they often point to statements such as Keynes made in 1937 in his *Quarterly Journal of Economics* response to his critics that regarding much of what will take place in the future, 'We simply do not know' (Keynes, XIV, p. 113). It is true, of course, that in situations of true uncertainty decision-makers do not know enough to form reliable probability judgements regarding future events. But that they do not is first and foremost a matter of the fact that the future will not sufficiently resemble the past so as to permit such judgements. Were, contrary to fact, the future to closely resemble the past, and were there still significant limitations in our capacity to process information (as clearly there are), uncertainty could then be modelled as behaviour under risk. What is required for radical uncertainty, then, is merely the fact that the future will not be like the past in important respects, that is, that historical data do not provide a reliable statistical basis for drawing inferences about future outcomes (Davidson, 1991; also cf. Hicks, 1979 and Davidson, 1994). When Keynes said that we cannot even begin to know what the future may hold, he simply meant to indicate that the future would be different in more ways than he or anyone else could imagine.

This emphasis may strike some as unnecessary, but saying that Keynesian uncertainty rests on the ontological proposition that the world is non-ergodic serves an important purpose. Namely, it encourages us to ask why cause-and-effect relations underlying the phenomena we observe should be thought to be historically specific. For Davidson, the answer is straightforward. Saying that the world is non-ergodic is equivalent to saying that it is transmutable, where this means the economic world may be transformed in fundamental ways as a consequence of human agency. That is, human beings are free to change not just the course of events (as orthodox thinkers allow), but are also free to change the very principles governing the economic process. It is this that produces radical Keynesian uncertainty regarding the future. We generally do not – cannot – know what the future will hold, because the future is yet to be determined, or better, will be determined in large degree by our actions. Uncertainty consequently cannot be treated as risk in all but the most trivial situations, because human action continually re-determines the frequency distributions of phenomena in which we are interested.

This does not imply, Davidson emphasizes, that economic policy is powerless. True, if economic policy is conceived of as designing specific courses of action that rely on accurate forecasts about what path the economy is likely to take, policy is unlikely to be successful. However, if economic policy is rather thought to have the design of institutional arrangements that tend to mitigate the undesirable effects of human action as its chief objective, then its prospects are more promising. Keynes's insight was that *laissez-faire* economies lack endogenous forces to drive them to full employment equilibria. Essentially the behaviour of individuals and the framework of free market institutions within which they operate permits series of mutually reinforcing contractions of demand that ultimately expire below full employment equilibria. However, different sorts of institutions may be devised that lack this character, and which rather tend to raise demand and employment. Keynes's call for 'a somewhat comprehensive socialisation of investment' (VIII, p. 378) was meant as just the sort of institutional reform that might accomplish this. Economic policy for Keynes and Davidson, then, aims at institutional change designed to improve patterns of interaction between individuals and the institutions within which they operate to achieve goals such as low unemployment.

At the same time, however, when individuals operate upon institutions in an effort to bring about policy goals, on a non-ergodic view of the world and economic policy we must also suppose that their actions will be influenced and conditioned by both the institutions they modify as well as new institutions that emerge. That is, a non-ergodic view of the world also tells us that social structure and individual agency have reciprocal effects on one another, so that individuals and institutions are continually evolving in relation to one another. In contrast, neoclassical economists suppose that the underlying principles operating in economic life are stable and unchanging, and thus generally also suppose that the nature of individuals and institutions in which they operate is set and unchanging. New Institutionalists do allow that institutions evolve, but still maintain that individuals are unchanging in nature, so that the institutional environment adapts to human action, but not the reverse. This suggests that on a non-ergodic view of individuals and institutions we ought to be able to demonstrate that in an historical economic process individuals are transformed along with institutions. Demonstrating this requires developing a new understanding of the individual alternative to that employed in neoclassicism – the subject taken up in section three below. Before turning to that task, the following section accordingly attempts to diagnose the problems inherent in the neoclassical conception of the individual to create guidelines for a better account.

THE NEOCLASSICAL CONCEPTION OF THE INDIVIDUAL

Two problems are diagnosed here: one concerning the standard characterization of individuals as collections of preferences, and the other concerning how individuals relate to social context.

(i)   Neoclassical economic theory assumes individuals are unchanging in nature. This implies that across any set of changes in an individual's environment, the theory must successfully demonstrate that any given individual remains in essence the selfsame individual. Alternatively, central to any conception of individuals as unchanging in nature is an account of what makes any individual consistently distinct from all other individuals. On the neoclassical view, of course, individuals are distinguished as distinct collections of preferences. But can this conception of the individual successfully distinguish individuals as distinct beings? In Davis (1995), I argued that for neoclassicism the idea of individuals having distinct collections of preferences is equivalent to saying that individuals have their *own* sets of preferences. In effect, since preferences themselves are defined entirely subjectively or only in terms of the individuals to whom they belong, they must always be some individual's *own* preferences. But using individuals' *own* preferences to distinguish individuals through change is question-begging in that it presupposes the very individuals those preferences are meant to distinguish. If a set of *own* preferences picks out some individual, they must naturally be that particular individual's preferences and not someone else's preferences. But if we have already picked out the individual to whom a set of preferences belongs in order to call these preferences that particular individual's *own* preferences, we cannot then turn around, and use those preferences as a criterion for distinguishing individuals from one another.

In short, neoclassical theory's criterion for distinguishing and defining individuals is circular and question-begging. The general problem with conceptualizing the individual as a collection of subjective preferences can be seen from a different perspective if we ask how the view holds up when we consider the possibility that individuals' preferences may change. Stigler and Becker (1977), in what has become the accepted position on the subject, sought specifically to rule out this case, insisting that preferences do not change. Their professed reason for doing so was entirely *ad hoc* in that they simply wished to explain choice solely in terms of changes in prices and incomes. But perhaps they were also aware that were an individual to be distinguished in terms of one set of preferences at one point in time, and then distinguished according to another set of preferences at another point in time, continuity of individual identity would require there to be something more to being an individual than just having preferences, thus demonstrating that individuals could not be explained solely in terms of preferences. Note that one common sense view of why preferences change is that individuals are influenced by their environment. Adults do not have the same preferences they had as infants, because of their subsequent experience. But this sort of answer is incompatible with characterizing individuals solely in terms of their subjective preferences. The Stigler–Becker strategy can thus be seen as a means of closing off investigation of the inadequacy of the neoclassical conception of the individual.

(ii) Another manifestation of the problems involved in the neoclassical approach to explaining individuals concerns the way that the call for microfoundations for macroeconomics tends to be addressed. For most proponents of microfoundations, the basic rationale behind the claim that macroeconomic relationships need to be grounded in microeconomic ones is that the latter concern the behaviour of individuals, whereas the former concern aggregative relationships based on the behaviour of groups of individuals. Individuals are ostensibly real entities, but groups of individuals are claimed to be mere conceptual constructions, and thus one step removed from the real. New classical and new Keynesian economists consequently favour what may be termed individualist–reductionist type explanations of macroeconomic relationships, supposing that good explanation is always explanation in terms of really existing things.

However, it is doubtful that individualist–reductionist microfoundational accounts of macroeconomic relationships can ever be successful. Not only do such accounts require that macroeconomic relationships be explained in terms of the behaviour of households and firms but they also require that the choices of households and firms ultimately be explained in terms of the choices of individuals within households and firms. This latter condition involves an analysis of individuals' strategic interaction, the province of game theory, where research has shown that determinate results are either available in only the most trivial situations or depend upon our assuming that conventions and institutions create a framework for individual interaction (Hargreaves-Heap and Varoufakis, 1995, pp. 204ff.). In the latter case, as we must presuppose conventions and institutions in order to explain individual choice, conventions and institutions cannot be said to be mere conceptual constructions, but must be, like individuals, real constituents of the world. Thus as individuals are not the only real things that exist, there is no reason to think that groups of individuals are not real as well, and consequently no special reason for an individualist-reductionism.

An alternative conception of the microfoundations project aims at reducing macroeconomic relationships to accounts of rational optimizing behaviour not associated with the choices of particular individuals. Representative agent models assume that the choices of any number of diverse individuals in a single sector of the economy can be treated as the choices of one 'representative' rational optimizing agent. What proponents of this approach might be said to assume is that microeconomics has a better developed structure than macroeconomics, and thus on unity of science grounds we should strive to make the latter conform to the former (Janssen, 1993). Of course in the face of such difficulties as the Sonnenschein–Mantel–Debreu results it is hard to believe that microeconomics either has a very well developed analytical structure or one obviously superior to macroeconomics. Moreover, it is hardly clear that the choices of representative agents coincide with aggregate choices of heterogeneous individuals (Kirman, 1992). And finally, the unity of science goal, while commendable in the abstract, may simply not apply to sub-disciplines of a subject that are fundamentally different in nature.

But more interesting for purposes of the discussion here is that proponents of this approach to microfoundations believe that rational optimizing behaviour need not be associated with actual individuals at all. Though the analysis was originally developed with actual individuals in mind, that the analysis can be used without reference to individuals suggests that it is not very closely tied to the task of characterizing real world individuals. In effect, then, rational optimizing could be said to not be a means of distinguishing actual individuals. This conclusion recalls the problem with individualist–reductionist microfoundational explanations. There the microfoundations project obscures the role of conventions and institutions that help to structure bargaining between individuals. In rational optimizing-reductionist explanations, on the other hand, whether conventions and institutions underlie rational optimizing is ultimately irrelevant, because that analysis need not even be about distinct individuals.

(iii)   The two sorts of problems with the neoclassical conception of the individual described in (i) and (ii) above may be said to be associated with two different types of considerations involved in developing an adequate conception of individuals. In (i), the issue is how we account for the subjectivity or subjective side of individuals. The neoclassical strategy of tying this aspect of individuals to *own* preferences clearly represents an unsuccessful way of getting at individuals' distinctiveness from one another. In (ii), the issue is how we account for the social embeddedness of individuals, or alternatively the issue is how we position individuals in social settings. This might be termed the objective side of individuals. Neoclassical theory was found wanting in this regard, in that its highly atomistic view of individuals either compels it to ignore individuals' social context or treat choice as disembodied.

A post Keynesian conception of individuals consequently needs to explain both what distinguishes individuals from one another – individuals' subjective side – and how individuals are positioned with respect to one another in social frameworks – individuals' social embeddedness or objective side. Moreover, it needs to do this in an account of a non-ergodic world in which individuals operate within and upon conventions and institutions. In the following section we first look at two locations in *The General Theory* in which Keynes addressed each of the two sorts of considerations involved here, and then turn to analysis of one post Keynesian approach to explaining individuals.

KEYNES AND POST KEYNESIANS ON INDIVIDUALS

(i) Keynes devoted the generally overlooked, ninth chapter of *The General Theory*, 'The propensity of consume: II. The subjective factors', to discussion of the subjective side of individuals. That the chief focus of the chapter is those 'motives or objects of a subjective character which lead individuals to *refrain from spending* out of their incomes' (VII, p. 107; emphasis added) demonstrates that Keynes was not looking upon individuals only in their capacity as consumers. Rather, since he was on the whole concerned with whether the economy's lower consumption was made up by higher investment, he was interested in the full range of motivations involved in individual economic behaviour from the perspective of their possible impact upon the propensity to consume. Indeed, following the list of eight motives that lead individuals involved in consumption to refrain from spending Keynes then appended four 'motives largely analogous to, but not identical with, those actuating individuals' on the part of those in 'Central and Local Government ... Institutions and ... Business Corporations' to refrain from spending.

The first eight motives are precaution, foresight, calculation, improvement, independence, enterprise, pride and avarice. The added four motives are enterprise, liquidity, improvement, and financial prudence (pp. 107–9). Besides compiling the list, Keynes briefly describes each motive. For example, improvement is characterized as the motive:

To enjoy a gradually increasing expenditure, since it gratifies a common instinct to look forward to a gradually improving standard of life rather than the contrary, even though the capacity for enjoyment may be diminishing.

Independence is characterized as the motive:

To enjoy a sense of independence and the power to do things, though without a clear idea or definite intention of specific action.

The four motives in the second list, in contrast, pertain directly to individuals' own appreciation or sense of the financial concerns of government and business in which they are employed.

One reason few readers of *The General Theory* have paid much attention to the book's ninth chapter is that what Keynes treats as objective factors determining the propensity to consume in the previous chapter are central to his 'fundamental psychological law' that individuals are disposed to increase their consumption as their income increases, but by not as much. Indeed in a comment upon how his subjective factors influence the propensity to consume, Keynes notes that, on account of slow change in society's organization, habits, capital, and distribution of wealth that form the 'main background' to these subjective factors, attention can be focused upon 'short-period changes in consumption [that] largely depend on changes in the rate at which income ... is being earned and not on changes in the propensity to consume out of a given income' (pp. 109, 110). But of chief interest here is how Keynes understands individuals' subjective side.

In contrast to the neoclassical conception, Keynes's motives are not treated as tastes entirely specific to particular individuals – thus as necessarily *own* preferences – but as types of motivations all individuals possess that may be observed in different combinations in particular individuals. To signal as much Keynes capitalizes the name of each motive ('Precaution ... Pride ... Extravagance'), as if to imply he is referring to widely observed character traits of individuals. The effect of this is to root the subjective side of individuals in the language of a highly familiar psychology, while yet particularizing individuals in terms of the specific combinations of motives they exercise. The circularity of the neoclassical account is avoided, because the language of motivation employed is not solely a matter of the isolated individual's mental contents. Precaution, Pride, and so on represent psychological orientations tied to types of circumstances in which individuals may find themselves. This implies that individuals are distinct from one another not just according to the combinations of motives they exhibit, but also according to the particular social–historical settings they occupy in which these various motives are exhibited. Two layers of content additional to what is found in the neoclassical conception of the individual thus individuate Keynes's economic actors: that they react in ways others may not according to the combination of motives they each exhibit, and that their doing so is occasioned by their own particular circumstances, where that includes the 'main background' to subjective motives in the form of social organization, habits, distribution of wealth, and so on.

(ii)   Turning from the issue of individuals' subjective side to the issue of their social embeddedness, or how individuals are positioned with respect to one another, we come to passages in *The General Theory* more familiar and more often quoted. In Chapter Thirteen Keynes explains uncertainty as to the future rate of interest as a foundation of liquidity preference. Recalling his *Treatise on Money* he notes that 'different people' – bulls and bears – 'will estimate the prospects differently' (p. 169), and:

> the individual, who believes that future rates of interest will be above the rates assumed by the market, has reason for keeping actual liquid cash ... whilst the individual who differs from the market in the other direction will have a motive for borrowing money for short periods in order to purchase debts of longer term. (p. 170)

That is, explaining liquidity preference, an attitude towards the importance of holding money in an uncertain environment, requires that we understand how individuals differentiate themselves with respect to others and the prevailing state of affairs, namely, market-determined interest rates. Relatedly, in the preceding twelfth chapter on investment and long-term expectation, Keynes states that speculators focus on the state of 'average expectation' (p. 151) regarding the worth of various investments, in order to figure out how to 'outwit the crowd' (p. 155), and do better than 'what average opinion believes average opinion to be' (p. 159). That is, individuals again position themselves with respect to established ways of seeing things, in order to mark out their own course of action.

In these passages and elsewhere in *The General Theory* Keynes addresses how individuals particularize themselves in institutional contexts. The contrast with neoclassical reductionist arguments is instructive. The latter aim to fully translate social–institutional economic settings into the choices of individuals, but either end up presupposing those settings (individualist-reductionism), or fail to account for the activity of individuals altogether (rational optimizing reductionism). Keynes's approach, on the other hand, situates individuals in conventional and institutional frameworks from the outset, and uses these frameworks to explain how individuals act differently from one another. This treatment of individual action as embodied in a social environment – rather than obscuring the place of individuals in the economic process, as might be claimed from a neoclassical perspective – serves to identify the specific impact and roles individuals have in concrete settings. It constitutes a non-reductionist form of explanation that acquires explanatory power by juxtaposing agents and institutions.

(iii)   For Keynes, then, individuals both possess a subjective side that exhibits shared human traits, and operate in social settings that distinguish them from one another in terms of their separate courses of action. How do these aspects of his thinking about individuals play into our conception of the economy as non-ergodic? Davidson characterizes a non-ergodic economy as one in which human action may transform basic cause-and-effect relationships, yet one in which individuals operate within and upon conventions and institutions. Relatedly, Lawson, in discussing the relationship between human agency and social structure in an uncertain world, emphasizes that 'human agency and social structure each presuppose the other, although neither can be reduced to the other, or identified with, or explained completely in terms of, it' (1995, p. 83). For both Davidson and Lawson, it thus seems fair to say, individuals and institutions maintain a relative autonomy which is central to our accounting for their reciprocal effects on one other. My argument regarding Keynes's thinking about individuals is that he places a similar emphasis on the relative autonomy of individuals (and institutions) to explain uncertainty in the economy. In the balance of the discussion in this section, then, I elaborate further on what relative autonomy implies, and how it operates in Keynes's characterization of individuals.

To further explain relative autonomy, it is best to contrast it with a stronger type of relationship between individuals and institutions that one school of post Keynesianism has recently advocated, namely, organic connection. The characterization of Keynes as an organicist dates to Brown-Collier (1985) and has more recently been defended in a 1995 collection of papers on Keynes and uncertainty by Carabelli, Dow, Hillard, Rotheim and Winslow, with Hillard asserting that it is 'now generally accepted among Post Keynesians that Keynes denied the atomistic ontology of classical economics and adopted an organicist mode of analysis' (1995, p. 257). Clearly post Keynesians agree that Keynes did reject a classical atomist ontology of economic agents. The passages above and their discussion indicate as much. But did he believe that individuals and social structures were organically related – a philosophical conception associated with the turn of the century British neoHegelian idealist thought of Bradley, Bosanquet and McTaggart, which Keynes's philosophical mentors Moore and Russell explicitly rejected? And is this proposition widely accepted among post Keynesians? Let us consider the nature of organicist thinking and its implications.

Organicism, or organic connection, is an ontological thesis concerning the nature of relations between things. Specifically, things are organically or internally related if their very natures depend upon or may be reduced to their relations to one another. More accurately, relations are real and exist, while the things they relate, their relata, are aspects of relations. In contrast, external relations exist between things if the latter are not reducible to their relations to other things. On this view, relations may be thought of as aspects of the things they relate, but they may also be thought of as real phenomena alongside real things, the latter sometimes distinguished as particulars (Strawson, 1959). A view sometimes taken for organicism is holism, a multilevel whole-part form of analysis that focuses on principles that apply only to the whole of some set of things, or are emergent at the level of the whole. However, holist arguments are typically not organicist, as the idea of principles emergent at the level of the whole, as for example when we say human thought is something over and above physico-chemical brain states, normally precludes our reducing talk about parts to talk about the whole, or that we translate our understanding of brain states into talk about human thought.

This difference between holist and organicist reasoning helps to isolate one of the chief characteristics of the latter. Like atomist reasoning, though in precisely the opposite sense, organicist views are reductionist. As things that are internally related to one another are only aspects of the relations that connect them, good organicist explanation is devoted to translating or reducing seemingly self-subsistent things into relata so as to explain the world as pure relation. Just as atomism has it that only individuals exist, the doctrine of organicism is that only relations exist. In contrast, holist argument involves a multi-level form of explanation. That human thought inheres in brain states, but is at the same time so unlike them, helps account for thought as a distinct principle over and above the collection of brain states which support it. Human thought, that is, involves a distinctive principle of the whole, just because it is closely associated with and also fundamentally different from the physico-chemical processes which underlie it. Thus holist argument operates on two levels, neither of which is reducible to the other, and both of which are required to explain the phenomenon in question.

A good case can be made for saying that Keynes used this holistic form of reasoning in important ways in *The General Theory*. Consider the paradox of savings as a multi-level explanation. The force of the paradox derives from the fact that individual savings behaviour produces contrary movements in aggregate savings. Thus two different concepts of savings are juxtaposed in the analysis. Now organicists might claim that the proper meaning of savings is that associated with the aggregate savings–income relationship, and that the concept of individual savings is derivative and ultimately reducible in some way to the aggregate notion. This claim does have a certain plausibility to it, but only when we stress linguistic meanings and interpretation as the appropriate level of analysis. Keynes, however, was not interested in debates over the linguistic interpretation of savings. Rather he believed one could isolate a real mechanism operating in the economy whereby increases in individual savings produced decreases in aggregate savings. Moreover, the mechanism he modelled depended upon individual and aggregate savings being irreducibly distinct phenomena. His paradox had force, that is, just because individuals could really do one thing, and something else really happened in the aggregate.

A number of the proponents of the organicist interpretation of Keynes represent organic connection as interdependence. Interdependence between two things might be said to exist when each has effects on the other, which then change the behaviour of each, so that they then have different effects on one another, which then again changes the behaviour of each, and so on. If we expand this picture to *n* number of things, it might be argued that the system of interdependent effects becomes so complicated that we may or must ignore detailed connections, and simply focus on a principle that describes the whole process. In effect, the parts reduce to the whole, because the parts have no real significance relative to the significance of the process of the whole. Interdependence on such a view collapses into organic relation.

This is a perfectly coherent and reasonable argument in regard to some processes. The question at hand, however, is whether Keynes employed it in *The General Theory*. Did Keynes regard all interdependent processes as collapsing into organic ones? Hillard (1995) argues that Keynes showed the flaws in classical economics when he demonstrated that investment and savings were (organically) interdependent via the latter's dependence on income. Rotheim (1995) argues that Keynes's entrepreneurs form expectations based on social factors rather than just information internal to the firm, and that this indicates the organically interdependent nature of the investment decision. But note that in both cases what Keynes does is give a better explanation of the mechanisms and the system of interdependence involved. Savings depend on income. Entrepreneurs attend to conventions. In neither case does Keynes reduce or translate concepts pertaining to the economy's parts into concepts pertaining to the economy as a whole. Rather he explains the economy as a whole specifically by exhibiting it as a particular system of interdependencies. This is a holist, not organicist, form of argument, and to call it the latter seems only to obscure the meaning of interdependence.

Returning, then, to the characterization of a non-ergodic economy offered by Davidson and Lawson as a process of reciprocal effects between agents and conventions, we need to ask whether this particular conception of interdependency ought to be taken as an example of organic connection. Clearly what bothers proponents of the organicist interpretation the most is the notion that the only alternative to their view is that Keynes held to a traditional atomist methodology (e.g. Carabelli, 1995, p. 141; Hillard, 1995, p. 257). Then, re-casting interdependence as organic connection, they conclude that individuals cannot be understood atomistically, because on the organic view things related are but aspects of the relations that involve them. But the premise of this argument – that without organic connection individuals must be conceived atomistically – is false, and not one entertained by Keynes.

As the discussion at the beginning of this section shows, in *The General Theory* Keynes not only used an understanding of individuals different from the one we find in neoclassical theory, but his conception has advantages over the neoclassical one in the way he frames individuals' subjective side and in the way he accounts for their social embeddedness. Indeed these strategies permit him to avoid the problems neoclassical theory encounters in its view of individuals as atomistic agents. Essentially, on Keynes's view individuals may be transformed in important respects according to change in the contexts in which they operate. On the neoclassical understanding, on the other hand, atomistic individuals are unchanging and uninfluenced in their basic nature by the contexts in which they operate.

This difference is significant for an understanding of the economy as non-ergodic. It means that we can analyse the historical evolution of the economy in terms of series of reciprocal effects that individuals and conventions/ institutions have upon one another. In particular, policies aimed at conventions and institutions can be designed to change individuals' interaction in ways that improve social well-being. At the same time, that individuals have effects on the way conventions and institutions operate tells us that policy design always involves unintended consequences. Basically, then, our grasp of the economy as an evolutionary process depends upon our grasping that there are two distinct poles or levels involved in the economy: agency and structure. Saying that the economy is non-ergodic means we need to trace how these evolve together in terms of their mutual impacts upon one another. On the other hand, saying that individuals and conventions/institutions are organically connected removes from view the project of sorting out this system of reciprocal effects.

KEYNESIAN UNCERTAINTY: CONCLUDING REMARKS

The project of explaining the economy as non-ergodic places thinking about historical process in the foreground. But an historical process is susceptible of analysis even when uncertainty and animal spirits are regularly observed. The charge of nihilism advanced by Coddington (1982) only applies if we do not have methods for explaining the state of uncertainty and animal spirits at different historical junctures. Runde (1991) has shown that for Keynes the impact of uncertainty varies according to different decision-making contexts, and thus that uncertainty need not imply unstable beliefs. On the view here, we may begin to understand variation in decision-making contexts and the consequent state of uncertainty at different points in time in terms of the evolution of interaction between individuals and the economic structures within and upon which they operate. More attention on my part to Keynes's thinking about expectations and the interaction between individuals and conventions appears in Davis (1994). Here attention is focused upon the nature of individuals as relatively autonomous agents on account of the importance of developing a post Keynesian analysis of agency.

Post Keynesians have emphasized the importance of conventions and institutions in the economy, but have given less attention to how to characterize the activity of individuals within this framework. Davidson's treatment of uncertainty in ontological terms suggests a way to develop this analysis. A non-ergodic economy is one in which individuals possess a relative autonomy that is exhibited in the system of reciprocal effects individuals and conventions/institutions have upon one another. To trace such a system of reciprocal effects, both the influence of agents upon economic structure and the reverse need to be explained. This chapter draws on Keynes to identify elements of a theory of the nature of the individual for this purpose.

REFERENCES

Brown-Collier, E. (1985), 'Keynes' View of an Organic Universe', *Review of Social Economy*, **13** (1), 14–23.
Carabelli, A. (1988), *On Keynes's Method*, London: Macmillan.
Carabelli, A. (1995), 'Uncertainty and Measurement in Keynes: Probability and Organicness' in S. Dow and J. Hillard (eds), *Keynes, Knowledge and Uncertainty*, Aldershot, Hants: Edward Elgar, 137–60.
Coddington, A. (1982), 'Deficient Foresight: A Troublesome Theme in Keynesian Economics', *American Economic Review*, **72**, 480–7.
Davidson, P. (1991), 'Is Probability Theory Relevant for Uncertainty?: A Post Keynesian Perspective', *Journal of Economic Perspectives*, **5**, 129–43.
Davidson, P. (1994), *Post Keynesian Macroeconomic Theory*, Aldershot, Hants: Edward Elgar.
Davidson, P. (1995), 'Uncertainty in Economics' in S. Dow and J. Hillard (eds), *Keynes, Knowledge and Uncertainty*, Aldershot, Hants: Edward Elgar, 107–16.
Davis, J. (1994), *Keynes's Philosophical Development*, Cambridge: Cambridge University Press.
Davis, J. (1995), 'Personal Identity and Standard Economic Theory', *Journal of Economic Methodology*, **2** (1), 35–52.
Dow, S. (1995), 'Uncertainty about Uncertainty', in S. Dow and J. Hillard (eds), *Keynes, Knowledge and Uncertainty*, Aldershot, Hants: Edward Elgar, 117–36.
Hargreaves Heap, S. and Varoufakis, Y. (1995), *Game Theory: A Critical Introduction*, London: Routledge.
Hicks, J.R. (1979), *Causality in Economics*, New York: Basic Books.
Hillard, J. (1995), 'Keynes, Interdependence and the Monetary Production Economy' in S. Dow and J. Hillard (eds), *Keynes, Knowledge and Uncertainty*, Aldershot, Hants: Edward Elgar, 244–63.
Janssen, M. (1993), *Microfoundations: A Critical Inquiry*, London: Routledge.
Keynes, J. M. (1971–89), *The Collected Writings of John Maynard Keynes*, vols I–XXX, ed. D. Moggridge. London: Macmillan.
Kirman, A. (1992), 'Whom or What Does the Representative Agent Represent?', *Journal of Economic Perspectives*, **6** (2), 117–36.
Lawson, T. (1995), 'Economics and Expectations' in S. Dow and J. Hillard (eds), *Keynes, Knowledge and Uncertainty*, Aldershot, Hants: Edward Elgar, 77–106.
O'Donnell, R. (1989), *Keynes: Philosophy Economics and Politics*, London: Macmillan.
Rotheim, R. (1995), 'Keynes on Uncertainty and Individual Behavior Within a Theory of Effective Demand' in S. Dow and J. Hillard (eds), *Keynes, Knowledge and Uncertainty*, Aldershot, Hants: Edward Elgar, 161–76.
Runde, J. (1991), 'Keynesian Uncertainty and the Instability of Beliefs', *Review of Political Economy*, **3** (2), 125–45.
Stigler, G. and Becker, G. (1977), 'De gustibus non est disputandum', *American Economic Review*, **67**, 76–90.
Strawson, P. (1959), *Individuals*, New York: Doubleday.
Winslow, T. (1995), 'Uncertainty and Liquidity Preference', in S. Dow and J. Hillard (eds), *Keynes, Knowledge and Uncertainty*, Aldershot, Hants: Edward Elgar, 221–43.

2. Social relations, social reproduction and stylized facts

Tony Lawson

INTRODUCTION

Paul Davidson is an important figure in recent heterodox economics – not only as a provider and inspirer of alternative perspectives to the not-altogether-successful mainstream project but also, through his expert stewardship of the *Journal for Post Keynesian Economics* in particular, as a facilitator of them. It is fair to say that heterodox economics over the last 20 years is significantly in his debt. I use this occasion to concentrate on a specific 'alternative' or 'heterodox' project, one indeed that has already been discussed in the pages of the *JPKE* (for example, Lawson, 1994b). It is a project that has been systematized within economics as *critical realism*. The project in question is broadly ontological in nature, it is concerned with social being, the nature of social reality. And this orientation ties in closely with much of Paul's own work. As many of his titles alone indicate, Paul has long insisted that insights into the nature of reality constrain our theories (for example, Davidson, 1972, 1978, 1992, 1996). His work on the relevance of the ergodicity assumption in social analysis is particularly important in this regard, as is his more recent focus upon the transmutability of reality (Davidson, 1996). Expressly tailoring the discussion which follows to an explicit theory of reality, then, should not be out of place here.

Ontology, by its nature, tends to be highly abstract. And a problem I have often encountered in arguing for the perspective I defend is the practical one of tying theoretical developments that are pitched at a highly abstract level, with substantive analyses that are sufficiently concrete to be illustrative of the abstract theory in question. To date I have mostly opted for emphasizing the former to the relative neglect of the latter. This emphasis has often been criticized. And only recently, at a meeting in London to honour Paul Davidson's work (November 1996), I encountered Paul insisting on the need, wherever possible, to connect proposals for new or 'alternative' approaches and orientations to substantive work which they bear upon. I have thus decided to take the opportunity provided by this forum to rectify the noted imbalance in material I have elsewhere presented, to relate *critical realism* to specific substantive study.

However, let me straightaway add a note of caution regarding this endeavour. Such a project as I am accepting to undertake here has the potential easily to mislead. This is due to the fact that abstractly formulated approaches can be consistent with a range of *competing* theories at the substantive level. Just as no one talks of *the* positivist or deductivist or even econometric theory of any substantive phenomenon, so there cannot be (or is unlikely to be) *the* critical realist one. In consequence, whatever may be the merits of the substantive analysis focused upon below, it should *not* be interpreted as providing grounds for, nor, in its concrete details, as being sanctioned by, the abstract perspective in question (or any other). The most that can be achieved in referring to substantive work when putting forward a particular theoretical or methodological approach is that the former can serve as an *illustration* of the latter. Illustrative argumentation, then, is my objective here. Before embarking on it, though, let me quickly set the context, starting with some relevant observations on the failure of the mainstream project.

A PERSPECTIVE ON SOCIAL SCIENCE AND EXPLANATION

The general untenability of the philosophical underpinnings of contemporary mainstream economics, and in particular of the latter's emphasis upon *deductivist explanation* with its associated *positivistic conception of science*, is, I think, becoming increasingly recognized. By deductivism, here, I mean the endeavour to 'explain' actual phenomena by way of deducing them from sets of initial conditions plus 'universal laws' of the form 'whenever event (type) *x* then event (type) *y*'. By positivistic science I mean precisely the attempts to elaborate universal laws of the noted event-regularity form. It is this conception of explanation and/or science which underpins the most common forms of econometric modelling as well as the 'economic theory' version of 'modelling' in economics. The limitations of the deductivist explanatory approach, and so of the formalistic modelling orientation it sponsors, turn on its central condition of relevance. This is simply that any system to which it is applied be *closed* in the sense that, within it, event regularities actually occur. The primary mistake committed by advocates of the deductivist explanatory approach is to suppose that the condition of relevance is everywhere satisfied. In fact such closures are extremely rare even in the natural realm, with interesting ones hardly occurring in the social realm. This observation, of course, is closely connected to Paul Davisons's repeated assessment that the ergodicity assumption underpinning much of mainstream modelling is largely irrelevant to the social domain.

A related deductivist shortcoming is a failure fully to recognize that successful science in any case has not concerned itself with seeking correlations at the level of events *per se*, but with identifying and understanding the structures, mechanisms, powers and tendencies that underpin them[1] (Bhaskar, 1978; Lawson, 1989, 1994a, 1997). Moreover, an acknowledgment of the relevance of this wider perspective, the acceptance of the fact of underlying structures and mechanisms as the primary objects of scientific knowledge, is fundamental to understanding those situations in which event regularities are sometimes uncovered in science, or more typically are *produced*. For basically, such event regularities as are significant in scientific understanding have been found to be restricted to situations wherein reasonably stable, but usually non-empirical, structures or mechanisms act in relative isolation. And outside astronomy such situations are found mainly to occur in conditions of experimental control (that is, in conditions of human intervention into, and controlled manipulation of, reality) – conditions that are rarely feasible in any meaningful sense in the social realm (see e.g. Bhaskar, 1978, 1979; Lawson, 1989, 1994a, 1994b, 1997).

I do not want to rehearse, here, the more detailed arguments against deductivism and the associated account of science or the structure of its results, but rather wish to concentrate on the alternative conception alluded to above. For in tandem with arguing against the former misconceived notions I have also been suggesting that social scientific endeavours, including economics, ought to aim, instead, to uncover the social structures (relations, rules, position, and so on) that underpin, condition, facilitate or produce, the identified phenomena of interest (see e.g. Lawson, 1989, 1994a, 1997). On this conception, indeed, economics can be seen to possess the potential to be scientific in exactly the sense of natural science. For just as the primary aim of natural science is not so much the describing of, say, patterns of falling leaves or movements in iron filings, as the identification of gravitational (or thermal or aerodynamic) and magnetic tendencies which govern them, so the primary task of economics can (and I am suggesting should) be to go beyond seeking to elaborate ever stricter patterns at the level of rates of unemployment, inflation or poverty, and so on, and to endeavour instead to identify (and perhaps to formulate ways of impeding) the causal mechanisms responsible (compare with Davidson, 1980, p. 158). In short, science, whether of nature or society, is *primarily* concerned *not* with such actualities which we may observe or otherwise experience (or even imagine), but with the conditions, structures and mechanisms or processes which underlie and govern them. Social *science*, on this account, is thus concerned with identifying the structures including relations and processes, that constitute society and economy; social *explanation* entails demonstrating how some configuration of social structures and/or mechanisms and processes came to make some social phenomenon of interest possible, and, indeed, produced it.

Now in arguing the case for this alternative conception of science and explanation in seminars, conferences, coffee-rooms, and so forth, I have noticed that certain responses are regularly induced – particularly among those who appear to be broadly sympathetic. It is with the addressing of these responses and the issues they raise that (in the context of a particular case-study to be elaborated upon below) I am primarily concerned here.[2]

A first such response that I have encountered, one that is almost always in evidence, is a querying of how any scientific or explanatory endeavour of the form here supported can get off the ground in the first place. If we allow that there may be few strict (including probabilistic) event regularities of an interesting kind to be uncovered or hoped for in the social domain, how do we know where to look if elucidating social structure is our aim? How can we begin to do anything of interest at all?

A second response is a demand that concrete examples be provided, particularly of possible *explanans*. More specifically still, in reaction to the fact that the emphasis of the position I defend is upon social relationships as, or as aspects of, explanations of social phenomena, the request is typically for further elaboration. It is not enough, it seems, to distinguish internal from external relations – which is usually all that is or can be attempted in highly abstract analysis.[3] There is a call for greater detail. And this *is* a reasonable request. Internal relations of the employer–employee type, for example, hold all over the place, yet the various activities which they govern are everywhere quite different. Is there ever anything more concrete about such relations to be said? In particular, can definite types of employer–employee relationships be distinguished?

The third response I want to consider here is perhaps the most interesting. However, it needs some elaboration. Broadly put, it is an expressed concern about certain central components or requirements of any adequate social scientific explanation concerned with elucidating social structure. I have argued elsewhere that social structures, unlike natural ones, not only facilitate human action, they also depend on it (Lawson, 1994a, 1994b, 1997). My driving home after work is facilitated by both the social rules which constitute the highway code and also the existence of gravity. However, the former, unlike the latter, depend in turn on human beings and their activities – if the human race were to disappear tomorrow, human society, its rules, relations and positions would go along with it. Social structure, then, is peculiar in that it is both condition and consequence of human action. This insight carries numerous implications for a putative social science of economics of which two, I think, stand out as fundamental.

The first of these is that the (relative) endurability (and/or eventual transformation) of social structure is something that will normally need to be addressed in any proposed explanation, and accounted for in terms of actions (including inactions) of human beings. If the existence of social structure depends upon always potentially transformative human agency then any longevity of structure is something that is made to happen, and it is this that needs to be understood. Notice that longevity *per se* requires definite social conditions with respect to natural objects as well. Planet earth, for example, has a definite space–time extension; its continuance rests on certain definite conditions. The same is true, for example, with regard to the existence of water on the earth's surface. Natural objects, then, are also only relatively enduring and space-time bound – just as, say, of the Roman Empire. The essential difference between natural and social objects is that longevity of social structures (but not natural structures) *always* depends upon human activity.

The second implication for social scientific research, is that there may be a need to identify how certain social structures and/or mechanisms of interest emerged in the first place – or, more generally, a need to investigate the conditions under which emergence and reproduction are possible. Thus while the existence and re-emergence of, say, water at different time–space locations on our planet is not particularly unusual, it seems unlikely that the Roman Empire will re-emerge. Of course, certain natural objects also require rather unique, or highly time–space restricted, conditions for their existence. But a reliance upon context-specific conditions seems always to be the case in this social sphere, with the consequence that very different social structures tend to come about and endure over different regions of time–space. Thus, the sorts of productive relationships that currently exist in, say, Northern Italy are quite different from those of, and seem unlikely to be reproduced in, contemporary Southern Italy, and are certainly not those of the same geographical region of the time of the Romans (or even of the pre-Second World War period); and so forth. The local context or conditions, then, appear to be essential to an understanding of why, or how, one or other set of structures including relations come about when and where they do.

The concern expressed in the third of the responses I am addressing, then, is simply that more detail on these components, or characteristic requirements, of social explanation be given. In seminar presentations committed to arguing the philosophical and general explanatory advantages of a rather abstract social theory, I have found it difficult to provide illustrations that are sufficiently detailed to be illuminating. Although concrete examples are requested regularly, they typically warrant more time for detail than is available.

Basically, then, the general problem I am alluding to which is manifest in all three of the noted 'responses', is the practical difficulty noted at the outset of combining a contribution that is pitched at a highly abstract level, and primarily oriented to elaborating a specific theory of ontology, with substantive analyses that are sufficiently concrete to be illustrative of the abstract theory in question. I recognize that, to date, I have opted for emphasizing the former, necessitating a relative neglect of the latter. I wish now to take the opportunity provided by this forum to rectify this. Specifically, I take the opportunity to *illustrate* central aspects of the abstract approach I have elsewhere defended by going through them in the context of a particular concrete case study.

Which study, however, should I focus upon? Although there are several that come to mind I hope I will be excused for drawing upon work that I myself have been involved with. In truth, I feel some compulsion to do so. For, along with an apparent hostility to methodology which emanates from many quarters of the economic's academy, there is a view, frequently expressed, that anyone presumptuous enough to offer suggestions bearing upon the conduct of economics should herself or himself be seen to follow such suggestions first. Indeed, when recently the UK Royal Economics Society allowed a debate in its Newsletter on the advantages and limitations of methodology in economics, it simultaneously reprinted, more or less without comment, the following statement by Irving Fisher to this effect contained in his 1932 Presidential Address to the American Statistical Association:

> It has long seemed to me that students of the social sciences, especially sociology and economics, have spent too much time in discussing what they call methodology. I have usually felt that the man whose essays tell the rest of us how to solve knotty problems would be more convincing if first he proved his alleged method by solving a few himself. Apparently those would-be authorities who are forever telling others how to get results do not get any important results themselves.

In short, according to the apparently influential view in question, any economist engaged in methodological reflection and criticism must be seen not only to illustrate their own approach (which is a reasonable request), but also actually to practice what it is that he or she, so to speak, preaches.

Although I reject the logic of this assessment (as I think will anyone who reflects upon it) I nevertheless recognize that it has proven (and continues) to be persuasive. I thus comply by attempting, in what follows to illustrate the sort of explanatory mode of analysis and conception of science and explanation above briefly elaborated, through drawing upon research with which I have previously been involved.

GETTING THINGS GOING – THE ROLE OF 'STYLIZED FACTS'

Now if, according to the perspective I am maintaining, the primary objective of science is to uncover some relatively enduring set of structures and/or mechanisms, how, first of all, can this be achieved in the social realm if we do not have access to event regularities which may indicate that something systematic is going on? This is the concern of the first 'response' noted above.

The point of relevance here is that the noted inability to engineer situations in which social structures or mechanisms can be insulated from the effects of other mechanisms does not rule out the possibility that the effects of some or other mechanism will come to dominate all others and to an extent 'shine through', at least over limited regions of time-space. In other words, the range of possible configurations at the level of events or actual outcomes is not exhausted by the polar extremes of strict (including probabilistic) event regularities on the one hand (that is the situation presupposed by, for example, deductivist endeavours including 'economic theory' and econometrics) and a non-systematic, inchoate, unintelligible, flux, on the other. Leaves do fall to the ground *much* of the time; women are *concentrated* in secondary sectors of labour markets; the UK's productivity growth performance has quite *frequently* been lower than that of other European industrial countries over the last hundred years. All such *stylized facts*, that is rough and ready, or partial, regularities, suggest that, in each case, something systematic is going on, that some mechanism is shining through, that some structural explanation is called for. Although attempts to turn such stylized facts into strict event regularities (for example, the 'Verdoorn Law' relating rates of change of measured productivity in manufacturing firms to rates of change of measured output, etc.) have notoriously failed (see for example Stanford, 1983) the degree of persistence of the phenomena in question, of certain rough and ready regularities, suggests that in each case there is something of significance to explain, that some important set of structures is in place.[4]

Now stylized facts, meaning or indicating partial event regularities, can be expected at any level of abstraction or generality. If we consider the just noted, and widely observed, experience of poor productivity performance in the UK, for example, it is to be anticipated that any set of structures and/or mechanisms responsible will have been common to a whole spread of British industry – conditioning a tendency which is operative throughout much of the economy at large. Indeed, in an earlier study of this phenomenon (Kilpatrick and Lawson, 1980), it was suggested that a major explanatory factor is the decentralized system of collective bargaining and job-based worker organization which has been unique to the UK's path of development. But there was no suggestion made in that study to the effect that the identified system had penetrated to the same extent, or taken the same form, in every workplace – even if a specific culture of industrial relations had been widely experienced. Each particular workplace is influenced by localized supportive, counteracting and other tendencies so that, even if the overall pattern is significant, each local situation is different. Of course, this recognition no more undermined the explanation in question than the unique path of each autumn leaf undermines the theory of gravity. Moreover, it is worth mentioning that exceptions to 'stylized facts', or observed partial regularities, may also themselves, even if highly space-time restricted or localized, constitute 'stylized facts' – that is be broadly persistent as exceptions and indicate once more that something systematic is going on, albeit something systematically at odds with, or acting to countervail, whatever broader, more space–time extended, tendency is in play. Indeed, the case study I want to focus upon here conforms precisely to this pattern. It concerns a firm and specifically a group of employees that, in their behaviour, departed significantly from a second broader stylized generalization that is (or has been) widely reported.

BACKGROUND TO THE STUDY

The broader stylized fact, or partial regularity, in question, one that had been widely reported in the *Labour Market Segmentation* literature (see for example papers in Wilkinson, 1981), is that dualism or segmentation in product market structures often coincides with dualism or segmentation in employment conditions. The recognition that primary sector or 'core' firms have tended to support primary (that is, better) employment conditions, arose with the early focus of the segmentation literature upon the development of 'monopoly capitalism' and the bureaucratization of control systems, including the growth of internal labour markets (see Burawoy, 1979; Edwards, 1975, 1979). Monopoly capitalism emerged with the expansion of consumption of standardized products, enabling certain firms to break down manufacturing processes into small individual cycles of activity capable of conversion into machine processes or 'semi-skilled' routines. As these firms grew in size the task of planning and monitoring was also frequently broken down into routines and inculcated as specialized management tasks. The system depended upon holding demand for a product steady enough for large lot or continuous flow production, and was often achieved through acquisition or merger designed to obtain a degree of market control.

For such 'core' firms stability in product markets in turn tended to give rise to a stable demand for labour. Thus, in order both to minimize 'turnover costs' and to achieve high productivity from the workforce, these firms were frequently party to the formalization of rules and procedures concerning pay determination and internal promotion structures, thus creating an 'internal labour market'. In many cases, however, this structure was also, in part, forced upon employers by a larger and more organized workforce, as the latter attempted both to benefit from better pay and promotion prospects and also to obtain protection from the vagaries of the 'external' competitive market.

Now if at some general level, and for the sort of reasons just suggested, a broad correspondence between segmented product markets and segmented labour markets was widely observed, the phenomenon that I chose to focus upon in the research in question, one that I took to be in need of an explanation, centred on the experiences of a specific firm which, as noted, were systematically at odds with the above noted stylized fact. The firm I refer to is Pye of Cambridge and, in the rest of the chapter, I draw upon research I was involved with several years ago when I spent a good deal of time (ranging over a few years) visiting the firm, talking with its members, going through archives, and so on (see Lawson, 1981b).

THE FIRM IN QUESTION

The firm in question started up in 1896 when the Cavendish Laboratory in Cambridge, owing to a lack of funds, ceased to employ its workshop superintendent W. G. Pye. At the time it made scientific instruments on a small scale for schools and laboratories and was constituted in the shed in the garden of the Pye family home. By the mid-1970s the Pye Group of Cambridge employed more than 25 000 people around the world, had an annual turnover of £200 000 000 and was successfully involved in many fields of high technology production. It was, for example, one of Britain's largest manufacturers of electronic equipment, with products and services ranging from transistor radios and television receivers to national broadcasting systems; from microcomputers to process control systems; from single laboratory instruments to systems for monitoring pollution across large cities; from moulding, bonding and specialist engineering services to financial services and data processing.

Moreover, during the inter-war and early post-war periods at least, the firm enjoyed a degree of market power despite experiencing substantial changes in product and process technology. Over this period product demand was strong enough to facilitate the introduction of mass production methods,[5] and to some extent was stabilized through the seeking out of bulk export orders and through the securing of fixed government contracts (particularly in war time). In addition many products were invented and technological advances developed as a result of Pye's own Research and Development activities, thus enabling the firm to maintain market leadership in various fields. Thus, by almost any definition, over the period in question Pye qualified as a 'core' or primary sector firm.

Yet throughout the company's history, employment conditions were distinctly 'secondary' for the majority of the workforce. In particular wages were low, promotion prospects tended to be severely limited and, for most of the firm's history, there was little evidence of a trend in the bureaucratization of employer–employee relations. In the late 1970s (the time of the study) unions had only recently begun to recruit on a significant scale and membership in many of the plants remained minimal. Moreover the majority of the workforce were female; a factor which itself would have reinforced the secondary nature of conditions and skill status (Philips and Taylor, 1980).

Despite this situation, however, much of the work could reasonably be described only as skilled (Payne, 1971), (although the word 'dexterous' was more commonly applied) while workers invariably revealed characteristics typically associated with those in primary employment conditions: in particular they displayed a loyalty and commitment to the firm and a high degree of job attachment. The latter was reflected in the low turnover rates plus the numerous recorded instances of workers remaining with the firm for over 30, and sometimes over 50, years.

The phenomenon I singled out for explanation, then, is how it was that Pye managed over a longish period of time – right up until the 1960s at least (whereupon it was taken over by a large overseas-based multi-national) – to combine, successfully, a primary product market structure with secondary employment conditions, while the general tendency in the economy at large was for product and employment conditions to correspond positively?

Paternalism

The proposed explanation of the noted phenomenon, the contributory or conditioning factor singled out in the research in question as significant, was the emergence and continual reproduction of a particular form of employer–employee relationship at Pye, a form of relationship that had long been observed to be in decline in the UK economy at large. It is this I wish to elaborate upon here. In doing so I take myself to be addressing both the second 'response' recorded above (the demand for more elucidation of explanatory social relations), as well as the third (the request for more to be said on how significant aspects of social structure can emerge and be continually reproduced and/or transformed). From here on, in fact, I shall not make further explicit reference to the 'responses' in question, or indeed to the theoretical framework which induced them, but merely focus on the case study as illustrative of the explanatory features in question.

What, then, is the employer–employee relationship which, in the earlier study, was held to be in some part responsible for the maintenance of secondary employment conditions in a firm operating in a primary product market? The relationship in question is one which is often described in the context of industrial society as *paternalism*. The notion of paternalism in this context, like, but not to be confused with, patriarchy or patrimonialism, derives from the structure of authority within the family. In a patriarchal society people are consciously related by blood ties, with males being the dominant forces in family relationships deciding who marries whom, and with property passing through male lines. In patrimonial society property still passes through male lines, although people do not think of their social relationships exclusively in terms of family. With paternalism the patrimony does not exist; property no longer passes legally from father to 'son'. Instead male domination depends on the male's role as 'guardian' and 'defender'. Nothing can be guaranteed for the family, but it is the father's 'duty' to protect, and if his advice is followed and his judgement accepted the 'best' outcome for all will ensue. Similarly paternal firms adopt the role of judge and protector acting in the worker's 'best interests'. In this way they seek employee attachment, attempting to create a communal cohesion and stability from which to obtain high productivity. Essentially paternal employers attempt to join the family and work symbolically with themselves as the authority. And this – via its provisions of clubs, of sports, transport and nursery facilities, right through to its repeated presentation of its achievements as a 'family affair' (see below) – is exactly what Pye strove to achieve.

There are, however, important conditions which need to be satisfied before paternalistic structures can be established. As will be clear from the discussion below these depend largely upon the nature and conditions of the local labour force. However, even when employee identification with the firm is attained which is of the form that those encouraging paternalistic relations hope to sustain, there remain difficulties that are inherent to the paternalistic mode of control. By emphasizing the view that workers and the firm have a common interest, the firm induces an expectation amongst the workforce concerning normal employer behaviour. Deference is maintained as a result of accord between management behaviour and employee expectation; the latter being the result of customs, traditions, past experience and the existing situation. The problems for the firm arise when the employer is encouraged, usually by product market conditions, to act outside the realm of employee expectations. For example, paternalism at 'Casterton Mills' (Martin and Fryer, 1973) was destroyed by the prospect of large-scale redundancies brought about by the decline of the product market.[6] In other circumstances paternalism has been undermined in different ways; the introduction of labour-displacing technology being an obvious example.[7] It is because paternalism involves such contradictions that it is usually considered to be a declining industrial form (for example, Norris, 1978, p. 484). The interesting issues facing the original study, then, all appeared to turn upon the question of how it was that paternalism had come about and survived at Pye.

The Production of Paternalism at Pye

> Have you heard his strong voice?
> Seen his silver-grey hair
> Or heard of his judgement
> Impartial and Fair
> At our dances and socials
> He'll wear a clown's cap
> Now who could help liking
> A Boss like that
> To his cheery speeches we all heartily clap
> And agree that 'old Robbo's a jolly fine chap.'

Poem by a Pye employee published in the internal *Pyradian Gazette*, in January 1930.

The Firm's Contribution: Business Efficiency, Employee Welfare and Scientific Progress

How did paternalism first come about at Pye? The record suggests that from early on, management consciously sought employee identification with the firm by highlighting the latter's links with the local region and emphasizing its concern both with the welfare of the workforce[8] and with the community as a whole.[9] Thus Pye, like paternalistic Quaker firms such as Cadburys, Rowntrees, Huntley and Palmers, and Clarkes before it, attempted to create a local culture based upon social responsibility and concern for its employees: 'The supreme principle has been the belief that business efficiency and the welfare of the employees are but different sides of the same problem' (E. Cadbury, quoted in Child, 1969, p. 37). In addition to this approach Pye repeatedly stressed the importance to society generally of the firm's contribution to 'scientific and technological advancement, and the workers' role in that success. In this way Pye developed its own distinctive scientific culture.[10] In such efforts the firm's close links with the university were exploited. And in all of this phrases like 'the Pye People' or 'the Pye Family' figured prominently whenever the firm addressed, or referred, to its workforce. Pye clearly wished to be viewed as a paternal employer.

The Workforce and Local Conditions

The generation and persistence of paternalistic employer–employee relations at Pye, however, were also significantly conditioned by the nature of the local labour market, the source of the labour supply and by the social history, values and aspirations of the local people.

Conditions in and around Cambridge in the early part of the twentieth century left much to be desired. Writing in 1912, Rackon, for example, observed that:

> there is in Cambridge much irregularity of work and resultant poverty; there are bad conditions of life, with their inevitable effects of enfeebled health and child suffering. There is much charity and desire to help – to a large extent irresponsible and unorganised, and confided it is to be feared, only to one section of the community. There is also a strong forming public opinion that the relief of suffering demands a wise charity well organised; there is an awakening on the part of the public authorities of the ever-widening powers they hold for social betterment; there is a keener conscience as to conditions of labour and the wise and fuller training of the young. (p. 36)

Further out in the Fen villages the picture was one of poverty and complete isolation (Shipley, 1973; Chamberlain, 1978). Social historians have widely portrayed an image of the untutored, docile and tractable labourer when exploring the nature of the poorly serviced areas where people lived, and continue to live; areas where people work in small isolated groups in an environment where the church has inculcated strict attitudes to discipline and obedience.[11]

The image of the isolated rural labourer as being relatively deferential or docile is, given the nature of the environment, undoubtedly correct. However, it is possible to take this conception too far; and as a characterization it needs to be heavily qualified. Indeed, the history of East Anglia includes moments of particular turbulence.[12] Moreover while the, largely female, workforce revealed a high degree of attachment and commitment to Pye it is quite likely that many people adopted a basically pragmatic acceptance of the firm's paternalism. Thus the 'family-like' environment may have been particularly conducive, especially with the associated provision of welfare benefits and social facilities. It need not be the case that workers are unaware of a conflict of interest; just that measures taken by the firm to produce an environment conducive to 'identification' create the impression among the workforce that they are better off than they would be elsewhere.[13]

It is also probable that most employees were completely dependent on Pye for any work opportunity at all. Indeed, Cambridge provides a rare example of a town where planning policy has sought actively to deter industrial expansion within its confines and to allow only limited employment growth in selected villages round about (Sant and Moseley, 1977). For example, IBM were refused permission to develop laboratories for electronic data processing at nearby Fen Ditton.

Moreover, Pye's tradition of providing buses to carry people from outlying hamlets and villages to work in Cambridge is a further factor that is likely to have reinforced worker dependency on the firm. Chamberlain (1978) observed in Gislea, a rural village where people commuted to Cambridge for work, that 'bicycles are, for most of the women, the only viable means of transport. The women's choice of work is therefore restricted to those factories which provide their own transport' (Chamberlain, 1978, p. 22).

The fact that Pye was one of the few Cambridge firms to set up a day nursery run by qualified staff also undoubtedly meant that for some parents it provided one of the few opportunities for work that existed. Others have probably been attracted by the opportunities to partake in the various sports clubs that play in local leagues; the inter-departmental tournaments; the Pye annual sports day; the company annual outings and so on.

Thus, there are a variety of reasons why workers may have revealed a high degree of attachment to a firm such as Pye. If employees appear to adhere to an employer's specific world view it does not necessarily follow that they adopt it for their own; they may perceive that by doing so they are acting in their own material best interests. In other words the defining character of deference is adherence to a particular world view, it is not the reasons for this adherence which are important (Martin and Fryer, 1975).

Even so, the extent of loyalty and worker attachment at Pye suggests that, for many employees, identification with the firm were of the type that 'traditional modes of control hope to engender' (Newby, 1977, p. 72). It may even have been the case that, in part, the paternalist strategy was forced upon the firm by the workforce.[14] It is, of course, understandable that workers may prefer an image of 'industrial harmony'; may wish to believe that their employer is acting in their best interests (especially the person who has spent many years in the firm's employ); and may accept that 'business efficiency and the welfare of employees are indeed but different sides of the same problem'. This view will be more readily adopted if, for example, there is regular face-to-face contact between management and workers; the two possibly being on first name terms. Moreover, with Pye being the largest employer in the locality, transporting the workforce to and from 'sheltered' locations, the limitations on workers' access to information concerning alternative employment conditions and interpretations was also probably important. Norris (1978), for example, argues that because of influences such as these 'paternalism will only be found in a locally based form' (p. 47).

As noted above, however, even if employee identification with the firm is of the form that 'traditional modes of control hope to engender' the system may be unstable; paternalism appears to be a fairly fragile form. Factors which serve to reduce worker dependency on the firm, or provide alternative 'world views', or which force management to act inconsistently with employee expectations, may all serve to undermine it: workers' consciousness and organizational solidarity may form very quickly. In addition, of course, even when the structure in question is less fragile, it is never fixed – it always has to be reproduced. My question, then, was how it was that, in a period of rapid growth and technical change, Pye managed successfully to maintain a paternalistic structure, particularly during the inter-war and early post-war period? The question of social reproduction, as we have seen, is as essential to an adequate explanation of any social phenomenon as identifying the crucial structure(s) governing the phenomenon of interest in the first place. The ability to reproduce such an intrinsically unstable structure in times of great uncertainty and change is certainly something that required an explanation in the original study and warrants some mention here.

Managing Paternalism at Pye

At least part of the answer lies in the use Pye made of small independent units of production; small groups of companies which provided the necessary flexibility to accommodate product market variability. When, for example, a new product went into production it was not unusual for a separate company to be created solely for its manufacture. Moreover this invariably enabled workers engaged in producing a declining product to be redeployed within the same firm, thus alleviating potential stresses and tensions, while the majority of the total workforce remained uninvolved.

In this way Pye seems to have been able to satisfy its employees' expectations of job security, while continued use of small separate production units did not threaten the efficacy of face-to-face interaction between management and worker. Thus Pye steered a course which helped sustain the paternalist relationship and employee identification in the form that 'traditional modes of control hope to engender'. At the same time Pye obtained a fragmentation of the workforce which, in any case, provided a major obstacle to collective worker organization.

It does not necessarily follow, however, that Pye steered this course solely for these reasons. For example Burns and Stalker (1961) argue that a similar strategy has been widely adopted by electrical engineering firms because it is most accommodating to management re-organization necessitated by changing technology (p. 8). Others have suggested, for example, that 'optimal' plant size for achieving technical economies of scale is, in many cases, not very large anyway; and often corresponds to output levels well below many existing plant sizes (Pratten, 1971).

Even so, it seems probable that Pye's concern to maintain paternalistic relations with the workforce *was* an important consideration. Evidence bearing on this is provided by events which occurred at the outbreak of the Second World War, when Pye became committed to the 'war-effort'; both producing and inventing war-time equipment. At this time the firm strongly resisted suggestions by the Government that it build 'without regard to cost' a giant shadow factory in the industrial West Midlands. The reason given by Pye was that it felt it would be less able to control its workforce. The firm's own 'history' of developments (Pye, 1956) indeed highlights how, when it was important to 'get the best' from its employees, 'it was vital that individual characteristics be recognised, and that war workers should be handled in the small groups in which they could best operate. Pye knew that the vast productive capacity of Cambridgeshire could be used – so long as they were left to work where their roots had been established for generations'.

The result was the establishment of village industries all over East Anglia 'wherever there was suitable labour'. 'Numerous units were formed and soon the most complicated electronic equipment was being made in every corner of the County' including in people's homes. Thus by the end of the war Pye had 14 000 so employed. 'The company's reliance upon the individual, rather than upon mammoth factories, was never disputed. In fact, early in the war, Pye gained a reputation for meeting hasty "crash-programme" orders with unrivalled speed and efficiency.'

Thus when forced to justify its policy to the war-time government Pye concentrated on the need to maintain a paternalistic structure in order to achieve high worker productivity. Indeed it claimed to have combined the needs of 'efficiency' with 'the no-less-important social needs of the community'.

In the period immediately following the war the small village industries in some cases began to grow substantially. However, a balance was actively maintained between operating large 'efficient modern plants' and the needs of maintaining employer–employee accord. Thus in Pye's words 'People still lived where they worked and the craftsman's individual identity, which the company had always fostered, was not lost.'

In short, the maintenance of paternalism at Pye was not independent of the social, technological and competitive environment in which the firm operated. In particular, the highly decentralized system of production units which facilitated this form of management–employee relationship was undoubtedly influenced by various other factors and considerations. But the direction of causation was not just one way and the firm's desire to maintain this form of control seems to have been one important factor determining the firm's total course of development.

The End of Paternalism at Pye? – Philips Takeover

The importance of the paternalistic relationship at Pye in maintaining a committed workforce in secondary employment condition is also revealed by later developments at the firm. During the 1950s Pye followed a course of growth by acquisition including expansion into a number of overseas subsidiaries. In 1960 the Pye and Ekco Group merged and in the same year Pye took over Telephone Manufacturing Company. Finally, following a further period of growth, Pye acquired the Ether Controls Groups in 1964. During this period the policy of maintaining decentralized relatively small independent production units was adhered to and the paternalistic nature of employer–employee relations was largely unchallenged.

In early 1967, however, the existing course of development was finally and fundamentally altered when Philips, an international group with headquarters in Eindhoven, Holland, acquired a majority shareholding in Pye. As a result the following years saw significant steps in the rationalisation of Pye's activities both internally and with Philips. By 1971 the Company was able to report (Pye, 1971) various 'improvements' including a reduction in the number of employees, an increased productivity 'through improved manufacturing and management techniques' and a restructuring of production so that 'a number of manufacturing facilities hitherto operating from multiple sites were concentrated on single sites, reducing administrative changes and improving factory loading ...' (p. 6).

The process of rationalization and centralization continued with the announcement in 1975 of plans to construct a new factory which was to be the 'largest building project ever undertaken by the Company and represents the largest single industrial investment of its kind in Cambridge' (Pye, 1975).

Accompanying this course of development was a steady reduction in the size of the workforce, a growth of trade union membership, more frequent industrial stoppages and a continuous restructuring of the system of management. Finally, following a steady process of rationalization and centralization over 12 years, Philips took full ownership and control in October 1979.

The reaction of Pye workers and lower management was perhaps predictable. Employees described how 'the women who have worked with Pye since before the takeover wish it was possible to go back to the sort of place it was then, when everyone was more friendly'. Management too became concerned about the re-organization which accompanied centralization: the latter especially led to increased uncertainty over day-to-day operations due to 'communications problems' with each company now forced to report to Philips Industries headquarters in London. One manager even indicated a willingness to join the union if it were possible.

Indeed, among the numerous factors noted in the original study to be operating to undermine paternalistic control were: increased centralization which had generated friction amongst layers of management and produced less attachment to the firm's goals; the accompanying increased average plant size which had given rise to a less friendly atmosphere, threatening the efficacy of face-to-face contact and facilitating worker organisation; and the increased remoteness from the locality of the decision makers which had undoubtedly led to less concern about, or less awareness of, employee expectations of normal employer behaviour in management decisions. Thus, Norris's argument that firms whose economic base is not primarily local, but national or international, attach less importance to 'legitimating their economic power at a local level in a peculiarly local form' (p. 477) appeared to be borne out at Pye.

In the period prior to the Philips takeover, Pye experienced increasingly severe competition in various product markets and on several occasions suffered declining profitability. The Philips takeover may therefore be viewed as an unavoidable 'defensive' strategy. It does not follow, however, that the subsequent course of developments was inevitable. Nor when the original study was carried out was it apparent whether paternalism at Pye would be displaced by substantially increased bureaucracy, or whether in fact it was just being subject to metamorphism. It seemed that the interesting question to follow up at that point, therefore, was whether there were identifiable forces acting in the economy that were working to undermine paternalism generally. Perhaps it is of some interest here to reproduce the sort of considerations that seemed of consequence at that stage. Certainly, from the perspective of methodology here at issue, it seems more insightful to elaborate upon the sorts of background tendencies that at that time appeared to be in play, rather than to list the actual outcomes that, with the advantage of hindsight, can now be seen to have taken place.

The Possible Decline of Paternalism: Employer Behaviour and Worker Expectations

What view, could be entertained at the time of the study with respect to the prospects for paternalism's longevity or decline? It follows from the preceding outline that factors which may be assumed to undermine paternalist structures basically fall into one or both of two categories: those which elicit manager responses which undermine the existing accord between management behaviour and employee expectation and those which directly affect the nature of the local labour supply, its interpretations and its degree of employer-dependency. Now the hypothesized influences which fall into the first category stem from the 'trend concentration of capital' thesis discussed above (for example, Norris, 1978, p. 482). It was not clear in the late 1970s, however, to what extent recent moves towards centralization *could* be viewed as a progressive or dominant tendency in the industrial economies. Indeed there were important examples of large companies decentralizing their organizations and establishing smaller largely autonomous production units (Ward, 1977; Brecher, 1979). Moreover, evidence for the UK gathered by Prais (1976) revealed almost no change over a 40-year period in the share of output produced by the 100 largest manufacturing plants.[15] Yet while between 1958 and 1972 the average number of plants run by the 100 largest companies rose from 27 to 72 the average number of workers per plant fell from 750 to 430.[16] Thus large firms tended to become multi-plant organizations, controlling plants which, on average, became smaller.

While a progressive tendency towards centralization of production seemed, in the late 1970s, not to be born out by observation, important tendencies of a countervailing sort were being induced by developments in 'new technology'. The most important example of the latter was the development of micro-electronic technology, which, through its often acclaimed pervasiveness, seemed likely to effect a substantial restructuring of large sections of industry; especially as larger firms attempted to increase flexibility. This development appeared likely not only to give rise to increased decentralization in large firms, however, but just as importantly, to provide an impetus to smaller firms and so reduce concentration (Mok, 1979, p. 4;[17] Gerschenkron, 1968, p. 252). This point was being made, of course, not because small firms must necessarily establish paternalistic relations.[18] Rather it was being argued that the necessary conditions for the maintenance of paternalism were not necessarily being eliminated.[19]

The Possible Decline of Paternalism: Factors Influencing the Local Labour Supply

It seemed on the face of things, however, that the most significant challenge to paternalism was more likely to come from factors which directly influenced conditions in local labour markets and the nature of the local labour supply. The most important influences of this kind, in addition to the general process of industrialization[20] and the concomitant changes in living standards, stemmed from the role of government and state institutions. In particular, the development of a national system of welfare provision was, at this point in time, often highlighted in this respect; with the widespread belief being that it removed 'significant element of working class dependency on the local bourgeoisie ...' (Norris, 1978, p. 414).

However, Britain had recently experienced the election of the first essentially 'non-corporatist'[21] government of the post-war period, with the result that, at a time when a world trade recession was depressing people's living standards, the government was enacting policies designed to reduce working class dependency on the state. Actions aimed at running down the national health service, cutting local authority grants, reducing public transport, shifting the emphasis of sick-pay provision to the firm, abolishing or limiting protective legislation concerning existing maternity rights, minimum rates of pay, unfair dismissal and so on, seemed bound to increase worker's dependency on their employers both within the firm and as part of the wider community. Thus, conditions were being created in which firms were able to re-establish a more 'exclusively beneficent role' in the community (Payne, 1974, p. 38) whilst their 'concern' for the workforce became a further sign of benevolence rather than a statutory commitment.

A final factor highlighted by Norris (1978) which was thought to undermine paternalism was the 'extension of the national mass media into most homes ...' making workers less sheltered from external views and interpretations. Certainly this influence seemed important and warrants further research. Chamberlain (1978) in a moving study of women's lives in a 'Fen Village' indicated, however, that the effect of the media may, in certain locations at least, have been minimal:

> the decline of transport and work is recreating the old isolation. Only this time television creates an illusion of the twentieth century of progress, change and communications, anaesthetizing the problems of the rural community in decline. But little has changed basically – only details, not fundamentals. Particularly for women. (p. 22)

In short, it was not clear from the various ongoing developments or tendencies considered back in the late 1970s that paternalism could be viewed, necessarily, as a declining industrial form in the UK. Of course, as with all relations of control it was bound to be subject to continuous metamorphosis. However, the prevailing situation was one in which the sorts of factors usually supposed to bring about its demise were to some extent being countered.

FINAL COMMENTS

It is usually supposed that because, or to the extent that, a primary sector firm is able to support primary employment conditions it will choose to do so; the argument being that this is the only way a large-scale firm can secure relatively high productivity from its workforce and at the same time minimize turnover costs. Secondary sector workers are assumed, instead, to reveal unstable work habits, high absenteeism and poor work rates. The experience at Pye, however, suggests that a primary sector firm may be able to secure both secondary employment conditions and a reliable, highly committed and loyal, workforce by maintaining a paternalistic relationship with its employees.

Let me just re-emphasize or make explicit a few of the issues of significant here. First, the possibility of maintaining the paternalistic relation was found to be significantly dependent upon context – in particular upon the nature of local conditions in which people live. Any study that, as with most orthodox 'economic theory', is formulated without regard to time and place will, for that reason alone, often miss connections that are crucial to explaining some identified phenomenon. Not only is the social world constituted by, among other things, internally related totalities, but the internal relations in question may involve highly localized, as well as historically specific, conditions.

In a similar vein, if the relationship here identified as crucial has been referred to as one of a type, that is as paternalist, it should be recognized that where it is found elsewhere it is bound to take a different form, or give rise to phenomena that are significantly dependent upon (local) context. Clearly paternalism at Pye in the post-war period will have been manifest differently from paternalism in, say, Quaker firms, in the nineteenth century. Similarly existing forms will be different in Britain to those operating in Japan or Mexico and so on. Thus, even given similar technological and competitive environments in these areas, there undoubtedly exists a vast array of occupational structures arising from combined complex processes of management–employee interaction, national and regional values or customs, national state policies, and so on.

A further point is that the nature of the relation identified, and so the whole patterning of outcomes, has been found to be significantly dependent upon the conceptions of the people involved. At the same time, it is clear that, despite the inability of the hermeneutic tradition to accommodate such a possibility, in situations such as described in the case-study in question many of the fundamental conceptions that people hold can be inadequate to their situations; the employer–employee relationship especially is frequently inappropriately understood. In consequence, of course, given the misunderstanding that employees can have of the relationships in which they stand, it is not surprising that studies of the paternalistic relationship find the latter to be something that can be quickly undermined, that employees often react with astonishment and anger, once the objective circumstances (product market, technological, conditions or whatever) provide reasons for employers to act in a manner that is transparently inconsistent with what employees have come to expect.

Can research such as reported here though – conducted as it is at a relatively concrete, space-time restricted, level – contribute to general understanding? I think so. At the time it was carried out the emphasis of UK industrial relations research (my own included – Kilpatrick and Lawson, 1980) focused primarily upon the form and consequences of industrial conflict – upon the significance of the production, reproduction and transformation of modes of collective worker organization along with the effect of conflict, and its threat, to industrial development at large. An implication of the research briefly sketched here is that a comprehensive understanding of industrial development is unlikely to be obtained if the focus of analysis is *exclusively* upon moments of conflict and the development of collective organization, significant though the latter considerations undoubtedly are. In particular, relations of trust and cooperation, whether or not correctly or adequately grasped by all the individuals involved, need also to be identified and understood.

NOTES

1. For an assessment of post Keynesian economics by Paul Davidson which corresponds to this conception see especially Davidson (1980, p. 158).
2. I am aware that my detailing and addressing recurrent 'responses' in the proposed manner is somewhat unconventional. Still it may be useful. Unlike with criticisms, many of which can be quite unsympathetic, requests for clarification and/or elaboration are unlikely to gain publication. Yet it seems unreasonable to ignore the latter for this reason alone, while the former usually get addressed as a matter of course.
3. A relation is said to be external where each of the relata are what they are independently of the relationship in which each stands to the other. Thus two passing ships, or bread and butter constitute examples. An internal relation, in contrast, holds where at least one of the relata is what it is, and can do what it does, only by virtue of the relation in question. A magnet and its field, or landlord and tenant, or employer and employee are examples that come easily to mind.
4. I use the term *stylized facts* here because, in the post Keynesian literature to which Paul Davidson has contributed so much, this is the accepted way of referring to what I have in mind. However, literally interpreted the term *stylized* means something like 'to cause to conform to a style of expression often extreme in character rather than the appearance of nature' (*Webster's Third New International Dictionary*). In other words, a 'stylized fact' is presumably a partial regularity reformulated as a strict one, that is reformulated as an empirical 'law'. Post Keynesians, of course, do see their emphasis on 'stylized facts' as a matter of presentation, taking any reference to such a 'fact' to indicate the site of a partial regularity and no more. Thus the role of such 'facts' is basically to signal an empirical phenomenon in need of an explanation. Increasingly, however, we can see mainstream deductivist modellers attempting to legitimize their 'whenever this then that' formalizations as stylized facts. In the circumstances the intention in using the phrase is likely to become increasingly confused. It is for this reason that I now prefer the terminology of demiregularities, or *demi-regs* (Lawson, 1997). It serves as a continual reminder that most empirical facts do not take the form of strict regularities, that they express phenomena to be explained not the end-points of research or mere devices to be build into formal systems.
5. One of the earliest example was a portable receiver, the Pye 555. Its mass production was achieved in 1925 (see for example Bussey, 1979, p. 5).
6. It was not the redundancies *per se* that created this reaction; various paternal firms have had to reduce their workforce but have still maintained this type of control. Rather it seems that at Casterton Mills the redundancies served to shatter employees' expectation –

'... a job at Casterton was a job for life, and hardly any one whether management, staff, or worker was ever dismissed' (p. 72).

7. In this chapter we shall focus on factors contributing to employee identification with the firm. However, within the (family) characterization of the paternalistic relations there appears to be an inherent tension, and it is upon this that studies of paternalism have frequently focused (for example, Newby, 1975; Norris, 1978, p. 472). The supposed problem lies in the firm's desire to achieve differentiation between employer and employee on the one hand (as head and member of the family) but to achieve employee identification with the firm (as members of the same family) on the other. Certainly for most of Pye's history the firm was large enough for this never to be a problem. Moreover, it is not obvious that this problem has ever been intractable (Newby, 1977, p. 71). For studies of paternalist employers and/or communities see, for example, Bell and Newby (1973), Birch (1960), Corley (1972), Davidoff (1974), Martin and Fryer (1973, 1975), Genovese (1974), Lane and Roberts (1971), McLaurin (1971).

8. Pye's apparent concern for the welfare of its workforce is best illustrated through the words of one of its own companies:

> And what of the people who make Pye receivers? The welfare of both male and female employees is at all times a very real concern of the Company. While at work their comfort and health has been studied to practical effect, but interest does not stop there. Industrial welfare as some modern manufacturers can interpret it can become a conception of far-reaching social purpose in conducing to the happiness of the work people. And, let it be said, happy workers are always the most efficient ...

So it is that, with one of the finest of modern radio factories and with a loyal and efficient staff, Pye, although not 'born great' have achieved greatness in their particular field (Pye, 1932).

9. Thus Payne (1974), for example, is impressed how:

> Pye through their Trust Fund help many registered charities appealing to them each year as well as needy former company employees. They have always been particularly keen to help old people, and various old people's homes in the city have been beneficiaries: Cancer Relief, the mentally handicapped, the RNLI flag day and the YMCA appeal are just some of the causes which have been helped. The university as a registered charity has received gifts earmarked for research. National appeals and national disaster funds are also considered by the board of trustees.
>
> That Pye are attuned to their changing role in the community is clear from their decision to appoint a community relations officer ... (p. 39).
>
> The company is also fond of pointing out that because of the nature of electronics production, Cambridge need have no fears of any environmental pollution. Both the atmosphere and the river is spared.
>
> Moreover the firm has gone so far as to promise the town – or rather the university – 'not to deface with an industrial monster a beautiful city which had given so much over the years to the Company' (Pye, 1956). Instead expansion was planned in small individual units.

10. Thus, for example, Pye's record especially concerning radio and TV or in wartime production was repeatedly singled out for attention, and various publications detailing the firm's history of success were distributed to the workforce. (See References for examples.) At the same time the repeatedly acclaimed 'tradition of precision manufacturing' associated with the firm was frequently presented to the workforce as something to which all members of the firm – 'the Pye Family' – should be proud. Thus, for example, it is noted how 'Pye employees made a great contribution to the war effort in World War II in providing desperately needed communications equipment of the Armed Forces ...' (Pye, 1978, p. 3) and elsewhere that '... the true strength of the Company built up over the years, lay in the special skills and crafts of its work people who have an intense pride in what they are doing ...' (Pye, 1962, p. 1).

Presumably the not infrequent visits to the firm by well-known 'dignitaries' including members of the royal family – events highlighted in internal Pye publications (e.g. Pye, 1932) – served as a means to strengthen any sense of pride and attachment.

11. There existed, however, a separation between attendance at church (Anglican) and chapel (Baptist) corresponding to some extent to social divisions. However, Blythe (1969) notes how chapel and church in an East Anglian village 'managed to practise ecumenicism for years' (p. 66). One 71-year-old farm-worker even told how his family would attend both: 'People believed in religion then which I think was a good thing because if we hadn't got religion there would have been a revolution. Nobody would have stuck it. Religion disciplined us and gave us the strength to put up with things' (p. 36).

12. These include the agrarian 'swing' riots of the early nineteenth century; the struggles for unionisation at the time of Joseph Arch's Agricultural Workers Union in the 1870's; and the struggles for unionization and better pay and conditions during the 1920s, culminating in the 1923 strike. However, all were brutally suppressed which must have had an impact on people's attitudes. A similar image of the Southern US cotton textile worker as a docile and tractable labourer has recently been convincingly criticised by Mclaurin (1971). He shows that paternalism survived in Southern textile mills not because the operators were satisfied or uneducated or subservient to mill management, but because management took to the offensive:

> Forced into the mills by economic necessity, the operative slowly began to adjust to industrialisation and to attempt to improve his newly acquired position. By playing on the operatives' old fear of the Negro, exploiting his xenophobia and using his individualism while ruthlessly applying the concepts of Social Darwinism through the paternalistic mill village system management defeated all such attempts. (p. xviii)

13. Certainly they will have felt better off than if working in the field gangs on the farms.

14. An employer in a second, smaller, Cambridge electronics firm in fact insisted that it was the workforce that 'forced' him into a paternal role and not vice versa.

15. 'Largeness' or 'smallness' here refers to the number of employees rather than the value of assets or size of turnover and so on, although the three variables seem to be highly related.

16. This and similar supportive evidence is also analysed, for example, in Hughes and Singh (1980).

17. Mok, for example, argued explicitly that 'small business will get a new impetus. In the old days, technological innovation was possible only at a certain minimal size, as in chemicals or oil. In the future small batch production – a strong point in British industry – will benefit from technology as well as the big firms used to do, so that we might see split-ups of British Leyland into Austin, Morris, Jaguar and the like!'

18. This point is made, for example, in a study by Curran and Stanworth (1978). As one worker in their study said: 'In a large firm you're just a number – in a small firm you're just a name.'

19. There was, of course, much evidence that small firms frequently adopted paternalistic policies, as was clear from the submissions to the Bolton Committee Report (1971), for example.

20. Including the proletarianization of the workforce.

21. The term 'corporatist' is here interpreted as, for example, in Harris (1972).

REFERENCES

Bell, C. and Newby, H. (1973), 'The Sources of Variation in Agricultural Workers' Images of Society', *Sociological Review*, **21**, 2.

Bhaskar, R. (1978), *A Realist Theory of Science*, 2nd edn, Harvester Press.

Birch, A.H. (1960), *Small Town Politics*, Oxford: Oxford University Press.

Blythe, A. (1969), *Akenfield*, Harmondsworth, Middx: Penguin.

Bolton (1971), 'Report of the Committee of Inquiry on Small Firms', Cmmd. 4811, London: HMSO.

Brecher, J. (1979), 'Roots of Power: Employers and Workers in the Electrical Products Industry' in A. Simbalist, *Case Studies on the Labour Process*, New York and London: Monthly Review Press.

Burawoy, M. (1979), *Manufacturing Consent*, Chicago and London: University of Chicago Press.

Burns, T. and Stalker, G.M. (1961), *The Management of Innovation*, London: Tavistock Publications.

Bussey, G. (1979), *The Story of Pye Wireless*, Pye Ltd.

Chamberlain, M. (1978), *A Portrait of Women in an English Village: Fenwomen*, London: Virago.

Child, J. (1969), *British Management Thought*, London: Allen and Unwin.

Corley, T.A.B. (1972), *Quaker Enterprise in Biscuits: Huntley and Palmers of Reading 1822–1972*, London: Hutchinson.

Curran, J. and Stanworth, S. (1978), 'Some Reasons Why Small Is Not Always Beautiful', *New Society*, December.

Davidoff, L. (1974), 'Mastered for Life: Servant Wife and Mother in Victorian and Edwardian England', *Journal of Social History*.

Davidson, P. (1972), 'Money and the Real World', *The Economic Journal*, **82**, March, 101–15.

Davidson, P. (1978), *Money and the Real World*, 2nd edn, London: Macmillan.

Davidson, P. (1980), 'Post Keynesian Economics', *The Public Interest: Special Edition*, reprinted in *The Crisis in Economic Theory*, edited by D. Bell and I. Kristol, New York: Basic Books.

Davidson, P. (1992), *International Money and the Real World*, rev. edn, London: Macmillan.

Davidson, P. (1996), 'Reality and Economic Theory', *Journal of Post Keynesian Economics*, **18**, (4), 479–508.

Edwards, R.E. (1975), 'The Social Relations of Production in the Firm and Labour Market Structure', *Politics and Society*, **5**, 83–108.

Edwards, R.E. (1979), *Contested Terrain*, New York: Basic Books.

Genovese, E. (1974), *Roll, Jordan Roll*, New York: Pantheon.

Gerschenkron, A. (1968), *Continuity in History and Other Essays*, Cambridge, Mass: Harvard University Press.

Harris, N. (1972), *Competition and the Corporate Society: British Conservatives, the State and Industry, 1945–1964*, London: Methuen.

Hughes, A. and Singh, A. (1980), 'Mergers, Concentration, and Competition in Advanced Capitalist Economies: An International Prospective' in *The Causes and Effects of Mergers: An International Comparative Study of Seven Nations*, edited by D. Mueller, chapter 1.

Lane, A. and Roberts, K. (1971), *Strike at Pilkington's*, London: Fontana.

Kilpatrick, A. and Lawson, T. (1980), 'On the Nature of Industrial Decline in the UK', *Cambridge Journal of Economics*, **4**, March, 85–102; reprinted in D. Coates and J. Hillard, *The Economic Decline of Modern Britain*, edited by C. Feinstein, Harvester Press, 1986; also reprinted in *The Economic Development of Modern Europe Since 1870*, Cheltenham, UK and Lyme, US: Edward Elgar, forthcoming.

Lawson, T. (1981b), 'Paternalism and Labour Market Segmentation Theory' in *Dynamics of Labour Market Segmentation*, edited by F. Wilkinson, London: Academic Press, pp. 74, 66.

Lawson, T. (1989), 'Abstraction, Tendencies and Stylized Facts: A Realist Approach to Economic Analysis', *Cambridge Journal of Economics*, March, 1989 reprinted in *Kaldor's Political Economy*, edited by T. Lawson, G. Palma and J. Sender, London, Academic Press, 1989; also reprinted in *Real Life Economics: Understanding Wealth Creation*, edited by P. Ekihs and M. Max-Neef, London and New York: Routledge, 1992.

Lawson, T. (1994a), 'A Realist Theory for Economics' in *New Directions in Methodology*, edited by R. Backhouse, London: Routledge.

Lawson, T. (1994b), 'The Nature of Post Keynesianism and its Links to other Traditions', *Journal of Post Keynesian Economics*, **16**, (4), 503–39.

Lawson, T. (1997), *Economics and Reality*, London: Routledge.

Martin, R. and Fryer, R.M. (1973), *Redundancy and Paternalist Capitalism*, London: Allen and Unwin.

Martin, R. and Fryer, R.M. (1975), 'The Deferential Worker?' in *Working Class Images of Society*, edited by M.I.A. Bulmer, London: Routledge and Kegan Paul.

Mclaurin, M.A. (1971), *Paternalism and Protest*, Connecticut: Greenwood Publishing Corporation.

Mok, A. (1979), 'Technological Innovation and Industrial Relations in the 1980's', Working Paper 162, University of Aston Management Centre.

Newby, H. (1975), 'The Deferential Dialectic', *Comparative Studies in Society and History*, **17**, 139–64.

Newby, H. (1977), 'Paternalism and Capitalism' in *Industrial Society: Class Cleavage and Control*, edited by A. Scase, London: Allen and Unwin.

Norris, G.M. (1978), 'Industrial Paternalist Capitalism and Local Markets', *Sociology*, **12**, (3), 469–89.

Payne, S. (1971), 'Production-line Blues', *Cambridge Evening News*, October.

Payne, S. (1974), 'Social Responsibility in Industry: Pye of Cambridge', *Care*, **3**, (3), March, 35, 39.

Philips, A. and Taylor, B. (1980), 'Sex and Skill: Notes Towards a Feminist Economics', *Feminist Review*, No. 6, pp. 79, 89.

Prais, S. (1976), *The Evolution of Giant Firms in Britain*, Cambridge: Cambridge University Press.

Pratten, C. (1971), *Economies of Scale in Manufacturing Industry*, Cambridge: Cambridge University Press.

Pye (1932), *Pye Radio Works – Cambridge: A Record of Achievement*, Cambridge: Pye Radio Ltd.

Pye (1956), *The Story of Pye*, Cambridge: Pye Ltd.

Pye (1962), *Scientific Instrument Centre*, W.G. Pye and Co. Ltd.

Pye (1971), 'Annual Report', Pye Holdings Ltd., Pye of Cambridge Ltd.

Pye (1975), 'Annual Report', Pye Holdings Ltd., Pye of Cambridge Ltd.

Pye (1978), *Employee Handbook*, Pye Telecommunications Ltd.

Rackon, C.D. (1912), 'Cambridge' in *Social Conditions in Provincial Towns*, edited by M. Bosanquet.

Sant, M. and Moseley, M. (1977), *Industrial Development of East Anglia*, London: GEO Books.

Shipley, C. (1973), 'Living Down a Fenland Drove: Women's Role at the Turn of the Century', *Cambridge and Huntingdon and Peterborough Life*, January, pp. 26, 27.

Ward, C. (1977), *Small Industries and Industrial Villages* in *The Politics of Technology*, edited by F. Boyles, D. Elliot and R. Roy, London: Longman.

Wilkinson, F.W. (ed.) (1981), *The Dynamics of Labour Market Segmentation*, London: Academic Press.

3. Rhetoric, paradigms and the relevance of the aggregate production function[1]

J.S.L. McCombie

INTRODUCTION

Paul Davidson is without doubt one of the foremost post Keynesians, as his numerous books and collections of essays (Davidson, 1990, 1991) bear eloquent testimony. But the importance of his role in establishing the *Journal of Post Keynesian Economics* (*JPKE*) and his editorship, initially with Sidney Weintraub, of the *Journal* should not be overlooked.[2] It is becoming increasingly appreciated that there is not a free market in ideas, where only the fittest survive. The academic market-place is more oligopolistic and dominated by the editors of the academic journals and their selected referees. Ideas, no matter how important, will not necessarily win through on their own merit. Much depends upon the paradigm within which they are written and their acceptability to the ideology of, especially, the editors of the key academic journals. It is here that the *JPKE* has performed such an important role. It has established itself as one of the most prestigious outlets for many views that are critical of, or unacceptable to, the mainstream orthodoxy, and which in other circumstances may well have gone unaired.

What determines whether a particular article becomes influential or, regardless of its intrinsic merit, becomes relegated, unread, to the library shelves has recently been addressed in terms of rhetorical analysis (McCloskey, 1985). The purpose of this chapter is to examine why some fundamental criticisms of the aggregate production function have been almost totally ignored in the literature. This is of particular interest as a good case could be made out for following Mendershausen's advice (although not necessarily for the same reasons) of nearly 60 years ago that the aggregate production function should be 'consigned to the wastepaper basket' (cited by Douglas, 1976).

There are two serious problems with the aggregate production function – so serious that the whole concept is deeply flawed. First, there is the 'aggregation problem' (Fisher, 1992). Secondly, there is the obstacle that, because of the underlying accounting identity, empirical estimation of the production function using value data cannot provide an independent test of its existence. Yet while both these shortcomings have been known for decades, they are either barely mentioned or totally ignored in the literature where aggregate production functions are discussed.

Here, I investigate why this is the case, drawing on recent developments in the methodology of economics and, in particular, on rhetorical analysis (McCloskey, 1985) and Kuhn's (1970) paradigms or disciplinary matrices. The latter has, in some quarters, become regarded as rather prematurely passé.

AGGREGATION AND THE PRODUCTION FUNCTION

Work on the conditions for the successful aggregation of micro-production functions suggests that they are so restrictive as to render the concept of the aggregate production function problematic, to say the least. The difficulties that aggregation poses for the aggregate production function have been known for a long time, and date from the 1940s (May, 1946, 1947; Nataf, 1948). Subsequent work includes Joan Robinson (1953–54), Solow (1955–56) and the research of Fisher (1969, 1992). Nor has there been an absence of warnings to the profession. Walters (1963a, p. 11), in a classic study of production and cost functions, came to the oft-cited conclusion that:

> After surveying the problems of aggregation one may easily doubt whether there is much point in employing such a concept as an aggregate production function. The variety of competitive and technological conditions we find in modern economies suggests that we cannot approximate the basic requirements of sensible aggregation except, perhaps, over firms in the same industry or for narrow sections of the economy.

More recent work on the aggregation problem has not altered this conclusion: 'Such results show that the analytic use of such aggregates as "capital", "output", "labour" or "investment" as though the production side of the economy could be treated as a single firm is without sound foundation' (Fisher, 1987, p. 55). While the conditions of successful aggregation are matters of logic or formal proof, whether or not the problems are sufficiently serious to warrant the abandonment of the use of the aggregate production function is a subjective matter. As Fisher continued in the above quotation, the aggregation problem 'has not discouraged macroeconomists from continuing to work in such terms'. A good example of this is Walters (1963b, p. 425) who, in the same year as publishing his survey cited above, also published the results of estimating an aggregate production function using

US time-series data. He justified this exercise on the grounds that 'there is no doubt that it is useful to rationalize data along these lines'.

The main reason must be that the aggregate production function 'works', in that statistical estimations generally (although not always) give close fits to the data and plausible values of the parameters. For example, the estimated values of the output elasticities are often close to the relevant factor shares. As Solow once remarked to Fisher, 'had Douglas found labor's share to be 25 per cent and capital's 75 per cent, instead of the other way around, we would not now be discussing aggregate production functions' (cited by Fisher, 1971). The empirical evidence has been interpreted as confirming the simple, not to say simplistic, neoclassical aggregate marginal productivity theory of distribution: 'A considerable body of independent work tends to corroborate the original Cobb–Douglas formula, but more important, the approximate coincidence of the estimated coefficients with the actual shares received also strengthens the competitive theory of distribution and disproves the Marxian' (Douglas, 1976, p. 914). However, as we shall see, this quotation is a *non sequitur*.

The defence of the use of the aggregate production function is usually based on the grounds of 'heroic abstraction', to use Samuelson's phrase. To quote Solow (1966), in a defence reminiscent of Friedman's (1953) instrumental position:

> I have never thought of the macroeconomic production function as a rigorously justifiable concept. ... It is either an illuminating parable, or else a mere device for handling data, to be used so long as it gives good empirical results, and to be abandoned as soon as it doesn't, or as soon as something better comes along.

Wang (1971, p. 97), for example, views the aggregate production function as an empirical law in its own right which is capable of statistical refutation. (See also Solow, 1974.) The same response was forthcoming from some neoclassicists with respect to the Cambridge Capital Theory Controversies – let the data decide whether the debate was, in retrospect, important. This defence was explicitly made by Ferguson (1971, p xvii.):

> Its validity [the Cambridge Criticism of neoclassical theory] is unquestionable, *but its importance is an empirical or an econometric matter that depends upon the amount of substitutability there is in the system.* Until the econometricians have the answer for us, placing reliance upon [aggregate] neoclassical economic theory is a matter of faith. I personally have faith. (emphasis added)

He then goes on to appeal to authority, citing the views of Paul Samuelson.

There is only one problem with this line of defence: as noted in the introduction, *the production function is not a behavioural concept that can be empirically refuted.* It is necessary to turn next to a justification of this assertion.

THE AGGREGATE PRODUCTION FUNCTION AND THE ACCOUNTING IDENTITY

The reason the 'aggregate production function' cannot be empirically refuted is that the regression estimates are merely reflecting the underlying accounting identity, namely $Q_t = w_t L_t + r_t K_t$, where Q, L, K, w, and r are value added, employment, capital, the wage rate and the rate of profit. (The argument applies equally to gross output.)

Thus, for purely definitional reasons, the estimation of a production function is likely to give a very close fit to the data, and factor shares *must* be approximately equal to the relevant output elasticities, notwithstanding Fisher's (1971) comment about Solow's remarks noted above. This close statistical correspondence has nothing to do with the validity of the aggregate marginal productivity theory of distribution.

This criticism was first put forward by Phelps Brown (1957) in the course of an extended critique of Cobb and Douglas's early estimations of the aggregate production function. His argument was buried in his paper and did not attract as much attention as it should have, possibly because it was directed at cross-industry regression analysis. Nevertheless, no less an authority than Joan Robinson commented in 1970 that the aggregate production function 'must have needed an even tougher hide to survive Phelps Brown's article on "The meaning of the fitted Cobb–Douglas function" than to ward off Cambridge Criticism of the marginal productivity theory of distribution'. This argument was formalized in a short note by Simon and Levy (1963), and later by Cramer (1969), again for cross-industry regressions, and it was not until 1974 that Shaikh extended the argument to cover time-series analysis. The whole issue was further aired by Simon in 1979. For expositional ease, attention will be confined initially to the Cobb–Douglas production function and time-series data, but any production function faces this problem.

Following Shaikh (1974), the value of total output (value added) at time t is defined as:

$$TC_t = Q_t = w_t L_t + r_t K_t \qquad (1)$$

where the terms have been defined above.

Equation (1) may be expressed in terms of instantaneous growth rates as:

$$\dot{Q}_t = \varphi_t + a_t \dot{L}_t + (1 - a_t) \dot{K}_t \qquad (2)$$

where $\varphi_t = a_t \dot{w}_t + (1 - a_t) \dot{r}_t$.

The variables $\dot{Q}$, $\dot{L}$ and $\dot{K}$ denote the growth rates of output, labour and capital; $\dot{w}$ and $\dot{r}$ are the growth rates of wages and the rate of profit; a_t is labour's share in total output.

The factor shares may, of course, change over time, which is why they have a time subscript. To begin with, though, let us assume that the shares are constant (that is, $a_t = a$). Furthermore, initially and for expositional convenience, it is postulated that $\dot{w}$ and $\dot{r}$ are both constant. But the argument in its general form does not depend upon either of these assumptions.

Integrating equation (2) with respect to time we obtain:

$$Q_t \equiv A_0 e^{\varphi t} L_t^a K_t^{(1-a)} \tag{3}$$

or

$$Q_t \equiv B_0 w_t^a r_t^{(1-a)} L_t^a K_t^{(1-a)} \tag{4}$$

where A_0 and B_0 are constants.

Compare equations (3) and (4) with the specification of the Cobb–Douglas production function with constant returns to scale, namely:

$$Q_t = A_0 e^{\lambda t} L_t^{\alpha} K_t^{(1-\alpha)} \tag{5}$$

where λ is the constant growth of total factor productivity and α and $(1 - \alpha)$ are the output elasticities of labour and capital. It may be seen that the equations are all formally equivalent. Under the assumption of perfect competition and the marginal productivity theory of distribution, the output elasticities should equal the relevant factor shares.

If, however, the equation:

$$lnQ_t = b_0 + b_1 t + b_2 lnL_t + b_3 lnK_t + \varepsilon_t \tag{6}$$

(where ε_t is the error term) were to be estimated, we should expect a perfect fit with the estimates of the coefficients b_2 and b_3 always equalling the values of the shares of labour and of capital respectively. This is because of the underlying identity which is given by equations (1) and (3). The coefficient b_1 will equal the weighted average of the growth of wages and of the rate of profit, namely φ. (The same argument holds if growth rates were used, which would be the correct procedure if the data were I(1) and not co-integrated.)

Since equation (1), $Q_t = w_t L_t + r_t K_t$, is compatible with *any* underlying production technology (for example, a fixed coefficients production function) or indeed with the complete absence of any well-defined production function, no inference can be drawn from the statistical results about, for example, the aggregate elasticity of substitution between the factors of production. Moreover, the close approximation of the output elasticities to the appropriate factor shares cannot be taken as providing any confirmation of the neoclassical theory of distribution, *pace* Douglas.

The argument may be generalized to the case where shares change over time, for example, where there is a CES production function, or a translog production function, with, for example, biased technological change, or, indeed, any production function (McCombie and Dixon, 1991; McCombie and Thirlwall, 1994, chapter 1). The reason why estimates of the translog production function do not always give a perfect fit is that although the weighted logarithm of the wage rate and the rate of profit closely follow a linear time trend, it may not be a close enough statistical fit. Thus, the estimated coefficients may be biased and have large standard errors. However, by choosing an appropriate non-linear time trend (Shaikh, 1980) or by adjusting the inputs for cyclical changes in capacity utilization (McCombie, 1996a), it should always be possible to improve the goodness of fit and hence more closely approximate the underlying identity.

It is necessary to amplify the implications of this. This argument does not mean that there is necessarily no underlying aggregate production function, merely that it is possible neither to test its existence nor to have any confidence in such parameters as the aggregate elasticity of substitution. The critique also explains the results of Fisher's (1971) simulation experiments which showed that the aggregate Cobb–Douglas relationship gives a very good fit even though the conditions for successful aggregation are deliberately violated, provided factor shares are constant (Shaikh, 1980).

RHETORIC AND ECONOMIC PARADIGMS

What is notable is the extent to which this potentially devastating critique of the aggregate production function has been simply ignored in the literature, notwithstanding that one of the critics, Herbert Simon, thought it important enough to mention it in his Nobel acceptance speech (in Lindbeck, 1992).[3] Blaug (1974, 1992), for example, has provided a succinct critique of the aggregate production function which he describes as 'measurement without theory', but he mentions neither Phelps Brown (1957) nor Shaikh (1974). Furthermore, he does not address the putative defence of the aggregate production function, namely, that empirical estimations of the production function suggest that the problem is not serious.

The critique is one of logic (a matter of 'the laws of algebra', as Shaikh (1974) puts it) rather than of subjective interpretation. Has it been ignored because the criticism is logically wrong or simply because the way it has been put forward has not been persuasive? Since the former is not the case, it must be the latter.

Recently, McCloskey (1985, 1994a,b) has argued that, to understand the development of economics, it is necessary to comprehend why some arguments have proved to be persuasive and others less so. This is the purpose of rhetorical analysis: not rhetoric used in its modern pejorative sense, but in the Aristotelian sense of 'wordcraft' or of an inquiry into argument. Using the techniques of literary criticism, McCloskey examines why certain papers have been so influential, including, interestingly for the purposes here, Solow (1957). Every economist practises rhetoric, whether it is in the form of a formal mathematical analysis, an applied econometric study or a more verbal analysis. Economics is a 'conversation'.

This view of economics as involving rhetoric, *per se*, would seem to be fairly uncontroversial. However, McCloskey goes further, arguing that rhetorical analysis is by itself sufficient and one can dispense with Methodology, with a capital M. This proposition has drawn, not surprisingly, a great deal of criticism from the methodologists (see, for example, Maki, 1988; Mirowski, 1988; Rappaport, 1988; Rosenberg, 1988; Hoover, 1995). There is not the space to discuss these views here. Nevertheless, to take one example, Blaug (1992), the 'unrepentant Popperian', seems to attribute to McCloskey the view that all econometric evidence and the predictive power of the model is irrelevant for theory appraisal. But econometrics is a part of rhetoric; it helps persuade but it cannot be the deciding factor, if only because of the problem of the auxiliary hypotheses.

But rhetoric alone is not enough. This may be seen by considering the question: 'What is good rhetoric?' It is one matter to identify the tropes in a passage; another to demonstrate that they provide good rhetoric. Of course, it is always possible to identify *ex post* influential articles, if only by recourse to the social sciences citation index. But as McCloskey (1994b, pp. 87–8) has so cogently put it:

> For students of science in the here and now it is naive to think that power, analogy, upbringing, story, prestige, style, interest, and passion cannot block science for years, decades, centuries. The naive view is that science is rational in a rationalist sense, that is, non-rhetorical and non-sociological, understandable in our rationalist terms now, not at dusk. The history and sociology and the rhetoric of science says it isn't so.

It is here that there is a shortcoming in McCloskey's approach, because he gives little indication of how to judge how and why rhetoric 'may block science for years'. The difficulty is that while it is easy to determine what is effective rhetoric in the narrow sense (for example, in terms of the number of citations and the development and elaboration of the arguments by subsequent scholars), it is far more difficult to ascertain whether this influential rhetoric has taken the subject up a blind alley. In other words, when is rhetoric, no matter how influential, what may termed 'pernicious rhetoric'?[4] Recourse to normative methodological canons might give us some objective criterion to enable us to decide whether economics has progressed, for example Lakatos's (1970) Methodology of Scientific Research Programmes [MSRP], but this has rightly been rejected by McCloskey (1994b, chapter 7). The only advice McCloskey gives is that competition among ideas will ensure that eventually progress will be made. In a revealing quotation cited by Mirowski (1988), McCloskey (1985, p. 29) argues that 'the overlapping conversations provide the standards. *It is a market argument.* There is no need for philosophical law-making or methodological regulation to keep the economy of the intellect running just fine' (emphasis added). As Mirowski has pointed out, there is a serious internal contradiction in McCloskey's argument. The sentence 'It is a market argument' used by McCloskey is a metaphor from *laissez-faire* (neoclassical) economics which he uses in defence of the dominant paradigm of economics, namely neoclassical economics. Just as impersonal market forces supposedly lead to the efficient allocation of resources (except for market failure) or the 'economic survival of the fittest' (Alchian, 1950), so the competition for ideas will lead to the survival of the most worthy. Thus, Mirowski (1988) argues that McCloskey, drawing on this metaphor, comes to the conclusion that 'if only economists would acknowledge that the persuasiveness of their arguments hinged upon rhetorical considerations, they would discover that orthodox theories now in the ascendent would be preserved, if not actually strengthened'. Yet it is precisely the modelling of capitalist economies solely as largely efficient exchange economies that many critics of neoclassical economics attack. McCloskey's metaphor has a serious self-referential shortcoming. (See Mirowski, 1992, for just one example where the so-called 'free-market of ideas' suppressed a conference paper unpalatable to the neoclassical orthodoxy.)

What is generally absent in McCloskey's analysis is any discussion of the context of the arguments outside of the text, *per se*. Here, the neoclassical McCloskey differs from Klamer (1984), who specifically addressed these questions in his *Conversations with Economists*. A useful comparison is with Lakatos's (1970) distinction between 'internal' and 'external' history. McCloskey confines himself to exegetical analysis or internal history. This is a major shortcoming because effective rhetorical analysis cannot be undertaken in the absence of consideration of social order and the intellectual climate in which the paper was written.

The problem, according to Mirowski (1988, p. 123), is that rhetoric is essentially inimical to the neoclassical paradigm:

> Of course, this would never do for his [McCloskey's] purposes, so in order to restrain and repress this tendency, McCloskey tried to restrict his definition of rhetoric to an atemporal consideration of the style of argumentation of economists independent of all historical context.

McCloskey (1994b, pp. 333–9) in his reply (with many interesting rhetorical twists – *argumentum ad hominem*, appeal to authority, and so on) misses the whole point of Mirowski's attack. It is not that Mirowski is arguing that rhetoric, *per se*, is in error; it is just the limited interpretation by McCloskey of rhetoric as merely style that is at fault. Thus McCloskey cites, *inter alios*, Milberg as an example of a radical use of literary criticism. But Milberg (1988) ironically bears out my above argument. Milberg uses deconstructionism to show brilliantly the ideological underpinnings of neoclassical economics present in the influential paper of Krugman (1979). Deconstructionism is a more recent development of literary criticism than that used by McCloskey. There are echoes of Mirowski in Milberg (1988, p. 36), when he writes from a different perspective that:

> McCloskey touches on but quickly avoids discussion of how language represents ideology. This is because he fails to acknowledge that language, and the meaning it creates, is a social construction. … Thus, while McCloskey correctly points to the active role of language in economic argument, he stops short of analyzing the social and unconscious dimensions of language.

Solow (1988a, p. 33) echoes some of these views: 'Some methods of persuasion are more worthy than others. That is what I fear the analogy to conversation tends to bury'. He raises the question, which McCloskey does not answer, as to 'what distinguishes a good metaphor from a bad one?' (Solow, 1988a, p. 34). But for Solow, a metaphor 'is not good or bad, it is more or less *productive*' (emphasis in the original). But a metaphor, and the accompanying rhetoric, may actually be damaging to the extent that it takes economics up a blind alley.

The deficiencies of reliance on rhetoric alone come out most clearly in McCloskey's discussion of the Cambridge Capital Theory Controversies, as Mirowski has pointed out. Agreement was reached in the mid-1960s that the possibility of reswitching and capital reversing logically existed and this was damaging to the theoretical foundations of the well-behaved aggregate production function (Samuelson, 1966). This consensus was not surprising, because the issues were essentially ones of mathematical proofs. For example, the claim by Lehavari (1965) to have proved that, under certain circumstances, reswitching was impossible was incontrovertibly shown by Pasinetti (1966), *inter alios*, to have been erroneous. See Harcourt (1972, chapter 4). (Lehavari's paper contained a mathematical slip.) Nevertheless, there was (still is) marked disagreement between the two camps as to the overall implications of the outcome of the debate. The capital controversies were seen by the post Keynesians of Cambridge, UK, as totally invalidating the notion of the aggregate marginal productivity theory of distribution (Harcourt, 1972, 1976). The importance of this was immediately belittled by some neoclassical theorists, such as Hahn (1975). The use of the marginal principle for factor pricing does not require the aggregate production function (true) which is only a pedagogical device (not true), as a casual perusal of any of the leading journals will quickly confirm. The parameters of the different functional forms of the aggregate production function are still widely estimated. Indeed, it is difficult to envisage what would be left of neoclassical macroeconomics if the concept of the aggregate production function were to be abandoned. For Cambridge, MIT, however, the result was merely a curiosum, and indeed even during the debate was not seen as being of great importance to neoclassical analysis: 'Nor was the debate, such as it was, a matter of central attention in the MIT department' (Fisher, 1992, p. xi).

McCloskey (1985) attempts to explain why, in spite of the logical contradictions Cambridge, UK, demonstrated, these arguments made little, if any, impact on the neoclassical economists. McCloskey is forced to conclude that the outcome of the debate was nothing more than a question of aesthetics:

> The combatants hurled mathematical reasoning and institutional facts at each other, but the important questions were those one would ask of a metaphor: Is it illuminating, is it satisfying, is it apt? How do you know? How does it compare with other economic poetry? ... The reason there was no decision reached was that the important questions were literary, not mathematical or statistical. The debate was equivalent to showing mathematically or statistically that a woman cannot be a summer's day. Yet no one noticed. The continued vitality of the idea of an aggregate production function (in the face of mathematical proofs of its impossibility) and the equal vitality of aggregate economics as practised in parts of Cambridge, England (in the face of statistical proofs of its impracticality) would otherwise be a great mystery.

As Mirowski points out, one would expect that rhetoric would shed some insights on precisely why the outcome was so inconclusive and would clarify the issues. 'There is no getting around it: Some parties are going to be criticized. Yet this is precisely the sort of analysis that McCloskey is not inclined to do' (Mirowski, 1988, p. 125).

The interesting point of the Cambridge Capital Theory Controversies is that they were about logical and mathematical points; and while there was some agreement on these issues, yet substantial differences remained over the implications of the debate. Cambridge, UK, saw it as much more than a mere technical point: it had implications for the appropriate way to analyse the whole functioning of the advanced capitalist economies (Harcourt, 1976).

For the neoclassical economists, there may have been logical problems, but the production function gives a good explanation of the output of an economy by the usual criteria of statistical significance (a point ignored by McCloskey). A complete explanation would require recourse to the sociology of knowledge. There is so much intellectual capital tied up in the production function that any defence is likely to be seized on with alacrity by the neoclassical economists. (After all, who is going to admit one's life's work has been based on a fundamental fallacy?) The effectiveness of rhetoric is a relative concept, being a function of the group to whom it is addressed. A neoclassical economist is likely to find an article written in the neoclassical idiom (agents maximizing objective functions subject to constraints) more plausible than, say, a Marxist who is accustomed to analysing the functioning of an economy in terms of social class, a concept that has no meaning for the neoclassicist.

The Cambridge Capital Theory Controversies were essentially about a clash of Kuhnian paradigms and, although in many respects the same economic language was used, there was bound to be a strong element of incommensurability. The combination of rhetoric and Kuhnian paradigms provides an incisive method of understanding the economic conversation. Kuhn's (1970) *Structure of Scientific Revolutions* was a major stimulus to methodological inquiry in economics, as in other disciplines. For example, it gave rise to such broad questions as whether or not it is possible to find Kuhnian revolutions – if they exist – in economics (the Keynesian revolution? the monetarist counter-revolution?) The intrinsic relativism of this approach was profoundly disturbing for some philosophers of science and indeed the Lakatosian approach of the MSRP can be seen as an attempt to rescue Popper in the light of Kuhn.

For Kuhn there are no canons by which we can judge objectively that science progresses; but, according to him, it does progress. If we look at two theories, Kuhn argues, it should be possible to tell easily which of the two is the more recent, so it may be inferred that science does progress. But it is impossible to give any objective criteria by which to judge theories. Lakatos, of course, does provide criteria by which he hopes to be able to discern the advance of science: the prediction of 'novel facts', and the replacement of one Scientific Research Programme by another with excess empirical content. The difficulty with this approach is that, if different schools of thought are to a certain extent incommensurable, there is no objective way of determining which one has excess empirical content.

The central tenet of Kuhn's work is that it is necessary to examine scientific practice to understand scientific endeavour. Indeed, Kuhn argues that if he were to rewrite the *Structure of Scientific Revolutions*, he would start with the structure of the scientific community:

[Paradigms] can be discovered by scrutinizing the behaviour of a given community's members. ... A scientific community consists ... of the practioners of a scientific
speciality. To an extent unparalleled in most other fields, they have undergone
similar educations and professional initiations; in the process they have absorbed
the same technical literature and drawn many of the same lessons from it. (Kuhn,
1970, pp. 176–7)

Each member of the community has been trained from textbooks that are
very similar to each other. This means that each member tends to respond to
arguments in much the same way.[5] The members of the community will
dispute the adequacy of a proposed solution to a puzzle – they will suggest
improvements, correct logical errors, but they will not question whether the
puzzle was worth doing in the first place. Moreover, 'the members of a
scientific community see themselves and are seen by others as the men
uniquely responsible for the pursuit of a set of shared goals, including the
training of their successors' (Kuhn, 1970, p. 177). Thus members of the same
community, for example the neoclassicists, are likely to be persuaded by the
same type of metaphors, if indeed they need persuading. The type of audience matters. To take an example: suppose, in a seminar, the presenter were
to write on the blackboard, as part of a formal model, the equations:

$$Q = F(L, K, t) = A(t)f(L, K)$$
$$F_K = r; F_L = w,$$
$$F_i > 0; F_{ii} < 0, \quad i = \text{either } K \text{ or } L.$$

This set of 'symbolic generalizations' (Kuhn, 1970, p. 182) would need no
justification, indeed no further explanation. As Kuhn notes, often such symbolic generalizations act as laws; in this case 'the laws of production'. But, as
he continues, they also function as 'definitions of some of the symbols they
deploy' (Kuhn, 1970, p. 183). Here, of course, it is especially $A(t)$, technical
change or total factor productivity, that is defined by the symbolic generalizations.

The disciplinary matrix protects economists from continually having to
question the fundamental tenets of their approach. Such fundamental problems as to what is meant by '$A(t)$' and 'K' may be conveniently ignored. This
does have the advantage in allowing puzzle-solving to occur without forever
becoming bogged down in fundamental conceptual problems.

Yet the danger is that in the social sciences, where empirical anomalies
(statistical results that conflict with the prevailing disciplinary matrix) can all
too easily be sidelined or explained away as problems with the auxiliary
hypotheses or with the *ceteris paribus* conditions, this can be a powerful
inhibitor of change or reassessment. Joan Robinson (1953–54) has put the
matter of symbolic generalizations with respect to the aggregate production
function with her usual eloquence as follows:

The student of economic theory is taught to write $Q = f(L, K)$ where L is a quantity of labour, K a quantity of capital and Q a rate of output of commodities. He is instructed to assume all workers alike, and to measure L in man-hours of labour; he is told something about the index number problem of choosing a unit of output; and then he is hurried on to the next question, in the hope that he will forget to ask in what units K is measured. Before he ever does ask, he has become a professor, and so sloppy habits of thought are handed on from one generation to the next. (The notation has been changed to be consistent with the text.)

THE ROLE OF EXEMPLARS

Given that symbolic generalizations are an important determinant of the disciplinary matrix, the question arises as to how members of a disciplinary matrix acquire the rules for acceptable scientific inquiry. In order words, what constitutes a legitimate puzzle?

Kuhn asks a slightly different question as for him the symbolic generalizations are 'uninterpreted, still empty of empirical meaning or application' (Kuhn, 1977, p. 464). The problem in this case is how scientists attach empirical meaning to them. The answer is not through the learning of any formal correspondence rules, but through a process of ostentation and of learning by doing. 'This is what the problems at the ends of chapters in science texts are particularly for.' The scientist (or economist) acquires experience of what constitutes good puzzle-solving through the use of textbooks and by solving the problems at the end of the textbook chapters. The latter Kuhn terms exemplars and, hence, textbooks play a vital role in determining the future shape of a discipline (Kuhn, 1970, chapter XI).

There is not the space here to examine in detail the treatment of the production function in the numerous economics textbooks, but a few examples will serve to make the point. Most students will be first introduced to the concept of the production function in a microeconomic textbook, since, after all, the production function is ideally a microeconomic concept. In the popular introductory textbook by Esterin and Laidler (1995), the student first meets the concept in chapter 11, 'Properties of the Production Function'. There is a brief mention of the difficulties of aggregation in a single paragraph, but these are quickly brushed aside: 'The results of the two input/output special case are both useful and often capable of being generalised, and therefore well worth the reader's attention' (p. 134). The student is then exposed to some simple exercises concerning marginal and average products (p. 170). The treatment of the production function in macroeconomic textbooks is virtually identical to that in microeconomic textbooks. See, for example, Dornbusch and Fischer (1994), with the exception that here there is no mention at all of the aggregation problem. This is true of even advanced textbooks, such as Barro and Sala-i-Martin (1995). Hence, the consideration of the production function moves seamlessly from the theory of the firm to the economy as a whole. The student progressively sees this as the best (only?) way of analysing, for example, the problem of economic growth. As Kuhn puts it: 'The student discovers a way to see his problem as like a problem he has already encountered. Once that likeness or analogy has been seen, only manipulative difficulties remain.' The rules of the game are acquired by demonstration; not by studying methodology. Kuhn borrows Polyani's phrase 'tacit knowledge' to describe this phenomenon.

But what can be almost as important as what is included in the textbook is what is left out. If it is not included, it cannot surely be very important, can it? To return to the aggregate production function, the fact that the criticisms of this concept are not included in the standard textbooks suggests to the student that they are not serious. This attitude then influences research papers, further reinforcing the belief that there is nothing fundamentally wrong with the aggregate production function.

This brings us back to the point made earlier: whether or not an argument is likely to be persuasive rhetoric will be partly determined by the audience to which it is addressed. It is not necessary to believe that disciplinary matrices are totally incommensurable to understand how different schools of thought can be seen to be 'talking past each other'.

THE RHETORIC OF THE AGGREGATE PRODUCTION FUNCTION

The production function has a long history and its empirical estimation dates back to the work of Cobb and Douglas (1928), although it is not often appreciated today just how hostile was the initial reaction to their work (McCombie, 1996b). There is little doubt that it was Solow (1957), however, who gave a major impetus to modern empirical work on the aggregate production function (Matthews, 1988, Prescott, 1988).

McCloskey (1985) cites Solow's (1957) paper as an excellent example of the role of rhetoric in influencing the acceptance of a particular set of arguments. Its impact was also enhanced by the fact that it was published immediately after the path-breaking papers on neoclassical growth theory by Solow (1956) and Swan (1956). Here was the demonstration that the simple theoretical models had an empirical counterpart.

So effective was Solow's (1957) paper that the substantial amount of previous work on productivity growth is now often overlooked (Griliches, 1996). The reason that it had such a great impact was the rhetoric of the paper. The fact that it used the aggregate production function (rather than just output/input indices) and explicitly used economic theory and the calculus meant it had a tremendous effect.

Solow begins the paper with the now familiar shared generalizations of the aggregate production function, $Q = F(L, K, t)$ and then introduces the more restrictive function $Q = A(t)f(L, K)$. After discussing the problems of attributing technical change to a shift in the production function, as McCloskey (1985, p. 85) puts it:

> Solow runs with it into a paragraph containing a little simple mathematics and a clever exploitation of the conventions of the economic conversation. By the second page of the article he has made his main point and persuaded most of the economists listening. He persuades them with the symmetry of the mathematics, and the appeal to the authority of scientific traditions in economics, and with the perspectival tropes: metaphor, metonymy and syndoche.

The metaphor used by Solow was the concept of the aggregate production function which 'asserts that the making of our daily bread is like a mathematical function. The jumble of responsibility, habit, conflict, ambition, intrigue, and ceremony that is our working life is supposed to be similar to a chalked curve on a blackboard' (McCloskey, 1985, p. 84). Put like this, it seems incredible that a function using only two arguments, K and L (together with a shift factor), can adequately represent the total output of an economy. 'Economists are so habituated to such figures of speech... to the point of not recognizing that they are, but noneconomists will agree that they are bold.' The metonymies are K and L. (A metonym lets 'a thing merely associated with the thing in question stand as a symbol for it, as the White House does for the presidency' (McCloskey, 1985, p. 84).) The use of the symbol K obviates the need for worrying about all the problems of the aggregation of such diverse capital goods as steel girders and personal computers. At least the use of such terms as leets, ectoplasm and jelly serves to remind rather more than K just how artificial the construct is. Indeed, as we have seen, the use of the shared symbolizations such as $Q = F(L, K, t)$; $Q = A(t)f(L, K)$; and $Q = A_0e^{\lambda t}L^{\alpha}K^{(1-\alpha)}$ immediately invokes a whole set of assumptions readily accepted by neoclassical economists and legitimizes their use without further explanation. Thus defining $A(t)$ as the complex phenomenon of technical progress is seen as a 'bold synecdoche' by McCloskey. (A synecdoche is a figure of speech in which a part is taken as representing a whole.) Here, the complex phenomenon of technical change is reduced to a shift in a mathematically simple function or reduced to an exponential function of time.

As has been noted above, the power of rhetoric is conditioned by the audience to which it is addressed. The Solow–Swan model opened up a whole new area of Kuhnian neoclassical puzzle-solving. The original exogenous assumption of a constant investment–output ratio could be endogenized in the utility maximizing Ramsey–Cass model, thereby satisfying one of the canons of neoclassical economics concerning the importance of optimizing models. Other puzzles were the optimal rule of growth, two-sector models, vintage models, endogenous growth theory, and so on. A paper has greater influence not only when it presents such opportunities for further work within the disciplinary matrix but also when it presents new results (or Lakatos's novel results) – the more counter-intuitive, the better! Models that merely tell us the obvious are not so memorable as those that do not. Solow's two papers certainly achieved the latter objective.

The counter-intuitive result of Solow (1956) was, of course, the finding that the proportion of GDP invested had no influence on the steady state rate of growth. In Solow (1957), the counter-intuitive result was equally 'startling' to use Solow's (1988b) words – 'gross output per hour of work in the US economy doubled between 1909 and 1949; and some seven–eighths of that increase could be attributed to "technical change in the broadest sense" and only the remaining eighth could be attributed to conventional increase in capital intensity'. This finding gave rise to the 'growth accounting approach' that attempts to whittle down the size of the residual (for example, Denison, 1967). (See, however, Harcourt, 1972, and McCombie and Thirlwall, 1994, for reasons why Solow's result can hardly be called 'startling'.) It should be noted that there was no mention in the above quotation of measurement errors and so on, which would make for poor rhetoric.

WHY HAS THE SHAIKH CRITIQUE BEEN SO WIDELY IGNORED?

I have already discussed how the disciplinary matrix sets the agenda for the research programme and how potential problems may be ruled out simply by being ignored. The question, though, arises why the Shaikh (1974) critique concerning the accounting identity was initially, and still largely is, ignored in the literature. At first glance, this is rather surprising as it appeared in the same prestigious journal as Solow's (1957) paper, namely, the *Review of Economics and Statistics* and not in some relatively obscure publication. One possible reason is that the critique may be thought to be limited solely to the case of the Cobb–Douglas, although we have seen that it is applicable to *any* putative production function. Another reason is the fact that paradoxically many time-series estimations of production functions either do not give very good statistical fits or show the estimated output elasticities differing considerably from the factor shares. This could have given the misleading impression that the production function was an empirical relationship, capable of being refuted. But it is likely that rhetoric again is a major reason, notably the effect of Solow's (1974) one page reply to Shaikh (1974). For example, Heathfield and Wibe (1987), one of the few textbooks to mention the Shaikh argument, simply comment: 'But see Solow (1974) for a critical comment' and 'For a rebuttal of this see R. M. Solow, 'Laws of Production and Laws of Algebra: The Humbug Production Function: A Comment' (1974)'.

Shaikh raised two objections to Solow's paper. The first related to the argument outlined above concerning the underlying accounting identity. The second was addressed to the specific procedure Solow followed in estimating various specifications of production functions (and one that was unusual to the extent that it has not been followed since). It was the latter point to which Solow's rejoinder was addressed and acceptance of Solow's points might well be mistakenly taken to be a rebuttal of the whole of Shaikh's argument.

There is little doubt that from the first sentence of Solow's rejoinder ('Mr Shaikh's article is based on misconception pure and simple') to the last ('The humbug seems to be on the other foot'), we find an example of an article that employs to great effect all the techniques of rhetoric. However, in order fully to appreciate the interchange, it is necessary briefly to review Solow's (1957) procedure. Solow starts with a general production function, differentiates it with respect to time, and uses factor shares to obtain an expression for the annual rate of technical progress:

$$\dot{A} \equiv \lambda \equiv \dot{q} - (1 - a_t)(\dot{k}) \tag{7}$$

where $\dot{q}$ and $\dot{k}$ are the annual growth rates of productivity and the capital–labour ratio.

The use of factor shares was justified by recourse to the assumption of the (aggregate) marginal productivity theory of factor of pricing.

Having calculated $\dot{A}$ using data for the US economy over the period 1909 to 1949, Solow then constructs an index for A taking A_{1909} equal to unity. This is then used to 'deflate' the level of output (that is, to correct it for the increase due to technical change) so that the production function is written as $q/A = f(k)$, where q is the level of output per head. Various specifications of this equation were estimated, all giving very close statistical fits (with R^2s of over 0.99). It was found that the Cobb–Douglas function gave a marginally better fit than the other specifications.

An early comment by Hogan (1958) pointed out exactly why these good fits were being obtained. It was simply that as the factor shares are roughly constant, then integrating equation (7) must give a Cobb–Douglas production function, for the reasons set out earlier. In other words, Solow's procedure is a tautology and the fact that high R^2 are obtained merely reflects this. Equation (7) is definitionally true and if $(1-a)$ is constant, then it can be integrated to give a Cobb–Douglas function, as has been shown above.

It is useful here to digress briefly in order to consider Solow's response to this.

Solow's (1958) reply to Hogan displays again all the hallmarks of persuasive rhetoric. His rejoinder is all the more emphatic for abandoning 'unheralded indirect speech', that is the conventional use of the passive tense in scholarly writing (McCloskey, 1994a, p. 324). The opening sentence sets a tone of both confidence and wit: 'Mr Hogan comes at me with a sugar-plum in one hand and a blackjack dangling from the other. It's a hard life and, since it is, I propose to do the natural thing: accept the sugar-plum and dodge the blackjack.' The essence of Solow's rejoinder is simply to argue that what Hogan pointed out is obviously true: so self-evident that it did not require elaboration in the original paper. There is a concession, but only a small concession, by Solow that he 'should have warned the reader explicitly that the method would automatically produce a perfect Cobb–Douglas fit if the observed shares were constant' (p. 412). True, the procedure was tautological ('how could the result of a chain of exact reasoning be otherwise?') but there are good and bad tautologies according to Solow. Since factor shares do vary, his approach is a good tautology. (If they were imposed as a constant, it would be a bad tautology, because this would have been the same as assuming a Cobb–Douglas production function in the first place and so there would be no point in estimating the latter.) It is a useful exercise to determine what the form of the production function might take. Thus, the procedure does tell us something useful if only that 'if the profile of calculated shifts were grossly implausible, one would conclude that a simple model was being asked to bear too heavy a weight' (Solow, 1958, p. 412). Presumably this would be the case if the shift was generally negative.

Hogan had already anticipated this as a likely reply from Solow. But the point Hogan was making was that the observed shares varied within a very narrow range so, given the tautological nature of the procedure (whether good or bad), it was not surprising that the R^2 was near unity. To the extent that the reader was likely to be impressed by the good statistical fits of the various specifications (a high R^2 and t-values are persuasive for most economists), this was an important point.

Hogan concluded his comment by writing that 'the plain fact is that we could insert any set of random numbers in the capital stock series and still get a production function, net of technical progress, with the same close fit'. Shaikh (1974) seems to have followed up this comment and constructed a hypothetical data set with the property that (a) shares were roughly constant and (b) the plot of productivity against the capital–labour ratio traced out the word HUMBUG. He then followed Solow's procedure in estimating a Cobb–

Douglas production function. Because of assumption (a), this hypothetical 'production function' inevitably gave a good statistical fit to the data.

The effectiveness of Solow's (1974, p. 121) reply can be judged from the following two opening paragraphs:

> Mr Shaikh's article is based on misconception pure and simple. The factor-share device of my 1957 article is in no sense a *test* of aggregate production functions or marginal productivity or of anything else. It merely shows how one goes about interpreting given time series if one starts by *assuming* that they were generated by a production function and that competitive marginal-product relations apply. Therefore, it is only not surprising but it is exactly the point that if factor shares were exactly constant the method would yield an exact Cobb-Douglas and tuck everything else into the shift factor. This is what one would *want* such a method to do.
>
> The point is even simpler than Mr Shaikh makes it out to be. It is hardly a deep thought that for any time series, g_q, g_k, and s (where g_x stands for the growth of x) [and s is capital's share] one can always write an *exact* relation of the form $g_q = sg_k + g_A$. It is only necessary to define the time series g_A to be $g_q - sg_k$. Once this is done, it is hardly surprising that $g_q - g_A$ should equal sg_k. The only empirical questions here are, first, whether s is related to k in any systematic way in the data, and second, whether g_A satisfies any natural a priori restrictions. Mr Shaikh ignores the first by discussing only the case where s is a constant or near-constant time series and begs the second in a sentence. They are, nevertheless, the important questions. (emphasis in the original)

Here, of course, Solow has turned Hogan's critique into a defence of his own method. But with respect to the first question, since Solow himself found the Cobb–Douglas to have been the best fit, it is hardly surprising Shaikh concentrated on this specification. With regard to the second question, it is difficult to find where Shaikh 'begs the question'. How does one determine 'whether g_A satisfies any natural a priori restrictions', especially when it captures measurement errors, and so on?

Solow continues:

> The cute HUMBUG numerical example tends to bowl you over at first, but when you think about it for a minute it turns out to be quite straightforward in terms of what I have said. ... If you ask any systematic method or any educated mind to interpret those data *using a production function and the marginal productivity relations*, the answer will be that they are exactly what would be produced by technical progress with a production function that must be close to Cobb-Douglas. (emphasis in the original)

This is persuasive if it is assumed that a production function does exist, and the purpose is not to test the existence of a function (as Solow clearly thinks can be done in principle). Given any data with constant factor shares, then the estimation must show that it must be a Cobb–Douglas, although in the case of the Humbug production function the residual is negative (which could be interpreted as technical regress). Shaikh has merely pointed out the obvious.

> All this has literally nothing to do with the question whether the empirical basis of aggregate production functions is strong or weak. When someone claims that aggregate production functions work, he means (a) that they give a good fit to input-output data without the intervention of data deriving from factor shares; and (b) that the function so fitted has partial derivatives that closely mimic observed factor shares. (omitting a footnote)

And to drive the point home, Solow freely estimates a Cobb–Douglas (that is, he estimates *lnq = c + at + blnk*, where *t* is a time trend) using the Humbug data, presumably as a test of whether it represents an aggregate production function. He finds the relationship to be statistically insignificant. There is no statistically significant relationship between output and inputs using the Humbug data, hence, according to Solow, the 'humbug is on the other foot'.

Solow's rejoinder has been quoted at length as an example of what might seem to be persuasive rhetoric. Unlike his reply to Hogan, the whole tenor of Solow's reply is that Shaikh's critique is trivial and hardly worth taking seriously. Consider the following expressions and phrases taken from the above quotations: 'misconception pure and simple'; 'even simpler'; 'hardly a deep thought'; 'the cute Humbug'; 'bowl you over at first'; 'but when you think about it for a minute'; and 'any educated mind'. Notice how the use of these unscholarly words have the effect of suggesting that we really do not have to take Shaikh's comment seriously – in other words, it is very effective rhetoric. Solow's rejoinder abounds with the use of verbal hierarchies (McCloskey, 1994b, chapter 23).

There was a reply from Shaikh (1980) in an appendix to an elaboration of his original paper, published in a book of articles by several authors. Thus, it is perhaps not surprising that the rejoinder went largely unnoticed. There were two strands to Shaikh's reply. First, he cited evidence from Solow's (1957) paper that could be interpreted as showing that Solow actually thought that he was *testing* the aggregate production function. This is not such convincing rhetoric since, regardless of what Solow actually had in mind, his methodology is certainly consistent with assuming the existence of the production function (Solow explicitly invokes the assumption of marginal productivity factor pricing) in the calculation of technical change. Shaikh's second strand was to question the need for a constant rate of 'technical change'. He shows that by fitting, *ex post*, a complex time trend which involves sines and cosines in its formula, it is possible to improve significantly the R^2 of the Humbug data and, as the fit improves, so the estimated slope coefficient approaches capital's factor share, as the identity suggests must happen. (The complex time trend is merely providing a closer approximation to the path of $alnw_t + (l - a)lnr_t$.)

More effective rhetoric would have perhaps been the use of irony, the 'trope of tropes', according to McCloskey. For example, let us commence by granting, for the time being, Solow his assumption that aggregate production functions can be tested and, using Solow's linear time trend and his data for the US, estimate a conventional Cobb–Douglas production function. (This is dealt with at length in McCombie, 1996a.) When the logarithm of productivity is regressed on a time-trend and the logarithm of the capital–labour ratio, the estimated coefficient of the latter is not statistically different from zero. By Solow's own criteria, his data reject the null hypothesis that there is a well-defined Cobb–Douglas production function. Estimating the specification in first difference form produces no better results. It is worth re-emphasizing the conclusions of this analysis. *Following Solow's procedure in estimating the Humbug production function and using his own data would lead us to conclude that there was no statistical relationship between output and the inputs.*

Consequently, if Solow (1957) himself had adopted his 1974 procedure and estimated a Cobb-Douglas production function directly without the intervention of factor shares, he would have found that the output elasticities bore little relationship to the observed factor shares. He would have been forced to conclude, by his own criterion, that there was no empirical basis for the aggregate Cobb–Douglas production function. This raises the interesting rhetorical questions: in these circumstances, would Solow have submitted the paper for publication and, if so, would it have been accepted? If it had been published instead of the original paper, would the intellectual history of the aggregate production have been very different?

The next point in the argument is to raise this question: if the fit is so bad, how is it we are estimating an identity? The *coup de grâce* would be to follow Shaikh but using Solow's data, and to demonstrate how, as we improve the fit (by including a non-linear time trend or other proxy that closely tracks $alnw_t + (1 - a)lnr_t$), the results converge to those given by the identity. (See McCombie (1996a) for a detailed discussion. Felipe (1996) discusses the accounting identity, the Cobb–Douglas production function and spurious regressions. Felipe and Holz (1996) further extend the analysis using simulation techniques.)

CONCLUSIONS

Rhetoric is indeed a useful method for discussing how economic ideas are accepted; but influential rhetoric can be pernicious in that it can 'block science for years', as the case of the aggregate production function shows. In order to understand why this can occur, we need to go beyond mere rhetoric and to study the relationship between rhetoric and the audience to which it is addressed, in other words, to the paradigmatic situation in which it is applied. Only by this method is it possible to understand fully how disputes between, for example, New Classical economists, neoKeynesians, post Keynesians, institutionalists and Marxists can persist for decades without any likelihood of a consensus being reached.

NOTES

1. An earlier and longer version of this chapter was presented at the 10th Malvern Political Economy Conference, August 1996. I am grateful to the participants, especially Geoff Harcourt and Steve Pressman, for their helpful comments.
2. Neither, of course, should the indispensable help of Louise Davidson.
3. Exceptions are some post Keynesians, such as, for example, Harcourt (1982) and Lavoie (1992).
4. For example, Lucas (1994) considers that students should not bother to read the *General Theory* as it misdirected macroeconomics for decades. From this view point the *General Theory* would be effective but pernicious rhetoric; but not, of course, to the post Keynesians.
5. In a postscript to Kuhn (1970), he proposes to reserve the term 'disciplinary matrix' for the earlier broad definition of paradigm as a particular community of specialists and their shared values. The term paradigm would be restricted to a 'shared example' or 'exemplar'. However, because the paradigm has been so widely interpreted as the former definition, the terms disciplinary matrix and paradigm are used here interchangeably.

REFERENCES

Alchian, A. (1950), 'Uncertainty, Evolution and Economic Theory', *Journal of Political Economy*, **58**, 211–21.

Barro, R.J. and Sala-i-Martin, X. (1995), *Economic Growth*, New York: McGraw-Hill.

Blaug, M. (1974), *The Cambridge Revolution: Success or Failure?*, London: Institute of Economic Affairs.

Blaug, M. (1992), *The Methodology of Economics, or How Economists Explain*, 2nd edn, Cambridge: Cambridge University Press.

Cobb, C.W. and Douglas, P.H. (1928), 'A Theory of Production', *American Economic Review*, **18** (supplement), 139–65.

Cramer, J.S. (1969), *Empirical Economics*, Amsterdam: North Holland.

Davidson, P. (1990), *The Collected Writings of Paul Davidson, Vol 1, Money and Employment*, edited by L. Davidson, Basingstoke: Macmillan.

Davidson, P. (1991), *The Collected Writings of Paul Davidson, Vol 2, Inflation, Open Economies and Resources*, edited by L. Davidson, Basingstoke: Macmillan.

Denison, E. (1967), *Why Growth Rates Differ: Postwar Experience in Nine Western Countries*, Washington: The Brookings Institution.

Dornbusch, R. and Fischer, S. (1994), *Macroeconomics*, 6th edn, New York: McGraw-Hill.

Douglas, P.H. (1976), 'The Cobb-Douglas Production Function Once Again: Its History, Its Testing and Some New Empirical Values, *Journal of Political Economy*, **84**, 903–15.

Esterin, S. and Laidler, D. (1995), *Introduction to Microeconomics*, London: Harvester Wheatsheaf.

Felipe, J. (1996), 'An Econometric Note on the Simon and Shaikh Critiques', The Hong Kong University of Science and Technology, mimeo.

Felipe, J. and Holz, C. (1996), 'On Production Functions, Technical Progress and Time Trends', The Hong Kong University of Science and Technology.

Ferguson, C.E. (1971), *The Neoclassical Theory of Production and Distribution*, Cambridge: Cambridge University Press.

Fisher, F.M. (1969), 'The Existence of Aggregate Production Functions', *Econometrica*, **37**, 553–77.

Fisher, F.M. (1971), 'Aggregate Production Functions and the Explanation of Wages: A Simulation Experiment', *Review of Economics and Statistics*, **53**, 305–25.

Fisher, F.M. (1987), 'Aggregation Problem' in *the New Palgrave: A Dictionary of Economics*, edited by J.L. Eatwell, M. Milgate and P. Newman, Basingstoke: Macmillan.

Fisher, F. M. (1992), *Aggregation: Aggregate Production Functions and Related Topics*, edited by J. Monz, London: Harvester Wheatsheaf.

Friedman, M. (1953), 'The Methodology of Positive Economics' in his *Essays in Positive Economics*, Chicago: Chicago University Press.

Griliches, Z. (1996), 'The Discovery of the Residual: An Historical Note', *Journal of Economic Literature*, **34**, 1324–30.

Hahn, F.H. (1975), 'Revival of Political Economy: The Wrong Issues and the Wrong Arguments', *Economic Record*, **51**, 360–4.

Harcourt, G.C. (1972), *Some Cambridge Controversies in the Theory of Capital*, Cambridge: Cambridge University Press.

Harcourt, G.C. (1976), 'The Cambridge Controversies: Old Ways and New Horizons – Or Dead End?', *Oxford Economic Papers*, **28**, 25–65.

Harcourt, G.C. (1982), *The Social Science Imperialists*, edited by P. Kerr, London: Routledge and Kegan Paul.

Heathfield, D.F. and Wibe, S. (1987), *Introduction to Cost and Production Functions*, Basingstoke: Macmillan.

Hogan, W.P. (1958), 'Technical Progress and Production Functions', *Review of Economics and Statistics*, **40**, 407–11.

Hoover, K.D. (1995), 'Why Does Methodology Matter for Economics?', *Economic Journal*, **105**, 715–34.

Klamer, A. (1984), *The New Classical Macroeconomics: Conversations with New Classical Economists and Their Opponents*, Brighton: Wheatsheaf.

Krugman, P. (1979), 'A Model of Innovation, Technology Transfer and the World Distribution of Income', *Journal of Political Economy*, **87**, 253–66.

Kuhn, T.S. (1970), *The Structure of Scientific Revolutions*, 2nd edn, Chicago: University of Chicago Press.

Kuhn, T.S. (1977), 'Second Thoughts on Paradigms' in *The Structure of Scientific Theories*, edited by F. Suppe, Urbana: University of Illinois Press.

Lakatos, I. (1970), 'Falsification and the Methodology of Scientific Research Programmes' in *Criticism and the Growth of Knowledge*, edited by I. Lakatos and A. Musgrave, Cambridge: Cambridge University Press.

Lavoie, M. (1992), *Foundations of Post-Keynesian Economic Analysis*, Aldershot, Hants: Edward Elgar.

Lehavari, D. (1965), 'A Non-Substitution Theorem and Switching of Techniques', *Quarterly Journal of Economics*, **79**, 98–105.

Lindbeck, A. (1992) (ed.), *Nobel Lectures: Economic Sciences 1969–1980*, Singapore: World Scientific.

Lucas, R.E. (1994), Interview in Snowdon B., Vane, H. and Wynarczyk, P. (1994), *A Modern Guide to Macroeconomics: An Introduction to Competing Schools of Thought*, Aldershot, Hants: Edward Elgar.

McCloskey, D.N. (1985), *The Rhetoric of Economics*, Madison: University of Wisconsin Press.

McCloskey, D.N. (1994a), 'How To Do Rhetorical Analysis, and Why' in *New Directions in Economic Methodology*, edited by R. E. Backhouse, London: Routledge, 1994.

McCloskey, D.N. (1994b), *Knowledge and Persuasion in Economics*, Cambridge: Cambridge University Press.

McCombie, J.S.L. (1996a), 'Solow's "Technical Change and the Aggregate Production Function" Revisited', Downing College, Cambridge, mimeo.

McCombie, J.S.L. (1996b), '"Are there Laws of Production?": An Assessment of the Early Criticisms of the Cobb-Douglas Production Function', Downing College, Cambridge, mimeo (*Review of Political Economy*, forthcoming, 1998).

McCombie, J.S.L. and Dixon, R. (1991), 'Estimating Technical Change in Aggregate Production Functions: A Critique', *International Review of Applied Economics*, **5**, 24–46.

McCombie, J.S.L. and Thirlwall, A.P. (1994), *Economic Growth and the Balance-of-Payments Constraint*, Basingstoke: Macmillan.

Maki, U. (1988), 'How to Combine Rhetoric and Realism in the Methodology of Economics', *Economics and Philosophy*, **4**, 89–109.

Matthews, R.C.O. (1988), 'The Work of Robert M. Solow', *Scandinavian Journal of Economics*, **90**, 13–16.

May, K.O. (1946), 'The Aggregation Problem for a One-Industry Model', *Econometrica*, **14**, 285–8.

May, K.O. (1947), 'Technical Change and Aggregation', *Econometrica*, **15**, 51–63.

Milberg, W. (1988), 'The Language of Economics: Deconstructing the Neoclassical Texts', *Social Concepts*, **4**, 33–57.

Mirowski, P. (1988), 'Shall I Compare Thee to a Mirowski–Ricardo–Leontief–Metzler Matrix?', reprinted in *The Consequences of Economic Rhetoric*, edited by A. Klamer, R.M. Solow and D.N. McCloskey, Cambridge: Cambridge University Press. (Originally published in *Economics and Philosophy*, 1987, **3**, 67–96.)

Mirowski, P. (1992), 'Three Vignettes on the State of Economic Rhetoric' in *Post-Popperian Methodology of Economics: Recovering Practice*, edited by N. de Marchi, Boston: Kluwer Academic Publishers.

Nataf, A. (1948), 'Sur la Possibilité de Construction de Certains Macromodèles', *Econometrica*, **16**, 232–44.

Pasinetti, L.L. (1966), 'Changes in the Rate of Profit and Switches of Technique', *Quarterly Journal of Economics*, **80**, 503–17.

Phelps Brown, E.H. (1957), 'The Meaning of the Fitted Cobb-Douglas Function', *Quarterly Journal of Economics*, **71**, 546–60.

Prescott, E.C. (1988), 'Robert M. Solow's Neoclassical Growth Model: An Influential Contribution to Economics', *Scandinavian Journal of Economics*, **90**, 7–12.

Rappaport, S. (1988), 'Economic Methodology: Rhetoric or Epistemology?', *Economics and Philosophy*, **4**, 110–28.

Robinson, J.V. (1953–54), 'The Production Function and the Theory of Capital', *Review of Economics Studies*, **21**, 81–106.

Robinson, J.V. (1970), 'Capital Theory Up To Date', *Canadian Journal of Economics*, **3**, 309–17.

Rosenberg, A. (1988), 'Economics is too Important to be Left to the Rhetoricians', *Economics and Philosophy*, **4**, 129–49.

Samuelson, P.A. (1966), 'A Summing Up', *Quarterly Journal of Economics*, **80**, 568–83.

Shaikh, A. (1974), 'Laws of Production and Laws of Algebra: The Humbug Production Function', *Review of Economics and Statistics*, **56**, 115–20.

Shaikh, A. (1980), 'Laws of Production and Laws of Algebra: Humbug II' in *Growth, Profits and Property*, edited by E.J. Nell, Cambridge: Cambridge University Press.

Simon, H.A. (1979), 'On Parsimonious Explanations of Production Relations', *Scandinavian Journal of Economics*, **89**, 459–74.

Simon, H.A. and Levy, F.K. (1963), 'A Note on the Cobb-Douglas Function', *Review of Economics and Statistics*, **39**, 93–4.

Solow, R.M. (1955–56), 'The Production Function and the Theory of Capital', *Review of Economic Studies*, **23**, 101–8.

Solow, R.M. (1956), 'A Contribution to the Theory of Economic Growth', *Quarterly Journal of Economics*, **70**, 65–94.

Solow, R.M. (1957), 'Technical Change and the Aggregate Production Function', *Review of Economics and Statistics*, **39**, 312–20.

Solow, R.M. (1958), 'Reply' [to Hogan, 1958], *Review of Economics and Statistics*, **40**, 411–13.

Solow, R.M. (1966), 'Review of Capital and Growth', *American Economic Review*, **56**, 1257–60.

Solow, R.M. (1974), 'Laws of Production and Laws of Algebra: The Humbug Production Function: A Comment', *Review of Economics and Statistics*, **56**, 121.

Solow, R.M. (1988a), 'Comments from Inside Economics' in *The Consequences of Economic Rhetoric*, edited by A. Klamer, R.M. Solow and D.N. McCloskey, Cambridge: Cambridge University Press.

Solow, R.M. (1988b), 'Growth Theory and After', *American Economic Review*, **78**, 307–17.

Swan, T.W. (1956), 'Economic Growth and Capital Accumulation', *Economic Record*, **32**, 334–61.

Walters, A.A. (1963a), 'Production and Cost Functions: An Econometric Survey', *Econometrica*, **31**, 1–66.

Walters, A.A. (1963b), 'A Note on Economies of Scale', *Review of Economics and Statistics*, **45**, 425–7.

Wang, H.Y. (1971), *Economic Growth*, New York: Harcourt Brace Jovanovich.

4. Keynes in retrospect

Robert W. Clower

INTRODUCTION

When I started college in the summer of 1946, my father – who had met Keynes at the Chicago Harris Foundation lectures in 1931 and thought him 'fascinating' – handed me a copy of *The Economic Consequences of the Peace*, evidently hoping it would dampen utopian thoughts about post-war political possibilities. Reading the book did nothing to dampen my youthful idealism, but I was captivated by Keynes's writing style, passion, impatience with opposing views and intellectual arrogance. I went on to read Marshall (1920), Smith (1776), Malthus (1798), Marx (Vol. 1), and Paul Douglas (1935), then to Keynes's *General Theory*, Mandeville, and Mummery and Hobson; so when in 1947 I decided to write an undergraduate honours thesis, fate dictated that I write on 'The Keynesian Contribution to Economic Positivism'. In the process I somehow managed to stumble through what then struck me as a maze of 'advanced economics' : Harris (1946), Tarshis (1947), Hansen (1938) and Klein (1947). When I finished, I was a dedicated 'Keynesian' and have been one since. So, like Paul, when I have occasion to peruse modern treatments of 'Keynesian' economics, I am invariably offended by the *ad hoc* theorizing that characterizes contemporary accounts of macroeconomic theory. It is *not* the Keynes I remember.

As we all now recognize, what was known in the 1940s and 1950s as the 'Keynesian Revolution' (Klein, 1947) was abortive. A book that opened with an attack on orthodoxy was converted by friendly interpreters – notably Harrod, Hicks, Reddaway and Meade – into an aggregative variant of Marshallian short-period partial equilibrium analysis (Clower, 1989). So it is not surprising that, 25 years later, in his Lekachman-volume survey of 'Post Keynesian developments' (Lekachman, 1964, p. 332), Paul Samuelson found it natural to remark: 'Had Keynes begun his first few chapters with the simple statement... that modern capitalistic societies had wage rates that were sticky ... downwards ..., most of his insights would have remained just as valid.' In short, the Keynesian Revolution and the controversy that accompanied it could be seen as a waste of time and effort (Leijonhufvud, 1983). That means that Samuelson's

'Neoclassical Synthesis' (1955, pp. 11, 212))[1] also was gratuitous because the thrust of the 'synthesis' was that the substantive portions of Keynes's *General Theory* contained nothing economists did not already know!

In this chapter I reconsider Samuelson's interpretation of Keynes in the light of my own understanding of *The General Theory*. Among other things, I show that Samuelson's conception of Keynesian economics, embodied in the 'Keynesian Cross' account of national income analysis that his 1948 text made a ubiquitous feature of later introductory books, owes its origin not to Keynes but to Alvin Hansen, and I argue that Samuelson's promulgation of Hansen's factitious version of 'Keynesian Economics' distorted the central message[2] of Keynes's *General Theory* and blunted its intellectual impact.

KEYNES'S MANIFESTO

The opening shot of what was to become Keynes's revolution was fired by Keynes in a British Broadcasting Corporation 'manifesto' of 1934[3], which directed attention to the 'gulf' between 'orthodox' believers in the self-adjustment capabilities of market economies and 'heretical' critics who consider the orthodox faith mistaken. Keynes ranged himself 'with the heretics', claimed to see 'a fatal flaw' in orthodox doctrine, warned that failure to redress the flaw would force us to confront 'the intolerable' [*sic*!], and concluded by indicating he had 'a better hope' – presumably referring to his soon-to-be-published *General Theory of Employment Interest and Money*.

In the event, Keynes paid little attention in *The General Theory* to the self-adjustment issue. The 'fatal flaw' identified in the 'manifesto' and there linked with a 'mistaken theory of the rate of interest' he identified in *The General Theory* (1936, p. 18) with the phrase 'Supply creates its own Demand', which he took to mean '... in some significant, but not clearly defined, sense that the whole of the costs of production must defined, sense that the whole of the costs of production must necessarily be spent in the aggregate... on purchasing the product'. Keynes cites no source[4] for this phrasing and interpretation, causing me to wonder how he might have 'translated' Adam Smith's celebrated anticipation of Say's *Loi de Débouchés*: 'It is not from the benevolence of the butcher, the brewer, or the baker, that we expect our dinner, but from their regard to their own interest' (Smith, 1976, p. 26). And how might Keynes have restated the modern *quid pro quo* proposition: 'There's no such thing as a free lunch'? Finally, what would Keynes have made of Walras' statement (Jaffe, 1956, p. 89) : '... one cannot demand anything without making an offer. Offer is only a consequence of demand'?

In pondering Keynes' varied accounts of 'Say's law' (see the index entries in *JMK*, XIV), I conclude that Keynes was unable analytically to express the self-adjustment doctrine. More particularly, I conjecture that Keynes confused Say's commonsense idea that 'products are paid for by products' with a problematic doctrine which, in my lectures on 'dead men', I call *The Classical Stability Hypothesis* (CSH). This doctrine takes for granted the coordinating action of an 'invisible hand' operating 'behind the scenes' to ensure short-run stability of market economies. In more technical jargon, CSH presumes that time-series representation of market economies lie 'almost always' in the neighbourhood of market-clearing equilibrium trajectories.

As for the evidentiary basis of the CSH, it rests on nothing more substantial than anecdote, casual historical knowledge, and ideology (Hansen, 1953, pp. 3–6). Thus it is hard to regard it as anything more than a metaphysical conception of 'reality' or perhaps a kind of superstition, as suggested by Mummery and Hobson's casual characterization of it (1889, p. 101) as '... confidence in... the automatic machinery of commerce'. However that may be, CSH surely is not a conjecture about formal properties of economic models. Keynes's apparent belief (*JMK*, VII, chapter 2, esp. p. 21) that 'Say's Law' was the classical theory's 'axiom of parallels' confused a disguised definition, named 'Say's Principle' by Clower and Due (1972, pp. 64–5) with a cosmological presumption (Leijonhufvud, 1985). Apparently Keynes beguiled himself into believing (incorrectly) that he had unearthed a logical flaw in orthodox doctrine. The rest (including Keynes's 'primer' on labour economics (chapter 2) and his 'technical' discussion of the dynamic stability of market economies (chapters 19 and 20) is history (cf. Tobin, 1988).

PRE KEYNESIAN ECONOMICS

Keynes was familiar with Walras's *Elements* (Hicks, 1982, p. 296 fn), but his family background, education, and life as Fellow of King's College were supportive of 'Marshallian' habits of thought. In any case, there was little reason for Keynes to regard Walras and Marshall differently; in the period 1900–36, it was natural for knowledgeable economists to regard both as interpreters of the classical tradition (Phillips, 1924, pp. 236–7; Schumpeter, 1955; Walker, 1987). In the *Elements*, for example, Walras wrote (Jaffe, 1956, pp. 83–4):

> Value in exchange ... arises spontaneously in the market as the result of competition. As buyers, traders make their *demands* by *outbidding* each other. As sellers, traders make their *offers* by *underbidding* each other. ... The more perfectly competition functions, the more rigorous is the manner of arriving at value in exchange. The markets which are best organized from the competitive standpoint are those in which purchases and sales are made by auction. ... Besides these markets, there are ... fruit, vegetable and poultry markets, where competition...

functions fairly effectively. ... City streets with their stores and shops of all kinds – baker's, butcher's, grocer's, tailor's, shoemaker's, etc. – are markets where competition, though poorly organized, nevertheless operates quite adequately.

Comparably, in Marshall (1920, p. 341) we read:

> ... the forces of demand and supply have free play... there is no... combination among dealers... and there is much free competition; that is, buyers generally compete freely with buyers, and sellers compete freely with sellers. But though everyone acts for himself, his knowledge of what others are doing is ... generally sufficient to prevent him from taking a lower or paying a higher price.

In modern writing, the contrast between so-called Marshallian and Walrasian perspectives is reflected in the treatment by 'Marshallians' of quantities as independent variables and demand and supply prices as dependent, whereas 'Walrasians' treat prices as independent variables and quantities demanded and supplied as dependent.[5] So Marshallian models are commonly described as 'quantity-into-price', while Walrasian models are described as 'price-into-quantity'. In this respect, the US literature, macro as well as micro, has a distinctly Walrasian twist. But there can be no doubt that, in terms of the categories just described, Keynes was a quantity-into-price Marshallian.

By 'classical economist', as Keynes tells us on the first page of *The General Theory*, he means the *followers*, not the predecessors of Ricardo. In truth, the followers he had in mind – Mill, Marshall, Edgeworth, Pigou – did not deviate much from Adam Smith. But neither did Walras – or, for that matter, Keynes before 1936. Indeed, we find a hint of Keynes's *General Theory* in book I, section vii. of *The Wealth of Nations*:

> The quantity of every commodity brought to market naturally suits itself to the effectual demand. It is in the interest of all those who employ their land, labour, or stock in bringing any commodity to market, that the quantity never should exceed the effectual demand; and it is in the interest of all other people that it never should fall short of that demand.

Of course Smith, like other writers before Keynes, was referring to a particular 'market' – or as Marshall would have styled it, 'industry'; but there is no reason why the same line of argument should not be applied to the economy as a whole by supposing that the economy consists of a multitude of firms all of which produce and sell a single commodity (Q) called *output* (of goods and services).[6]

Now suppose short-period output is initially at Q_0, so the (unit) supply price of output, P^s, is indicated by P_0^s, as shown by the Aggregate Supply (Price)[7] Curve labelled $S(W_0)$ in Figure 4.1. The curve $S(W)$ is here drawn

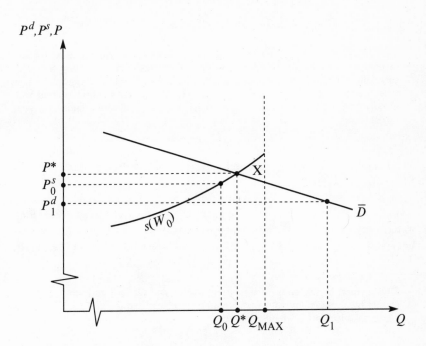

Figure 4.1   The Marshallian macrocross

upward-sloping with a discontinuity at 'capacity' output (Q_{MAX}): cost rises[8] up
to capacity.[9]

Suppose next that when aggregate output is Q_1 the [unit] demand price is
P_1^d as shown by the Aggregate (output-adjusted)[10] Demand (Price) Curve $P^d \equiv$
$\bar{D}\{Q, \dot{A}\}$[11] in Figure 4.1. Given the supply and demand relations illustrated in
Figure 4.1, we define *equilibrium* price, P^*, and *equilibrium* quantity, Q^*, by
the coordinates of the point of intersection of S with D (the point X in Figure
4.1). As Marshall argued (1920, p. 345) :

> When... the amount produced... is such that the demand price is greater than the
> supply price, then sellers receive more than is sufficient to make it worth their
> while to bring goods to market to that amount; and there is at work an active force
> tending to increase the amount brought forward for sale. On the other hand, when
> the amount produced is such that the demand price is less than the supply price,
> sellers receive less than is sufficient ... so that those who were just on the margin
> of doubt as to whether to go on producing are decided not to do so, and there is an

active force... tending to diminish the amount brought forward for sale. When the demand price is equal to the supply price, the amount produced has no tendency either to be increased or decreased; it is in equilibrium.

Analogously, in Walras (Jaffe, 1956, p. 224, section 187) we read:

in the real world ... purchases and sales takes place according to the mechanism of competitive bidding. When you go to a shoe manufacturer to buy a pair of shoes he acts as an entrepreneur delivering the product and receiving the money. If more products are demanded than supplied, another consumer will outbid you; if more products are supplied than demanded another producer will underbid your shoe manufacturer.

These different views, one quantity-into-price, the other price-into-quantity, are so similar that a hasty reader might find it hard to decide which writer is Marshall and which Walras.

In both Marshall and Walras we find a hint of the Classical Stability Hypothesis. Indeed, belief in the clearance of commodity markets seems long to have been common among economists, and may even have some evidentiary support (Tobin, 1980, pp. 788–92); but when Marshall (1889, p. 16) writes:

The position of the point of intersection [of S and $\bar{D}$] ... [represents] approximately the average amount which would be produced and the average price about which the mean price would oscillate.

he is presuming merely short run clearance, which (Keynes's several *General Theory* insinuations to the contrary notwithstanding) is a far cry from the Classical Stability Hypothesis. Similarly, when Walras (op. cit., section 188) writes:

Equilibrium in production... is an ideal and not a real state.[12] It never happens in the real world that the selling price... is absolutely equal to the cost.... Yet equilibrium is the normal state... towards which things spontaneously tend under a régime of free competition.

he is concerned only with clearance of individual commodity markets.[13]

A KEYNESIAN CROSS

Though the macroeconomic literature contains numerous accounts of the so-called 'Keynesian Cross', no textbook writer appears to have constructed a 'cross' according to Keynes's description in chapter 3 of *The General Theory*.[14] I propose to construct such a 'cross' here.

Focusing on Keynes's initial account of aggregate demand and supply (*JMK*, VII, 24–32), we start by identifying *Aggregate Supply*, the function $Z(Q) \equiv P^sQ\{N\}$ shown in the two-quadrant diagram Figure 4.2, as a curve that shows for each given level of employment and output 'the expectation of proceeds [which will] just make it worth the while of entrepreneurs' to maintain the given level of output.[15] This definition mimics Marshall's description of normal supply price for the representative firm, namely, 'the price the expectation of which will just suffice to maintain the existing aggregate amount of production' (Marshall, 1920, pp. 342–3). More succinctly, $Z(Q)$ is aptly characterized as 'a reconcoction of our old friend the supply function' (*JMK*, XIII, p. 513).

Analogously, we identify *Aggregate Demand*,[16] the function $E(Q, \dot{A})$ ($\equiv P^d$ $(F(N), \dot{A})F(N))$ in Figure 4.2, as a curve that shows for any given level of output (and employment) 'the proceeds which entrepreneurs expect to receive from the employment of N men' (*JMK*, VII, 25), a definite twist on the later definition (p. 30) where he writes '... which the entrepreneurs *can expect* to get back' (my italics). The latter phrase would make $E(Q, \dot{A})$ another 'reconcoction', this time of the Marshallian demand curve; the former phrase is puzzling (see Robertson's 3 February, 1935 letter to Keynes, *JMK*, XIII, 497–8), but may be just one of those things Keynes omitted to alter in the final draft of *The General Theory*.[17]

Suppose, next, that employment is initially at N_0 and output at Q_0 so that $E(Q_0) > Z(Q_0)$: Aggregate Demand exceeds Aggregate Supply. On standard maximization assumptions (compare Keynes's letter to Kahn, *JMK*, XIII, 422–3), some producers will increase employment and output. Dropping further explicit reference to employment, we argue conversely that for Q such that $E(Q) < Z(Q)$, where Aggregate Supply exceeds Aggregate Demand, output will decline. We then conclude that the *equilibrium* level of output (to be faithful to Keynesian terminology we should call this the *effective* or, going back to Adam Smith, the *effectual* level of output) is Q^*, where $E(Q) = P^dQ = P^sQ = Z(Q)$. In general, moreover, and regardless of the manner in which marketers set prices, it is concordant with the thought of both Marshall and Keynes to presume that market price typically lies between demand price and supply price, so we conclude that equilibrium price P^* in Keynes's system is defined jointly with equilibrium quantity Q^* by the intersection of Aggregate Demand and Supply (point E in Figure 4.2), and that here we have $P^d = P^* = P^s$.

On the above showing, Keynes's theory of effective demand is a straightforward variant of Marshallian short-period demand and supply analysis.[18] Taking the preceding account as a valid representation, Keynes's remark, namely, that '... "Supply creates its own demand" must mean that $f(N)$ and $\phi(N)$ are equal for *all* values of N...' is nonsense; but if, instead, we take

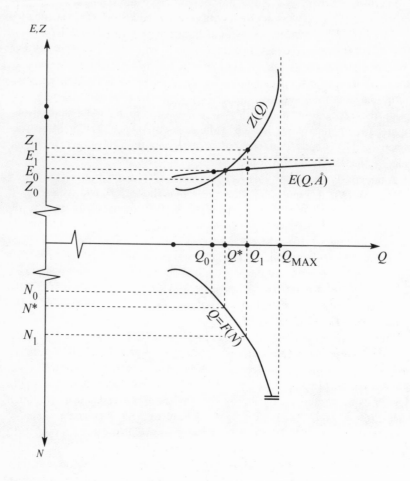

Figure 4.2   A Keynesian cross

Keynes to mean what he writes in the next sentence, *viz.* 'The classical theory assumes... that the aggregate demand price... always *accommodates* itself to the aggregate supply price... [my italics]', then both Keynes's argument and my restatement of it makes sense. In all that follows I shall adopt this charitable interpretation of Keynes's several descriptions of 'Say's Law'.

Let us next consider a special case that derives from Alvin Hansen's review of *The General Theory*. In that review (Hansen, 1938, 321) Hansen wrote: 'So long as there are unused resources, every increase in demand is matched by an increase in supply.' If the proposition *Supply Creates Its Own Demand*[19] is to be called '*Say's Law*', then we may with equal justice translate Hansen's assertion as *Demand Creates Its Own Supply* and label that proposition '*Hansen's Law*'.

To convert Hansen's Law into a proposition about aggregate supply, let us suppose that marketers set (full cost)[20] reservation prices slightly above levels at which they stand ready to sell whatever quantities buyers are willing to purchase. Then writing the aggregate asking price index as P_0 we may define the corresponding Aggregate Supply Function, call it Z^H, as $Z^H \equiv P_0 Q$, and graph it as shown in Figure 4.3. Combining this revised Aggregate Supply Function with the Keynes Aggregate Demand Function $E = P^d Q$, defined as before, earlier argument may be used to define equilibrium output, Q^*, by the intersection of Z^H with E (the point $E' = (Q^*, P_0 Q^*)$ in Figure 4.3). Note that shifts in $\dot{A}$ shift only the equilibrium level of output in Figure 4.3: the 'equilibrium' asking price, P_0, is fixed at a preassigned level 'by the theorist' *outside* the model (the equilibrium value of demand price is, of course, affected by shifts in $\dot{A}$, but P^d is not 'observable' in the special 'Hansen's

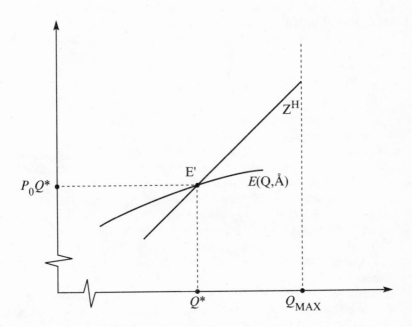

Figure 4.3   The Hansen cross

Law' case of Keynes's model. To all intents and purposes, the Hansen's Law case consists in the *elimination* of business price-making decisions from the model of J. M. Keynes.

THE FUNDAMENTAL EQUATION OF KEYNES'S ECONOMICS

I next restate Keynes's theory of effective demand as a fixed-point (45° – line) proposition. As Aggregate Demand and Aggregate Supply are both functions of Q, we may for any given value of $\dot{A}$ write E as a parametric function, F, of Z:

$$[H] \qquad E(Q, \dot{A}) = F(Z\{Q\})$$

Then the point of 'effective demand' (*JMK*, VII, p. 25), that is the point E in Figure 4.3, corresponds exactly to the point $A = (Z^*, E^*)$ in Figure 4.4,[21] where the curve F (Z) intersects the identity relation $E = Y$ (that is, the 45° line; cf. Samuelson (1939, p. 790). Thus the point $A = (Z^*, E^*)$ in Figure 4.4 is a *fixed point* of the mapping F (Simmons (1963), pp. 337–43; Arrow and Hahn, 1971, p. 28]; that is Z^* is a solution to the equation $Z - F(Z) = 0$.

If we confine attention to values Q^* of Q that *solve* (*H*), then for alternative given levels of $\dot{A}$, we obtain the *identity*:

$$[K] \qquad E\{(Q^*), \dot{A}\} \equiv F\{Z(Q^*)\}$$

hence, for each alternative value of the 'animal spirits' vector $\dot{A}$, the expenditure-income *identity* $E^* \equiv Z^*$ is seen to hold. As a result of the central role that Keynes assigns to this hypothesis (*JMK*, VII, 25) – '... this is the substance of the General Theory of Employment...' – I shall henceforth refer to (*K*) as The Fundamental Equation of Keynes's economics.[22]

The identity **[K]** *defines* Keynes's *point of effective demand* (*JMK*, VII, 25). *It holds, of course, only for hypothesized equilibrium states*. It is only by supposing that commodity markets are always in equilibrium, so that 'effective demand' is the same thing as 'realized' income and expenditure, that one can make sense of the comparative statics multiplier exercises that one finds in macroeconomics texts.

Evidently modern macroeconomic texts are based not on Keynes's theory of effective demand but upon the Hansen's Law case from which Paul Samuelson conceived the so-called 'Keynesian cross' that dominated elementary expositions of national income analysis for at least 30 years after it appeared in Samuelson's *Economics* (1948a).

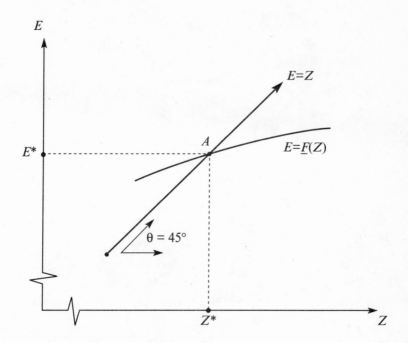

Figure 4.4   Keynes's fixed point cross

In Figure 4.5 the expenditure curve $E = E (Q) = H (P_0Q, \dot{A}) = H (Y)$ is shown with income (Y or GNP) as the sole independent variable on the assumption that aggregate output in the Hansen special case is measured in units such that, at the predetermined reservation price P_0, one unit of money will buy just one unit of output; hence $P_0Q \equiv Y$ (or GNP). Then the intersection of $H (Y)$ with the 45° line (the identity relation $E = Y$) defines a fixed point (shown as point A' in Figure 4.5) of the mapping H, that corresponds exactly with the point $E'(Y^*, P_0Q^*)$ in the Hansen cross of Figure 4.3

In his presentation of 'the simple mathematics of income determination' in the Hansen festschrift volume (Metzler, 1948, pp. 134–5) Samuelson seems to confound the conditional equilibrium condition $E = F (Z)$ – equation **[H]**, above – with the national income accounting identity $Y \equiv C + I$, thereby converting a conditional equation in one unknown into an identity that holds for every value of Y (the latter identity asserts that 'the market value of output' is literally a synonym for 'national income').

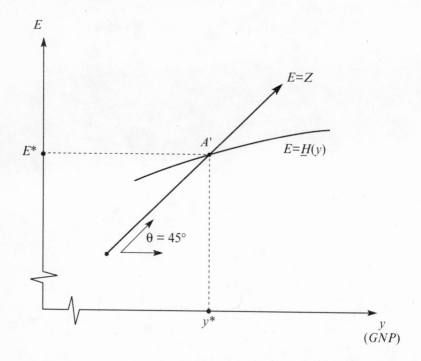

Figure 4.5   Hansen fixed-point cross

Perhaps Samuelson had in mind the fundamental equation **[K]**, for then his 'Keynesian' cross could be regarded as a special case of the fixed-point diagram in Figure 4.4. But as usually described,[23] the 'Keynesian' cross defines merely a particular quantity solution (assuming output units are chosen so that $P_0 = 1$) to the household expenditure function. As the Hansen Cross effectively dispenses with the business sector of the economy (reducing it to a 'placeholder' for Y, I, $\dot{A}$, and other independent variables and/or parameters), the Hansen's Law Cross cannot logically be used to determine 'equilibrium' business decisions respecting output.[24] Given a solution to the household expenditure problem, aggregate output is trivially determined by Hansen's Law (*Demand Creates Its Own Supply*). Samuelson's three proofs (graphical, tabular, algebraic)[25] notwithstanding, the Samuelson version of Keynes's cross does not permit us to define a 'J. M. Keynes' equilibrium for output and employment in the economy as a whole. So when Joan Robinson dubbed the Hansen–Samuelson *et al.* income analysis 'Bastard Keynesianism'[26]

(Robinson, 1962) she was not using foul language: she was merely voicing her literal opinion of the doctrinal illegitimacy of the Samuelsonian 'School'.

CONCLUSION

The history of macroeconomics is a story of repeated attempts to extract from Keynes's *General Theory* more than it contains: formally valid argument that would substantiate its disputed revolutionary *claims* and simultaneously rationalize its undisputed revolutionary *impact*. All that appears to have been established after some 60 years of exegesis and debate is that Keynes's *General Theory*, like Copernicus's *De Revolutionibus* four centuries earlier, was a 'revolution-making' but not a 'revolutionary' book (Kuhn, 1957, p. 135).

No one disputes the novelty of Keynes's aggregative approach to economics, but many have questioned the comparative-statics framework that Keynes adopted. As Patinkin (1982, p. 88) hinted, had Keynes not been an already acknowledged economic guru, his choice of method, stripped of extraneous polemical 'dust' (*JMK*, XIII, 548), might well have caused his 'revolution' to founder.

The central question raised by Keynes's book – which did, after all, impart a remarkable burst of energy to a nearly moribund discipline grown stale with subjectivist platitudes – is, 'How can professional economists best make theoretical sense of contemporary 'free-market' economies?'. To this question, Keynes's book provides no answer; but the book contains myriad insights, one of which merits comment before this essays ends.

Most macroeconomics texts are obsessed with the idea that every 'sensible' macromodel must define a full employment or natural unemployment solution – usually styled 'full employment' equilibrium, 'market-clearing' equilibrium, or 'maximum potential output' equilibrium. This perspective seems to be part and parcel of the landscape of the Newtonian conception of science; and such an outlook is probably unavoidable if we conceive of 'explanation' in terms of classically defined 'causal' systems described by differential or difference equations.

From a doctrine-history perspective, much of the controversy that has plagued macrotheory since its inception reflects the frustration of writers who have attempted unsuccessfully to make sense within existing doctrine of Keynes's outwardly self-contradictory notion of 'less than full employment' equilibrium. How has such a snippet of analytical jargon produced so much fuss? The explanation is straightforward: the fuss arises out of a preconceived commitment to conventional equilibrium dogma.

Keynes adumbrated a different vision. I have specifically in mind the isolated passage in chapter 18 of *JMK*, VII where Keynes at one stroke eliminates the involuntary unemployment conundrum. He says (p. 249):

> ... it is an outstanding characteristic of the economic system in which we live that, whilst it is subject to severe fluctuations in ... output and employment, it is not violently unstable. Indeed, it seems capable of remaining in a chronic condition of sub-normal activity for a considerable period without any marked tendency either towards recovery or towards complete collapse.

We may restate this vision by saying that, in a Poincaré phase portrait of the economic system there exists *no* stationary point, but there *does* exist a *region of stability* within which all trajectories are strictly Brownian (motions which Keynes and Marshall might have called 'neutral' equilibria, and which modern systems analysts would describe as 'noncontrollable'). Outside this

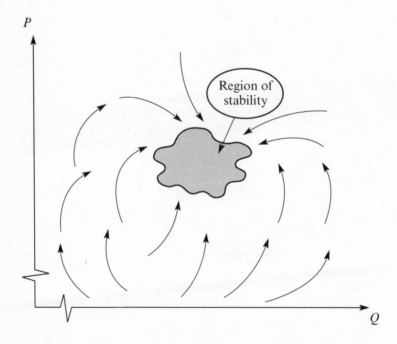

Figure 4.6   Non-controllable motions: region of stability

region of stability, all trajectories are governed by attractive forces. A two-dimensional illustration of such a portrait is shown in Figure 4.6.

If we insist that every 'sensible' model economy contain a full employment equilibrium solution then we commit ourselves to preconceptions about the working of economic systems that are unsupported by either logic or fact, so we are likely to chase red herrings that lead to endless confusion. If instead we leave moot the equilibrium issue by adopting the broader vision adumbrated by Keynes, then 'unemployment equilibrium' and related ideas become topics not, as now, for aimless disputation but for serious research. Such a change in conceptual perspective presaged the Copernican and Einsteinian revolutions and emptied earlier 'science' of myriad self-imposed perplexities. A similar mind-shift is long overdue in economics.

NOTES

1. The term 'neoclassical' seems first to have appeared at p. 11 of the third (1955) edition of the text, but the same idea is expressed, in an almost identical passage, at p. 11 of the second (1951) edition.
2. The 'central message' theme is central to Patinkin's *Anticipations of the General Theory?* (1982, Part I). On the same topic, see Clower (1991), pp. 246–7 and pp. 256–7.
3. *JMK*, XIII, 486–9; a revised version of the 'manifesto' appeared 20 February 1935 in *The New Republic*, pp. 35–7, with the title 'A Self-Adjusting Economic System?'. The string JMK[ROM#] identifies the specified volume of Keynes's *Collected Writings* (1971) and later dates).
4. He quotes Mill, but the passage quoted appears to have been 'lifted' from Mummery and Hobson (1889) who themselves offer an interpretation of Mill that is flatly contradicted by material at the end of the quoted passage. See Davis and Casey (1977), Kahn (1984) for further comment.
5. For early comment on the origin of this differentiation, see Edgeworth (1925, vol. III, p. 169).
6. Marshall used an aggregate output variable called 'gross real income of a country' (g), in his (unpublished) 'Notes on The Theory of Economic Growth' (see Whitaker, 1975, Volume 2, p. 309).
7. 'Price' may be thought of as a scalar representation of an index of a distribution of prices, perhaps a distribution over prices at a point in time, possibly a dated distribution of a single price. It might be familiar function (mean, median, mode) or index number (CPI, WPI, GNP Deflator, and so on). On this, see Clower and Due, 1972, pp. 50–1; also Bushaw and Clower (1957, p. 180).
8. Figure 4.1 and later diagrams represent magnified expansions (not necessarily the same scales vertically and horizontally) of corresponding full-size diagrams that would be required if units were measured on an absolute scale. Hence, in the diagrams as drawn no significance attaches to slopes, curvatures, and so on.
9. There is a complication here (Knight, 1938, p. 102); unless we suppose that, at the fixed money wage rate, W_0, unemployed workers are available for all levels of output less than Q_{MAX}, we cannot coherently treat the level of the supply price curve as given independently of the volume of output as a whole because for all industries, taken together, we can hardly suppose that increases in employment don't sooner or later put upward pressure on the money wage rate.
10. Elsewhere I have called $\bar{D}$ the *mutatis mutandis* demand curve. For details about the

relation between $\bar{D}$ and more familiar *ceteris paribus* demand (price) curves, see Clower (1989, 136fn).

11. The symbol $\hat{A}$ denotes a 'shift parameter' which might refer to a row vector representing such imponderables as 'the state of confidence', 'autonomous expenditure', 'uncertainty about future economic conditions', and so on. Thus $\hat{A}$ is analogous to the 'portmanteau' shift parameter occasionally called 'animal spirits' (Howitt and McAfee, 1992, pp. 502–3; *JMK*, VII, 24, 91–6, 148–9).

12. For a treatment that emphasizes the confused state of much contemporary 'supply and demand' analysis, see Haavelmo (1978, pp. 31ff.). In fairness to Walras, one should also consult Don Walker's account of the Edgeworth–Walras controversy about price-making in theory and practice.

13. Given Marshall's views on competition, it seems natural to suppose that actual market (transaction) prices lie generally in the neighbourhood of equilibrium points, and this 'naturalness' is the source of potential confusion (see Haavelmo, 1958).

14. The closest approach is probably Davidson and Smolensky (1964, p. 145 and Fig. 10.3); but their construction treats employment as the sole independent variable and so leaves the connection between employment and output in the background. Phelps (1985, p. 525) draws a two-quadrant diagram that allows us to see directly the connection between employment and aggregate demand and supply, but Phelps's graph is a fixed-point diagram similar to that developed later in this paper, not a Keynesian Cross in any customary sense. Hansen (1953, pp. 30–1) also attempts a graph, but either his discussion rests on some curious and unstated assumptions, or his diagrams are seriously in error.

15. Patinkin (1982, pp. 142–50) identifies several ambiguities and/or confusions here. I do not here attempt to deal with these and related issues in doctrine history. For earlier comment, see Clower (1991, p. 255).

16. I replace Keynes's D with the symbol E to make it clear that Aggregate Demand in the present context is an expenditure magnitude, not a quantity or price.

17. This conjecture is based largely on Keynes's letter to Hawtrey of 8 November 1935 (*JMK*, XIII, 602–3): 'The demand which determines the decision as to how much plant to employ must necessarily concern itself with expectations. And I am in this respect simply trying to put more precisely what is implicit in most contemporary economics.'

18. This conclusion accords with Amadeo's view (1989, p. 150) that '... the price versus quantity dichotomy should not be taken as the basis for a comparison between [the *Treatise on Money* and *The General Theory*]...'. For another view, see Patinkin (1982, pp. 88–9); Clower (1991, pp. 245–5).

19. The proposition now called Say's Law in macroeconomic texts appears to have been first so stated by Keynes (*JMK*, VII, 18) who, as intimated earlier, never seemed able to decide just what it meant (for his many remarks about the notion, see the index to *JMK*, XIV).

20. See Andrews and Brunner (1975, p. 29); also Okun (1981, pp. 178–81).

21. In Figure 4.3, I have set the parameter $\hat{A}$ to some initial level $\hat{A} = \hat{A}^*$, to fix the position of the aggregate expenditure curve.

22. With apologies to Axel Leijonhufvud, whose *Keynesian Economics and the Economics of J.M. Keynes* (1968) distinguishes between 'Keynesian economics' and 'The Economics of J. M. Keynes' in a quite different way than my formulae **[H]** and **[K]**.

23. Klein (1947, pp. 51–2) asserts an inventory-adjustment 'theory' of output adjustment, thus introducing a business sector of sorts into his 'Keynesian cross' model: but he omits consideration of such possibilities as prohibitively costly stock-out problems, carrying charges, and so on.

24. Klein (1947), Parkin (1990) and other authors adopt a mechanical theory of output determination according to which output increases if inventories decline and output declines if inventories increase. On that theory, one can talk about output 'equilibrium' in terms of equality of production and sales alone. The problem then is to square such a view of output adjustment with the most elementary cost and revenue considerations of everyday business experience.

25. See, for example, Samuelson (1948, pp. 258–64), who even has a text section labelled '...Income Determination: A Third Restatement'. This is reminiscent of Carroll's Bellman

in *The Hunting of the Snark*, who proclaims early in that long poem: 'What I tell you three times is true.'
26. Bruce Littleboy (1990, p. 308, fn 113) comments: 'Perhaps a less offensive and more modern term, "love-child Keynesians" could be used instead.'

REFERENCES

Amadeo, E.J. (1989), *Keynes's Principle of Effective Demand*, Aldershot, Hants: Edward Elgar.

Andrews, P.W.S. and Brunner, E. (1975), *Studies in Pricing*, London: Macmillan.

Arrow, K.J. and Hahn, F. (1971), *General Competitive Analysis*, San Francisco: Holden-Day.

Bushaw, D.W. and Clower, R.W. (1957), *Introduction to Mathematical Economics*, Homewood, Ill.: Richard D. Irwin.

Clower, R.W. (1989), 'Keynes' *General Theory*: the Marshall Connection' in *Perspectives in the History of Economic Thought*, edited by Walker, Volume II, Aldershot, Hants: Edward Elgar, pp. 131–47.

Clower, R.W. (1991), 'Ohlin and the *General Theory*' in *The Stockholm School of Economics Revisited*, edited by Jonung, New York: Cambridge University Press, pp. 245–62.

Clower, R.W. and Due, J.F. (1972), *Microeconomics*, Homewood, Ill.: Richard D. Irwin.

Davidson, P. and Smolensky, E. (1964), *Aggregate Supply and Demand Analysis*, New York: Harper and Row.

Davis, J.R. and Casey, F.J., Jr (1977), '"Keynes" Misquotation of Mill', *Economic Journal*, **87**, June, 329–30, further comment in *Economic Journal*, September, 658–9.

Douglas, P.H. (1935), *Controlling Depressions*, New York: Norton.

Edgeworth, F. Y. (1925), *Selected Papers in Political Economy*, Volume 3, London: Macmillan.

Haavelmo, T. (1978), 'What Can Static Equilibrium Models Tell Us?', *Economic Inquiry*, April 1974, 27–34.

Hansen, A.H. (1938), *Full Recovery or Stagnation?*, New York: Norton.

Hansen, A.H. (1953), *A Guide to Keynes*, New York: McGraw-Hill.

Harris, S.E. (1946), *The New Economics*, New York: Knopf.

Hicks, John (1982), *Money, Interest and Wages, Collected Essays in Economic Theory*, Volume 2, Oxford: Blackwell.

Howitt, P.W. and McAfee, R.P. (1992), 'Animal Spirits', *American Economic Review*, **82**, (3), June, 493–505.

Jaffe, William (1956), English language translation of Walras's *Elements*, London: Allen and Unwin.

Kahn, R.F. (1984), *The Making of Keynes' General Theory*, New York: Cambridge University Press.

Keynes, John Maynard (1934), 'Poverty in Plenty: Is the Economic System Self-Adjusting?', *Listener*, **12**, November, 850–1; reprinted in *JMK*, XIII, 485–92.

Keynes, John Maynard (1936), *JMK*, VII.

Keynes, John Maynard, *Collected Writings*, 30 volumes, varying dates, 1971–90, London: Macmillan, for the Royal Economic Society.

Klein, Lawrence R. (1947), *The Keynesian Revolution*, New York: Macmillan.

Knight, F. (1938), 'Unemployment: And Mr. Keynes's Revolution in Economic Theory', *Canadian Journal of Economics and Political Science*, 100–23.

Kuhn, T.S. (1957), *The Copernican Revolution*, New York: Vintage Books.

Leijonhufvud, Axel (1968), *On Keynesian Economics and the Economics of Keynes*, Oxford and New York: Oxford University Press.

Leijonhufvud, Axel (1983), 'What was the Matter with IS-LM?' in *Modern Macroeconomic Theory*, edited by J.-P. Fitoussi, Oxford: Blackwell, pp. 64–90.

Leijonhufvud, Axel (1985), 'Ideology and Analysis in Macroeconomics' in *Economics and Philosophy*, edited by Peter Koslowski, Tübingen: Siebeck, pp. 182–207.

Lekachman, R. (1964), *Keynes' General Theory Reports of Three Decades*, New York: St Martin's Press.

Littleboy, Bruce (1990), *On Interpreting Keynes*, London: Routledge.

Malthus, T.R. (1798), *First Essay on Population*, London: Macmillan, 1926.

Marshall, A. (1889), *The Pure Theory of Domestic Values*, London: University of London (reprint of Scarce Tract, 1949).

Marshall, A. (1920), *Principles of Economics*, 8th edn, London: Macmillan.

Metzler, L.A. (1948), *Income, Employment and Public Policy : Essays in Honor of Alvin Hansen*, New York: Norton.

Mummery, A.F. and Hobson, J. (1889), *The Physiology of Industry*; reprinted in 1989, Fairfield, N.J.: Kelley.

Okun, A. (1981), *Prices and Quantities*, Princeton, N.J.: Princeton University Press.

Parkin, Michael (1990), *Economics*. Reading, MA: Addison-Wesley.

Patinkin, D. (1982), *Anticipations of the General Theory?*, Chicago: University of Chicago Press.

Phelps, E.S. (1985), *Political Economy: An Introductory Text*, New York: Norton.

Phillips, H. (1924), *'The Theory of Social Economy*, by Gustav Cassel', review of McCabe translation of 2nd end (1921) of Cassel's 1918 (Leipzig) *Theoretische Sozialökonomie, Economic Journal*, **34**, June, 235–41.

Robinson, Joan (1962), 'The General Theory after 25 Years', review of Harry Johnson's *Money, Trade and Economic Growth, Economic Journal*, **72**, 690–2.

Samuelson, Paul A. (1939), 'A Synthesis of the Principle of Acceleration and the Multiplier', *Journal of Political Economy*, **47**, December, 786–97.

Samuelson, Paul A. (1948), *Economics*. New York: McGraw-Hill.

Samuelson, Paul A. (1951), *Economics,* 2nd edn, New York: McGraw-Hill.

Samuelson, Paul A. (1955), *Economics,* 3rd edn, New York: McGraw-Hill.

Samuelson, Paul A. (1973), *Economics,* 9th edn, New York: McGraw-Hill.

Schumpeter, J.A. (1955), *History of Economic Analysis*, London: Allen and Unwin.

Simmons, G.F. (1963), *Introduction to Topology and Modern Analysis*, New York: McGraw-Hill, Appendix One, pp. 337–43.

Smith, Adam (1776), *An Inquiry into the Nature and Causes of the Wealth of Nations*, Campbell and Skinner edition in 2 volumes, edited by W.B. Todd, Oxford: The Clarendon Press.

Tarshis, Lorie (1947), *Elements of Economics*, New York: McGraw-Hill.

Tobin, J. (1980), 'Are New Classical Models Plausible Enough to Guide Policy?', *Journal of Money, Credit and Banking*, **12**, 788–99.

Tobin, J. (1986), 'The Future of Keynesian Economics', *Eastern Economic Journal*, **XII**, (4), October–December.

Walker, D.A. (1987), 'Edgeworth versus Walras on the Theory of Tâtonnement', *Eastern Economic Journal*, **13**, (2), April–June, pp. 155–65.

Walras, Léon (1874), *Elements of Pure Economics*, Jaffe Translation – see Jaffe (1956).

Whitaker, J. (1975), *The Unpublished Writings of Alfred Marshall*, 2 volumes, New York: Free Press.

5. Consumption and investment when bankruptcy is not a fate worse than death

M.J. Gordon and S.P. Sethi

INTRODUCTION

What happens to the consumption or the dividend payments of a capitalist expressed as a fraction of income or net worth as income or net worth rises? A capitalist here is a proprietor, a portfolio investor or a corporation. What happens to the allocation of a capitalist's net worth between risky productive assets (or shares of stock that are surrogates for such assets) and risk-free loans, as net worth rises? These are important questions in the Keynesian theory of employment and output, where employment and output are determined by aggregate demand, and aggregate demand is equal to the sum of consumption and investment demand in a closed capitalist system without government. If the consumption and investment of capitalists expressed as fractions of income or of net worth vary inversely with these variables, capitalist behaviour contributes to stability in the short run by absorbing random disturbances, and it creates the possibility of stagnation in the long run.

Keynes (1936) argued that consumption and investment both depend materially on how expectations about the future are arrived at, and on how decisions are made in order to cope with the problems created by uncertainty about the future. Recognition of this problem by Keynes motivated consideration of the consumption-investment behaviour of a portfolio investor, whose objective is to maximize the expected utility of future consumption. The conclusion reached in this literature, where the possibility of bankruptcy was largely ignored, is that consumption and investment expressed as fractions of net worth could rise, fall or remain unchanged, depending upon the investor's utility function.

A series of papers coauthored by S.P. Sethi from 1979 to the present and collected in Sethi (1997) investigated the consumption-investment behaviour of a portfolio investor, who maximizes the expected utility of future consumption, under a wide range of assumptions with regard to bankruptcy and the other variables of the model. In Gordon and Sethi (1997) we investigated a portfolio investor's consumption and investment behaviour under assumptions with regard to the other variables that have economic relevance, and under all HARA utility functions, the functions widely used in expected utility models. We found that the work in which bankruptcy is ignored and in which behaviour depends upon the parameters of the utility function, it is implicitly assumed that bankruptcy is a fate worse than death. It must be avoided at all cost. When it is recognized that there is life after bankruptcy, the maximization of expected utility makes consumption and investment, expressed as fractions of net worth, vary inversely with net worth under a very wide range of assumptions with regard to the investor's utility function, except for a few cases of questionable practical relevance.

The main purpose of this chapter is to present the findings in a manner that concentrates on the economics and avoids the mathematical detail to the extent possible. The next two sections will present our decision model and discuss the meaning of bankruptcy. The subsequent three sections will show how the recognition of bankruptcy in a realistic manner leads to very strong conclusions on how the fractions of net worth consumed and invested in a risky asset by a portfolio investor vary with net worth. For a post Keynesian explanation of the dividend financing and investment behaviour of corporations see Gordon (1994). The final two sections comment on the generality of our conclusions on how consumption and investment vary with net worth and on their macro implications.

Some post Keynesians, including perhaps Davidson (1991), may be uncomfortable with our use of the probability calculus and utility theory to explain consumption and investment behaviour. However, these instruments of analysis should not be rejected because they have been misused by others. Keynes demonstrated that the neoclassical theory of investment under the assumption that the future is certain is invalidated by the recognition of uncertainty. However, many neoclassical economists were reluctant to accept this conclusion. Their contribution to the counter-attack on Keynes was to replace the fantastic assumption that the future is certain with the fantastic assumptions of the Modigliani–Miller theory of corporate finance and the Arrow–Debreu state preference theory, in order to show that the recognition of uncertainty leaves unchanged the utopian properties of a perfectly competitive capitalist system. Exercises in the fantasy that we need only overcome one market imperfection or another to arrive at the promised land of a perfectly competitive capitalist system, should not blind us to the use of the probability calculus and utility theory to explain the world in which we live. The last two sections on the macro implications of our findings with respect to consumption and investment behaviour will illustrate some of their benefits.

THE DECISION MODEL

A portfolio investor with an initial net worth of $W \geq 0$ is represented in the literature as making a decision with regard to the rate of consumption $C(t)$ per unit time and a decision with regard to the fraction $\pi(t)$ of net worth $W(t)$ invested in a risky share portfolio at time t, $t \geq 0$; let $W(0) = W \geq 0$ denote the initial net worth. The objective in these decisions is to maximize the expected utility of future consumption, so that

$$J(W, C(\cdot), \pi(\cdot)) = E\left[\int_0^T e^{-\beta t} U(C(t))dt + Pe^{-\beta T}\right]. \tag{1}$$

Here (i) E is the expected value operator, (ii) β is a discount rate that converts utility *not* money on any date in the future to its present value, (iii) $U(C)$ is the utility of consumption $C \geq 0$, with the nature of the function to be specified later, and (iv) P is the utility of what the investor receives in the event of bankruptcy, which takes place at time T as soon as $W(t)$ falls to zero.

The investor's life is assumed to be infinite, but a finite life can be recognized in some measure by varying the discount rate β; see Presman and Sethi (1997c). The date T at which bankruptcy takes place is uncertain, but it depends in part on the consumption-portfolio decisions over time, and they depend in part on what the investor receives in bankruptcy. It has been found mathematically convenient to model share prices over time as diffusion processes, and consequently to have net worth change with time according to the following stochastic differential equation:

$$dW(t) = (\alpha - r)\pi(t)W(t)dt + (rW(t) - C(t))dt + \sigma\pi(t)W(t)dZ(t),$$
$$W(0) = W. \tag{2}$$

Here, α is the mean return on the risky share portfolio,[1] r is the interest rate on a risk-free loan, σ^2 is the variance of the risky returns, $\alpha > r$, $\sigma > 0$, and $Z(t)$ is a standard Brownian motion on the given probability space. The net worth $W(t)$ is assumed to change continuously over time according to the mathematics of Brownian motion. Thus, $W(t) \geq 0$, $0 \leq t \leq T$.[2]

The utility functions that are widely used to solve the above decision problem are called HARA utility functions. They have the power function form:

$$U \overset{*}{=} \frac{|\delta|(C+\eta)^\delta}{\delta}, \quad \delta < 1, \quad \delta \neq 0, \tag{3}$$

or the logarithmic form (when $\delta = 0$)

$$U = \ln(C + \eta) \tag{4}$$

When $\eta < 0$, the restriction $C \geq -\eta$ must be imposed on (3) and (4) for them to be defined.

Arrow (1965) and Pratt (1964) showed that when the argument of the utility function is net worth, W, *not* C, the investor has decreasing absolute risk aversion, because the investment in the risky asset increases with net worth. The investor is described as having decreasing absolute risk aversion, since the measure of absolute risk aversion is $1/(W + \eta)$, and the *amount* invested in the risky asset increases with net worth. The measure of relative risk aversion is $W/(W + \eta)$, and the investor is said to have increasing, constant or decreasing relative risk aversion, depending on whether η is positive, zero or negative, since the *fraction* of net worth invested in the risky asset then falls, remains unchanged or rises as net worth rises. However, no immediate inference can be drawn about how the fraction of net worth consumed or invested varies with net worth, when consumption is the argument of the utility function. What is needed is the investor's derived utility of wealth $V(W)$, which is the maximum value of the expected utility in (1) over the class of investor's consumption and investment policies. This derived utility of wealth has been obtained explicitly in Karatzas, *et al.* (1986) and Sethi, *et al.* (1992), and analysed further in Presman and Sethi (1991, 1997a, b). These form the basis of our further discussions.

MEANING OF BANKRUPTCY

How a capitalist behaves under any utility function depends materially on what she expects with regard to the conditions under which bankruptcy takes place and what will be the consequences of bankruptcy. On the first of these two questions, it is widely accepted in theoretical work that bankruptcy takes place when net worth falls to zero. That is a reasonable assumption for a portfolio investor, and it will be made here. However, it should be noted that for proprietors and for corporations, necessary but not sufficient conditions for bankruptcy are: (1) the individual or corporation does not find it possible or expedient to meet debt obligations as they fall due; (2) debt obligations in total are greater than the market value of assets; and (3) a receiver is appointed to decide what should be done.[3] Bankruptcy then takes place, when and if the receiver declares the individual or corporation bankrupt, disposes of the assets, distributes the proceeds among the creditors in some way and wipes out the creditor claims against the individual or corporation. If a stroke of good fortune is experienced somewhere along the way, the receivership is terminated and life continues as before.

Hence, bankruptcy is not so fearful a prospect for proprietors and corporations as it is for portfolio investors.

To elaborate on when bankruptcy takes place for a portfolio investor, assume that an investor with $W = \$100$ decides to borrow $\$1\,000\,000$ and invest $\$1\,000\,100$ in the share portfolio. The investor has $\pi(W) = 10\,001$ and $1 - \pi(W) = -10\,000$. If the investor, on the other hand, had decided to invest $75 and lend the remaining \$25, he would have had $\pi(W) = 0.75$ and $1 - \pi(W) = 0.25$. However, with $\pi(W) = 10\,001$, the interest paid on the loan, the amount consumed, and a fall in the value of the portfolio, all totalling just $100 would reduce the investor's net worth to zero. In the very short time that this took place, the stock portfolio would be liquidated and the proceeds used to pay off the debt in full. The investor would be bankrupt as defined here and she would enter a new state – beggar, welfare recipient, or worker.

When bankruptcy takes place, the investor enters a state in which consumption is forecast to be at the rate $B(t)$, for t from T to ∞, with the time of bankruptcy T uncertain until it arrives. For simplicity we let P represent the discounted utility at T of that consumption stream, and its expected utility discounted to $t = 0$ is $EPe^{-\beta T}$. If $B(t) = B$ for all t from T to ∞, then $P = U(B)/\beta$. A special case of particular interest is the utility at T from the worst possible forecast of consumption thereafter, that is $B = \max [0, -\eta]$. We then have $P = \tilde{P} = U(B)/\beta$, which is $-\infty$ when $\eta \leq 0$ and finite when $\eta > 0$. Note also that when $U(C) = \ln C$, we get $P = 0$ when $B = 1$.[4]

Bankruptcy may carry with it negative or positive psychic income, the former to the extent that shame attaches to going bankrupt or living on the dole. The psychic income may be positive for devoutly religious people who believe that poverty is a blessing, and perhaps for others. In what follows we ignore psychic income, so that the difference between P and $\tilde{P}$ arises solely from the forecast consumption in bankruptcy. The value of P in bankruptcy depends upon whether the investor expects to become a beggar, go on the dole, become a thief, or find some other kind of employment. In earlier times bankruptcy could result in imprisonment, slavery or even death.

The behaviour of investors who are represented with HARA utility functions can be classified according to whether $\eta = 0$, $\eta > 0$ or $\eta < 0$. The next section is devoted to $\eta = 0$.

η EQUAL TO ZERO

The graph in Figure 5.1 shows the relation between $\pi(W)$ and W, when $\eta = 0$ and P takes on various values. This is a particularly important case, since we may presume $\eta = 0$, when there is no reason to believe it is different from zero. When $P = \tilde{P} = U(0)/\beta = -\infty$, that is when the investor receives nothing in

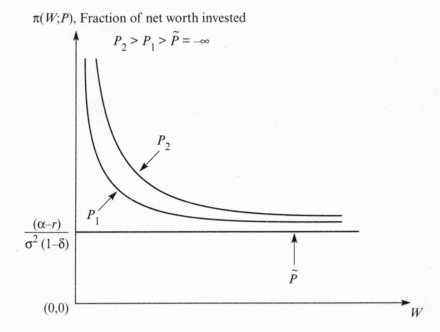

$\pi(W;P)$, Fraction of net worth invested

Figure 5.1 *Fraction π(W; P) of net worth invested in the risky asset, when net worth is W, the utility of bankruptcy is P, and η = 0*

bankruptcy, the utility of that state is minus infinity, and the fraction of net worth invested in the risky portfolio is independent of net worth. It is:

$$\pi(W; \tilde{P}) = \pi^* = \frac{(\alpha - r)}{\sigma^2(1-\delta)}. \qquad (5)$$

Note that when $\delta = 0$, that is when $U = \ln C$, π^* is the excess of the expected return on the risky portfolio over the risk-free interest rate, divided by the variance of the return on the risky portfolio.

As the consumption in bankruptcy rises above the zero level, so that P rises above $\tilde{P}$, the fraction of net worth invested in the share portfolio at $W = 0$ rises above π^*. Furthermore, as $W \to \infty$, the value of π approaches π^* asymptotically from above as drawn in Figure 5.1. Hence, when consumption in bankruptcy is merely positive and its utility is greater than minus infinity, the fraction of net worth invested in the risky portfolio decreases with net worth. Moreover, the fraction increases with P, the utility of the payoff in bankruptcy.

Figure 5.2 graphs the relation between consumption and net worth for various values of P with $\eta = 0$. $C(W; P)$ is consumption when net worth is W and the utility of consumption in bankruptcy is P. When $P = \tilde{P}$, consumption is a fraction of W that is independent of W. More specifically:

$$C(W; \tilde{P}) = \frac{\psi}{(1-\delta)^2} W, \tag{6}$$

with

$$\psi = r\delta^2 - \delta(r + \gamma + \beta) + \beta, \tag{7}$$

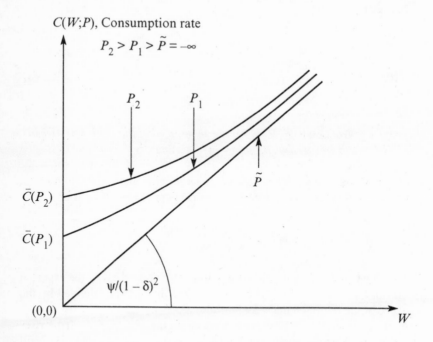

Figure 5.2   Consumption C(W; P) *when net worth is* W, *the utility of bankruptcy is* P, *and* $\eta = 0$

and $\gamma = (\alpha - r)^2/2\sigma^2$. Note that when $\delta = 0$, in which case the investor has logarithmic utility, $\psi = \beta$, and the fraction of net worth consumed is β, the rate at which utility is discounted.

As P rises above $\tilde{P}$, C at $W = 0$ rises above zero, and $C(W; P)$ rises above $C(W; \tilde{P})$ for each value of W. As $W \to \infty$, $C(W; P)$ approaches $C(W; \tilde{P})$ from above asymptotically. Hence, C/W like π decreases with W and increases with P.

There is a simple economic explanation for the variation in investment and consumption with net worth shown in Figures 5.1 and 5.2. With $\eta = 0$, the marginal utility of consumption at $C = 0$ is infinite. Hence, when $C = 0$ in bankruptcy, bankruptcy is considered a fate worse than death. It is to be avoided at all cost. Specifically, when $P = \tilde{P} = -\infty$, $C(W; \tilde{P}) = W\psi/(1 - \delta)^2$ and $\pi(W; \tilde{P}) = \pi^*$ for all W. Both ψ and π^* are independent of W, and we then have consumption and risky investment go to zero as net worth goes to zero, in a way so as to ensure that the investor never goes bankrupt. If the net worth falls to the equivalent of one kilo of rice, only a part of it is consumed, and the remainder is not all planted. Another part is set aside to guarantee that there is some rice to consume and seed for the next crop if this one fails.

As P rises above $\tilde{P}$ and the prospects of life after bankruptcy become less terrifying, the investor becomes more willing to risk bankruptcy. When net worth is low, the low consumption dictated by the no bankruptcy policy becomes increasingly intolerable by comparison with the consumption available in bankruptcy, and the fraction of net worth consumed rises. Similarly, the conservative investment policy that avoids bankruptcy at all cost, offers little prospect of any improvement in net worth, and what is called a 'go-for-broke' policy becomes increasingly attractive. The probability of soon going bankrupt and the probability of soon getting rich are both increased by moving to a very high debt-equity ratio.

It is easy to see why $C(W; P)/W$ and $\pi(W; P)$ move asymptotically towards $\psi/(1 - \delta)^2$ and π^* respectively, as W becomes large, regardless of the value of P. As W becomes large, bankruptcy becomes increasingly remote and irrelevant.

It may be noted that Samuelson (1969), Merton (1969, 1971) and others after them ignored bankruptcy. See, e.g., Richard (1979) and Ingersoll (1992). In doing so they implicitly assumed that consumption in bankruptcy will be zero and the utility of zero consumption when $\eta = 0$ is minus infinity. Hence, the implicit assumption in this literature for HARA utility functions with $\eta = 0$ is that bankruptcy is a fate worse than death.[5]

η GREATER THAN ZERO

It will be recalled that when net worth and *not* consumption is the argument of an investor's utility function, $\eta > 0$ would represent increasing relative risk aversion, in that the fraction of net worth invested in a risky asset falls as net worth rises. What happens when consumption is the argument of the utility function cannot be described so simply. As η rises above zero, utility for each value of C including $C = 0$ rises, while the marginal utility at each value of C falls, with $U'(C)$ falling *strictly* below infinity at $C = 0$. The economic interpretation of $\eta > 0$ is that the pleasure from consumption for any level of C rises with η, while the pleasure from increasing C at each level of C declines as η rises. Also, with marginal utility finite at $C = 0$, the fear of bankruptcy falls as η rises, and the investor with $\eta > 0$ does not take the drastic measures to avoid bankruptcy that are employed by the investor with $\eta = 0$.

Figure 5.3 plots the relation between C and W for various values of P when $\eta > 0$ and $r < \psi/(1 - \delta)^2$. What happens when $r > \psi/(1 - \delta)^2$ will be discussed shortly. In Figure 5.3, $\bar{W}(P_1)$ is the net worth up to which $C = 0$ when $P = P_1$. It can be seen that when $P = \tilde{P}$, that is when the investor faces zero consumption after bankruptcy, $C = 0$ up to some positive value of W, call it $\bar{W}(\tilde{P})$. As W rises above $\bar{W}(\tilde{P})$, C rises above zero and asymptotically approaches from below $C(W; P^*)$, where $C(W; P^*) = W\psi/(1 - \delta)^2$.

The value of $\bar{W}(P)$ increases with η and decreases with P. Hence, as P rises above $\tilde{P}$, the value of $\bar{W}(P)$ moves towards zero, and it becomes zero at some value of P, designated P^* in Figure 5.3. For $P > P^*$, consumption is positive at $W = 0$, and C rises with P at $W = 0$. Also for $P > P^*$, C rises with W, asymptotically approaching $W\psi/(1 - \delta)^2$ from above. Note that in Figure 5.3, there is a value $\hat{P} > P^*$ for which $C(W; \hat{P})$ is a straight line with its intercept on the C-axis. The latter is true for $\eta > 0$ when $r < \psi/(1 - \delta)^2$. When $r > \psi/(1 - \delta)^2$, $\hat{P} > P^*$, and the straight line $C(W; \hat{P})$ has its intercept on the W-axis. In this case we still have $C(W; P)$ positive at $W = 0$, when $P > P^*$. Initially, $C(W; P)$ is equal to zero when $W > 0$ for $P < P^*$, as in Figure 5.3. In the border-line case $r = \psi/(1 - \delta)^2$, $\hat{P} = P^*$, and $C(W; \hat{P})$ passes through the origin, meaning that $C(W; \hat{P}) = C(W; P^*) = W\psi/(1 - \delta)^2$.[6]

What can we say about how consumption varies with W when $\eta > 0$? First, we can rule out the case of $P < P^*$, where $C = 0$ up to some positive wealth. Clearly, it makes no sense to set $C = 0$ and starve with $W > 0$. This is particularly true when $P > \tilde{P}$ and positive consumption is available in bankruptcy. Next, when $r < \psi/(1 - \delta)^2$ and $C(W; \hat{P})$ has its intercept on the C-axis, $C(W; \hat{P})/W$ falls continuously as W rises, and this inverse relation also holds between $C(W; P)/W$ and W for all values of $P > P^*$. When $r > \psi/(1 - \delta)^2$ and $C(W; \hat{P})$ has its intercept on the W-axis, we still have the intercept of $C(W; P)$

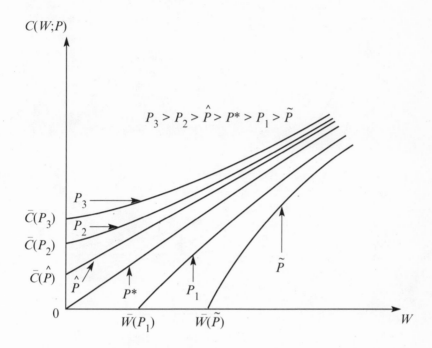

Figure 5.3 Consumption C(W; P) *when net worth is* W, *the utility of bankruptcy is* P, *and* η > 0

on the C-axis for $P > P^*$ as noted earlier. Now, $C(W; P)/W$ for $P > P^*$ falls up to some value of W and then rises, asymptotically approaching the slope of $C(W; \hat{P})$ as $W \to \infty$. The larger the value of P, the longer this interval of W over which C/W falls as W rises. Hence, the inverse relation between C./W and W is not true only for $r > \psi/(1 - \delta)^2$ and W above some value, a value that increases with P.

Figure 5.4 depicts the relation between $\pi(W; P)$ and W for a given $\eta > 0$ and as P rises above $\tilde{P}$. When $P = \tilde{P}$, $\pi > \pi^*$ at $W = 0$. As η rises with $P = \tilde{P}$, Presman and Sethi (1997a) show that the value of π = at $W = 0$ rises and the interval of W over which π remains constant increases. As W rises above zero, π remains unchanged over some interval of W that corresponds to the interval of W over which $C = 0$ in Figure 5.3. As W rises above this value, π falls asymptotically towards π^*. As P rises above $\tilde{P}$ the value of π at $W = 0$ tends to infinity, and the rate at which π falls towards π^* increases.

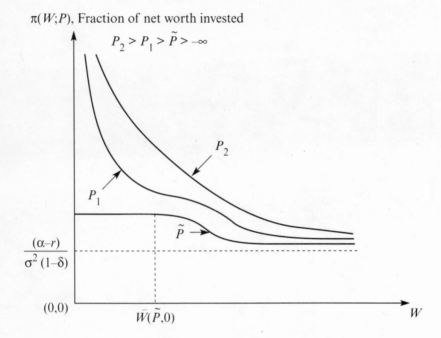

$\pi(W;P)$, Fraction of net worth invested

$$P_2 > P_1 > \tilde{P} > -\infty$$

*Figure 5.4   Fraction $\pi(W; P)$ of net worth invested in the risky asset, when
net worth is W, the utility of bankruptcy is P, and $\eta > 0$*

Recall that when net worth is the argument, a utility function with $\eta > 0$
implies increasing relative risk aversion. That is, as the investor's wealth
increases, aversion to risk is satisfied by putting a smaller fraction of net
worth in the risky asset. Hence, the above behaviour is even more reasonable
for $\eta > 0$ than for $\eta = 0$. Consequently, for sufficiently large values of P, $\eta > 0$
is qualitatively the same as $\eta = 0$ with respect to consumption and investment
policy. Consumption and investment, expressed as fractions of net worth,
both fall as net worth increases. The only difference between $\eta = 0$ and $\eta > 0$
is that for any pair of values for W and P, C is smaller and $\pi(W; P)$ is larger as
η rises above zero.

η LESS THAN ZERO

Recall that when net worth and *not* consumption is the argument of an investor's utility function, $\eta < 0$ means that the investor has decreasing relative risk aversion, because the fraction of net worth invested in the risky portfolio rises with net worth. However, when consumption is the argument of the utility function, the interpretation of how consumption and investment vary with net worth is considerably more complex.

With $\eta < 0$, $U(C)$ is not defined for $C < -\eta$, just as it was not defined for $C < 0$ when $\eta = 0$. The economic interpretation of ruling out $C < 0$ when $\eta = 0$ is that negative consumption is not possible. The economic interpretation of ruling out $C < -\eta$ when $\eta < 0$ is that the investor finds it quite impossible to even contemplate living on $C \leq -\eta$. That is, $C \leq -\eta$ is a fate worse than death, and $P = \tilde{P} = -\infty$ when the periodic consumption after bankruptcy is $S = -\eta$. Mathematically, with $\eta < 0$, the marginal utility of consumption at $C = -\eta$ is infinite. By comparison with $\eta = 0$, the investor with $\eta < 0$ gains less satisfaction from any level of C, and she gains more satisfaction from increasing C at each level of C, while attaching the greatest importance to ensuring that C does not fall below some minimum level. Perhaps $S = -\eta$ should be called a bare subsistence level, with consumption below S, intolerable for an investor with $\eta < 0$.

Consider first the case of a consumption rate in bankruptcy of S or less, in which case $P = \tilde{P} = -\infty$, and bankruptcy is a completely unacceptable state. If $W \leq S/r$, every feasible solution for $C(t)$ and $\pi(t)$ is equally optimal from a mathematical point of view, since they are all equally bad. Bankruptcy is completely unacceptable, but nothing can be done to avoid with certainty the terrible consequences of bankruptcy. Casual empiricism suggests that most people in this situation will set $C(t) > S$ and $\pi(t)$ large, since it offers some hope of escape from bankruptcy. If the investor is fortunate enough to have $W > S/r$, she can and will consume S plus $\psi/(1 - \delta)^2$ times the excess of W over S/r, thereby making it certain never to go bankrupt.

The relation between C and W for various values of P is graphed in Figure 5.5 for a given value of $S = -\eta > 0$. As $S = -\eta$ is raised, $C(W; \tilde{P})$ in Figure 5.5 shifts higher and to the right and $\overline{W}(\tilde{P}, S)$ increases. There are some people for whom $-\eta$ is quite large. They find it impossible to live unless it is lived royally, and that is what they do as long as the money lasts. For most people with a personality represented by $\eta < 0$, however, $-\eta$ is likely to represent at most a very modest standard of living, if not a bare subsistence standard of living, in which case the consumption rate in bankruptcy is likely to be greater than $-\eta$, or in other words $P = \tilde{P} = -\infty$. In that event $C(W; P)$ is positive at $W = 0$, and its intercept on the C-axis is greater than S, as drawn in Figure 5.5. Consumption at $W = 0$ is greater than $-\eta$, since it makes no sense

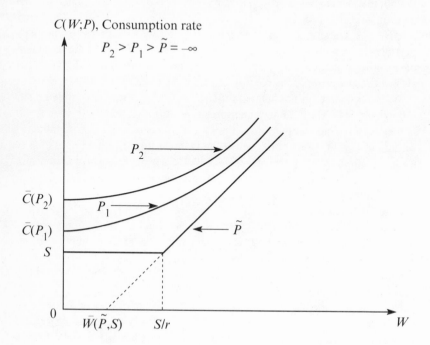

Figure 5.5   Consumption C(W; P) when net worth is W, the utility of
bankruptcy is P, $\eta < 0$, and the minimum possible
consumption is S = $-\eta > 0$.

to consume less in order to avoid bankruptcy. Consumption then rises with W, asymptotically approaching from above the value $C(W; \tilde{P})$.

In Figure 5.5, $C(W; \tilde{P})$ is drawn on the assumption that $r < \psi/(1 - \delta)^2$. Its intercept here is on the W-axis, in contrast with Figure 5.3, where the intercept is on the C-axis when $r < \psi/(1 - \delta)^2$ and $\eta > 0$. The value of the intercept $\bar{W}(\tilde{P}, S) = S[1/r - (1 - \delta)^2/\psi] > 0$. In Figure 5.5, $C(W; P)/W$ is infinite at $W = 0$, it falls over some intervals of W that increases with P, and thereafter it rises with W, asymptotically approaching $W\psi/(1 - \delta)^2$. On the other hand, when $r > \psi/(1 - \delta)^2$, the intercept of $C(W; P)$ is on the C-axis, and $C(W; P)/W$ falls continuously as W rises.

Figure 5.6 graphs the relation between π and W for various values of P. Not on Figure 5.6 is the relation between π and W when $P = \tilde{P}$ and $W < S/r$. As noted earlier the mathematics fail us in this case, since all solutions are

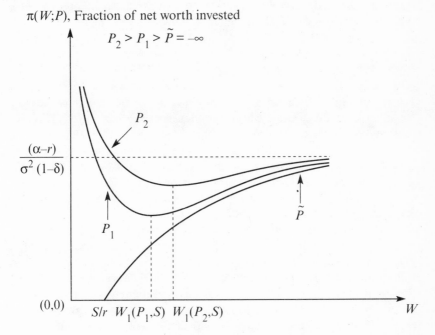

$\pi(W;P)$, Fraction of net worth invested

Figure 5.6 *Fraction $\pi(W)$ of net worth invested in the risky asset when $\eta < 0$ and $S = -\eta$ and various values of P, the utility of bankruptcy.*

Note: In this figure, we do not know precisely the relative locations of $W_1(P_1, S)$ and S/r. But this knowledge is not essential for the purpose of this chapter.

equally unacceptable. With $P = \tilde{P}$, as W rises above S/r, π rises above zero, approaching $\pi^* = (\alpha - r)/\sigma^2(1 - \delta)$ asymptotically from below as $W \to \infty$. The value of π like the value of C is constrained by the objective of not letting the wealth fall below S/r. The investor in this case exhibits decreasing relative risk aversion in that the fraction of net worth in the risky asset increases with net worth. The strange thing about this solution is that this investor with decreasing relative risk aversion puts less in the risky asset at all values of W than the investors with $\eta \geq 0$.

The most interesting and difficult case is the relation between π and W as P rises above $\tilde{P}$, that is when the consumption in bankruptcy is more or less greater than the investors' bare subsistence level. We see in Figure 5.6 that when $P > \tilde{P}$, π falls as W rises until W reaches W_1, and thereafter it rises asymptotically approaching $\pi^* = (\alpha - r)/\sigma^2(1 - \delta)$. Consequently, the investor exhibits increasing relative risk aversion initially, and then decreasing relative risk aversion once W rises above W_1. The value of π tends to infinity at $W = 0$. While W_1 increases with P, we do not have an explicit formula for W_1.

CONSUMPTION BEHAVIOUR

The previous pages have investigated the consumption and investment behaviour of a portfolio investor who maximizes the expected utility of future consumption under a utility function that is plausible and widely used in theoretical work. We saw that when it is recognized that there is life after bankruptcy, the fraction of net worth consumed decreases with net worth under a wide range of combinations of parameters of the utility function. As one might expect, the less unattractive the investor's prospects in bankruptcy, the greater the tendency to make the fraction of net worth consumed fall as net worth rises. Furthermore, for any given utility in bankruptcy, the lower the investor's net worth, the larger the fraction of net worth consumed and the greater its variation with net worth.

Portfolio investors represent only one class of economic actors. Other classes are proprietors, workers and corporations. Proprietors are real persons like portfolio investors, and they also can be represented as maximizing the expected utility of future consumption in their consumption-investment decisions at each point in time. The market for the assets of a proprietor is not as liquid as the market for the assets of a portfolio investor. Hence, the transaction costs of moving from one capital structure to another make it more difficult for proprietors to implement the consumption-investment policy that maximizes the utility of future consumption. However, proprietors share this objective with portfolio investors, and higher transaction costs should not result in qualitative differences in their behaviour.

Corporations present a radically different problem in that they are not real persons and do not consume. They pay dividends, but the dividends they pay cannot be treated like the consumption of a real person. Hence, our model cannot explain the dividend policy of corporations.

Bodie *et al.* (1992) established the consumption and investment that maximize expected utility for a person whose net worth is $W = W_1 + W_2$ with W_1 portfolio assets and W_2 non-traded human capital derived from prospective employment income. They argue that it is possible to trade around human capital, so that the distinction between the two types of assets can be ignored in maximizing expected utility.[7] In reaching this conclusion, Bodie *et al.* assumed that the individual has a known life and bankruptcy can be ignored.

When the latter assumption is withdrawn, the problem of taking possession of someone else's human capital arises. This can be seen by reducing the value of Jones's risky capital from $1 500 to $500 in footnote 7, in which case his net worth falls to zero, and creditors face the problem of taking possession of $900 worth of human capital. To the extent that it is possible to trade around human and illiquid capital, the conclusions reached here are not confined to persons whose income is from nonhuman capital.

Among Keynes's most important contributions to economic theory was his consumption function, under which the fraction of income consumed varies inversely with income. Our finding that the same relation exists with net worth replacing income as the independent variable generalizes and provides further support for Keynes's theory. However, theories of consumption at odds with the Keynesian consumption function have contributed significantly to two Nobel Prizes, one to Milton Friedman and the other to Franco Modigliani. Friedman's (1957) permanent income hypothesis makes the positive constant term found in linear regressions of consumption on actual income consistent with having the fraction of income consumed independent of income, when permanent income is the independent variable. In fact, permanent income is proportional to wealth. Hence, our conclusion is at odds with Friedman's theory. The explanation is quite simple. His theorem was developed 'under conditions of complete certainty' (Friedman, 1957, p. 7).

After establishing the truth of his hypothesis under certainty, Friedman (1957) acknowledged that he had no answers to the questions posed by the presence of uncertainty, and he concluded as follows (p. 15):

> The introduction of uncertainty thus blurs the sharp lines of the above analysis, and suggest additional factors that may produce departures from the shape of the consumption function specified in (2.5). However, on the present level of analysis, there seems no way to judge whether these factors would tend to make consumption a larger or a smaller fraction of wealth the higher the absolute level of wealth. Accordingly, this effect of uncertainty establishes no presumption against the shape assigned to the consumption function, and thus casts no shadow on the "simplicity" that recommends it.

It would seem that the time has arrived to abandon the 'permanent income' hypothesis. See also Deaton (1992).

In the Modigliani–Brumberg (1954) life cycle theory of consumption, its relation to income depends materially on age. People save during their productive years in order to consume during their retirement, and consumption and income are equal over the individual's entire life. Consequently, the aggregate relation between consumption and income depends upon such variables as the age distribution and the growth rate of the population. Clearly, this theory abstracts from uncertainty, uncertainty about how long the individual will live as well as future income. Our model deals explicitly with uncertainty about future income, and our assumption that the investor has an infinite life is more realistic than the assumption of a known finite life and no concern for descendants. Merton (1971), Richard (1975) and Presman and Sethi (1997c) have proposed various ways to recognize a finite life, none of them completely satisfactory. However, it is not likely that the satisfactory recognition of an uncertain finite life with a bequest function would change radically our consumption function.

INVESTMENT BEHAVIOUR

With respect to investment, we found an inverse relation between the fraction of net worth invested in the risky asset and net worth for all HARA utility functions, except those with $\eta < 0$, that is decreasing relative risk aversion. Even then we have the same relation between the fraction of net worth invested in the risky asset and net worth up to some value of net worth. Only after net worth rises above some value, does the fraction reverse itself and rise with net worth. Then, as $W \to \infty$ the fraction approaches as an upper limit the same value that the fraction falls to on the part of investors with constant or increasing relative risk aversion.

What is the theoretical basis for questioning the conclusion that the fraction of net worth invested in risky assets falls as net worth rises? When Keynes (1936) was being written, the neoclassical theory of investment under certainty was the prevailing theory. Under it the individual or firm maximized net worth, with the investment that equates its marginal rate of return with the interest rate, and that investment is independent of the investor's net worth. Keynes (1936, Book IV) expressed great dissatisfaction with the theory because it failed to recognize the presence of uncertainty, but he provided no alternative theory.

The postwar development of neoclassical theory under uncertainty distinguished between real and corporate persons. Corporations invest in real assets, and they maximize net worth as before, except that the cutoff rate is the expected rate of return on the risky asset, α. The risk premium $\alpha - r$ is large enough to persuade portfolio investors to hold the outstanding quantities of risky shares and risk-free loans. Real persons are now portfolio investors who invest πW in risky shares and put $(1 - \pi)W$ in risk-free loans, with the objective of maximizing expected utility. The value of π that maximizes expected utility increases with the risk premium $\alpha - r$. With bankruptcy unrecognized nothing can be said on how π varies with net worth.

The conclusions reached here for portfolio investors on investment would seem to hold for proprietors as well. Here as with dividend policy, there is no simple extension of our model to explain the behaviour of corporations. However, if corporations maximize market value, they respond to the behaviour of portfolio investors, because their investment varies inversely with α. In fact, corporations compromise concern for market value with concern for long-run survival. Gordon (1994) has shown that dividend, financing and investment policies reflect the latter concern, and corporate policies have much in common with our findings for portfolio investors.

At the start of this chapter it was stated that the consumption-investment behaviour of portfolio investors established here helps explain two important characteristics of capitalist systems. One is their ability to absorb exogenous changes in demand, and the other is their tendency to experience excess supply. We will now provide the basis for these statements, without constructing a complete macro model.

First, it should be clear that in capitalist systems the supply of output does not generate its own demand, due to the way in which individuals find economic security in capitalist systems. In pre-capitalist systems, people dealt with the problem of uncertainty about future harvests and about supply in general by storing the objects of consumption. Hence, supply generated its own demand, whether it be for consumption or for storage. Storage also takes place in capitalist systems, but such storage is specialized in firms that do so for profit and not for security. These firms like all other firms and like individuals find security by increasing the fraction of net worth held in the form of loans, both interest and non-interest bearing loans, that are free of default risk. The macro supply of output insofar as it is undertaken for the purpose of acquiring such assets does not generate its own demand for the output. It also does not increase the supply of risk-free assets in a closed system. Risk-free loans are a wonderful instrument for security on the micro level. Holding them earns a positive instead of a negative interest rate. Furthermore, they have negative betas, in that their real value rises as the economy declines, when calling these loans becomes needed to supplement current income. However, the use of nominal risk-free loans for economic security wreaks havoc with the relation between supply and demand on the macro level. In the long run, the desire to increase economic security as wealth increases is satisfied by increasing the fraction of net worth in risk-free loans, and that makes excess supply a chronic problem of capitalist systems. They experience secular stagnation, without the more or less regular introduction into the system of new capitalists, who have extraordinary profitable investment opportunities, and who borrow heavily to take advantage of them. Otherwise the desire for security and the maintenance of aggregate demand are satisfied most effectively by growth in the public debt.

In the short run, the use of risk-free nominal loans to provide security creates a problem of instability. An individual or firm can make demand greater than supply by drawing on liquid assets or borrowing, and an excess of supply over demand can be devoted to liquid assets or debt retirement. This creates a problem of stability, because an exogenous rise in real investment by corporations raises profitability, the rise in profitability raises investment, and so on. This upward spiral is restrained and reversed to the extent that the investment cut-off rate α is raised as the return on investment function is shifted up. A rise in the interest rate serves that objective. In addition, the rise in net worth with investment and profitability also curbs the expansion, because the inverse relation between $\pi(W)$ and W makes the risk premium in α rise with W.

NOTES

1. If there are a number of risky securities available, they can be replaced by a single mutual fund. The result is known as the mutual fund theorem or the Tobin separation theorem; see Tobin (1958), Merton (1971), and Karatzas *et al.* (1986).
2. It has been shown that such a restriction on net worth precludes arbitrage opportunities; see, for example, Dybvig and Huang (1988).
3. See also Senbet and Seward (1995).
4. The unit of consumption may be looked on as some multiple of one, say $10\,000$ with one year the unit of time.
5. Merton (1973), Richard (1979), Breeden (1979), and others used the 1971 Merton model in their development of dynamic capital asset pricing models. In doing so they, like Merton (1971), ignored bankruptcy. Karatzas, Lehoczky and Shreve (1987), Cox and Huang (1989), Cadenillas and Sethi (1997) and others generalize the wealth equation (2) to allow for random market coefficients, but with the exception of Cadenillas and Sethi, they do not model bankruptcy explicitly and they have the investor consume nothing after his wealth reaches zero. Karatzas, Lehoczky and Shreve (1990) and others develop equilibrium models via the construction of a single representative agent. No consideration is given to bankruptcy in these models. For additional references, see Sethi (1997, 1998) and Duffie (1996).
6. $C(W ; P)$ approaches $C(W; \hat{P})$ asymptotically as $W \to \infty$ for all values of P including P^*. However, the relation between C/W and W depends on the relation between r and $\psi/(1 - \delta)^2$. When $r < \psi/(1 - \delta)^2$, $C(W; \hat{P})$ has its intercept on the C-axis, and the inverse relation also holds between $C(W ; P)W$ and W for all values of W when $P > P^*$. Also, recall that when $\delta = 0$ and we have logarithmic utility, $\psi/(1 - \delta)^2$ reduces to β. Hence, r is then above (below) $\psi/(1 - \delta)^2$ when r is above (below) β. When $\delta > 0$, the relation between r and $\psi/(1 - \delta)^2$ does not reduce to the relation between r and β.
7. For instance, let Smith and Jones be identical, except that Smith has $W_1 = \$1\,000$, and $W_2 = 0$, while Jones has $W_1 = \$100$ and $W_2 = \$900$ with the latter risk-free. They both want to put $\$1\,500$ into a risky portfolio. Smith as well as Jones can do this, the former can do so by borrowing $\$500$ and the latter by borrowing $\$1\,400$.

REFERENCES

Arrow, K.J. (1965), *Aspects of the Theory of Risk-Bearing (Yrjo Jahnsson Lectures)*. Helsinki, Finland: Yrjo Jahnssonin Saatio.

Bodie, Z., Merton, R.C. and Samuelson, W.F. (1992), 'Labour Supply Flexibility and Portfolio Choice', W. P. #3954, Cambridge, Mass.: NBER.

Breeden, D.T. (1979), 'An Intertemporal Asset Pricing Model with Stochastic Consumption and Investment Opportunities', *Journal of Financial Economics*, **7**, 265–96.

Cadenillas, A. and Sethi, S.P. (1997), 'The Consumption-Investment Problem with Subsistence Consumption, Bankruptcy, and Random Market Coefficients', *Journal of Optimization Theory and Applications*, **93** (2), and in S. P. Sethi (1997), chapter 12.

Cox, J.C. and Huang, C.-F. (1989), 'Optimal Consumption and Portfolio Policies When Asset Prices Follow a Diffusion Process', *Journal of Economic Theory*, **49**, 33–83.

Davidson, P. (1991), 'Is Probability Theory Relevant for Uncertainty?', *Journal of Economic Perspectives*, **5**, 129–44.

Deaton, A. (1992), *Understanding Consumption*, Oxford: Clarendon Press.

Duffie, D. (1996), *Dynamic Asset Pricing Theory*, 2nd edn, Princeton, NJ. Princeton University Press.

Dybvig, P. and Huang, C.-F. (1988), 'Non-negative Wealth, Absence of Arbitrage, and Feasible Consumption Plans', *Review of Financial Studies*, **1**, 377–401.

Friedman, M. (1957), *A Theory of the Consumption Function*, New Brunswick, N.J.: Princeton University Press.

Gordon, M. (1994), *Finance Investment and Macroeconomics: The Neoclassical and a Post Keynesian Solution*, Brookfield, Vt.: Edward Elgar.

Gordon, M.J. and Sethi, S.P. (1997), 'A Contribution to the Micro Foundation for Keynesian Macroeconomic Models' in S.P. Sethi (1997), chapter 11.

Ingersoll, J.E. Jr (1992), 'Optimal Consumption and Portfolio Rules with Intertemporally Dependent Utility of Consumption', *Journal of Economic Dynamics and Control*, **16**, 681–712.

Karatzas, I., Lehoczky, J., Sethi, S.P. and Shreve, S. (1986), 'Explicit Solution of a General Consumption/Investment Problem', *Mathematics of Operations Research*, **11**, 261–94.

Karatzas, I., Lehoczky, J. and Shreve, S. (1987), 'Optimal Portfolio and Consumption Decisions for a Small Investor on a Finite Horizon', *SIAM Journal on Control and Optimization*, **25**, 1557–86.

Karatzas, I., Lehoczky, J. and Shreve, S. (1990), 'Existence and Uniqueness of Multi-Agent Equilibrium in a Stochastic, Dynamic Consumption/Investment Model', *Mathematics of Operation Research*, **15**, 80–128.

Keynes, J.M. (1936), *The General Theory of Employment, Interest, and Money*, New York: Harcourt Brace.

Merton, R.C. (1969), 'Lifetime Portfolio Selection under Uncertainty: The Continuous-Time Case', *The Review of Economics and Statistics*, **51**, 247–57.

Merton, R.C. (1971), 'Optimal Consumption and Portfolio Rules in a Continuous-Time Model', *Journal of Economic Theory*, **46**, 213–14.

Merton, R.C. (1973), 'An Intertemporal Capital Asset Pricing Model', *Econometrica*, **41**, 867–87.

Modigliani, F. and Brumberg, R. (1954), 'Utility Analysis and the Consumption Function: An Interpretation of Cross-Section Data' in *Post-Keynesian Economics*, edited by K. Kurihara, New Brunswick, N.J.: Rutgers University Press, pp. 388–436.

Pratt, J.W. (1964), 'Risk Aversion in the Small and in the Large', *Econometrica*, **32**, 122–36.

Presman, E. and Sethi, S.P. (1991), 'Risk-Aversion Behavior in Consumption/Investment Problems', *Mathematical Finance*, **1** (1), 100–24.

Presman, E. and Sethi, S.P. (1997a), 'Risk-Aversion Behavior in Consumption/Investment Problems with Subsistence Consumption and Bankruptcy' in S.P. Sethi (1997), Chapter 8.

Presman, E. and Sethi, S.P. (1997b), 'Consumption Behavior in Investment/Consumption Problems in S. P. Sethi (1997), Chapter 9.

Presman, E. and Sethi, S.P. (1997c), 'Equivalence of Objective Functionals in Infinite Horizon and Random Horizon Problems', in S.P. Sethi (1997), Chapter 10.

Richard, S.F. (1975), 'Optimal Consumption, Portfolio and Life-Insurance Rules for an Uncertain lived Individual in a Continuous Time Model', *Journal of Financial Economics*, **2**, 187–203.

Richard, S.F. (1979), 'A Generalized Capital Asset Pricing Model', *TIMS Studies in the Management Sciences*, **11**, 215–32.

Samuelson, P.A. (1969), 'Lifetime Portfolio Selection by Dynamic Stochastic Programming', *The Review of Economics and Statistics*, **51**, 239–46.

Senbet, L.W. and Seward, J.K. (1995), 'Financial Distress, Bankruptcy and Reorganization' in *Finance*, edited by R.A. Jarrow, V. Maksimovic and W.T. Ziemba, Amsterdam: Elsevier, 921–61.

Sethi, S.P. (1997), *Optimal Consumption and Investment with Bankruptcy*, Boston, Mass.: Kluwer Academic Publishers.

Sethi, S.P. (1998), 'Optimal Consumption-Investment Decision Allowing for Bankruptcy: A Survey' in *World Wide Asset and Liability Modeling*, edited by W.T. Ziemba and J.M. Mulvey, Cambridge: Cambridge University Press, in press.

Sethi, S.P. and Taksar, M. (1992), 'Infinite Horizon Investment Consumption Model with a Nonterminal Bankruptcy', *Journal of Optimization Theory and Applications*, **74**, 333–46.

Sethi, S., Taksar, M. and Presman, E. (1992), 'Explicit Solution of a General Consumption/Portfolio Problem with Subsistence Consumption and Bankruptcy', *Journal of Economic Dynamics and Control*, **16**, 746–68.

Tobin, J. (1958), 'Liquidity Preference as Behavior Toward Risk', *Review of Economic Studies*, **26**, 65–86.

6. Marx, Keynes and class warfare in America

Wallace C. Peterson

In the last chapter of *The General Theory* Keynes wrote: 'The outstanding faults of the economic society in which we live are its failure to provide for full employment and its arbitrary and inequitable distribution of income and wealth' (Keynes, 1936, p. 372). Unfortunately as Keynesian economics was developed post Second World War by mainstream economists, the second part of his basic critique of the economy was all but forgotten. It is only with the emergence of post Keynesian economics, largely the result of the labour of Paul Davidson, that the economics profession is beginning to understand that distributional matters are and should be a major concern of macroeconomics. Thus, it is entirely appropriate that the issue of wealth and income distribution be addressed in this *Festschrift*.

Class warfare is an idea that frightens Americans, provoking images of bands of armed and angry workers rising up in a violent and bloody revolution to overthrow the existing social and economic order. It is an image that American conservatives invariably invoke when they fear too much attention and curiosity is being aroused about the real distribution of wealth and income. It is a tactic that succeeds brilliantly most of the time, partly because the normal state of America is a denial of reality when it comes to class – almost everyone claims middle class status irrespective of their real economic status. A second reason for the success of this tactic was the 40-plus years of the *Cold War*, a time when America believed she stood nearly alone against the worldwide spread of the Marxist system that emerged in Russia after the violent overthrow of the Czarist government in 1917. President Ronald Reagan's one-time description of the USSR as an 'evil empire' fell on receptive ears. Finally, it succeeds because the abandonment of Keynes – especially those aspects of Keynes championed by the post Keynesians – by mainstream economics allowed the stealth-like class war of conservatives to take place without any serious academic criticism. Mainstream economists are as much infatuated by the 'magic of the marketplace' as any hard right conservatives.

KARL MARX AND CLASS WARFARE

Modern ideas about class war come primarily from the writings of Karl Marx, an angry and embittered German Jew, who spent most of his adult life in England writing his great masterpiece, *Das Kapital* (Capital), an exhausting analysis and scathing indictment of 19th century capitalism. Marxism, as his system of analysis is usually called, rests upon two fundamental ideas. The first is that the bedrock foundation of every society is *economic* – how it organizes itself to produce and use the goods and services essential to sustain human existence. Everything else – the system of politics, moral and religious ideas and beliefs, literature, all the ways people behave – are but a superstructure built upon an economic (or material) base. This is Marx's 'materialist conception of history'.

The second key idea in Marxism is that of the class struggle or class warfare. All history, Marx believed, is a struggle between two classes, those who own and control the *means* by which goods and services are produced, and those without such control. In the language of economics, the 'means of production' consist of material things such as land and machines (capital) and the human beings (labour) which must combine and work together to produce everything needed for people to live and reproduce. Ownership is crucial, because it determines how the total output of society is divided among all the members of society.

In feudal society, for example, land, the primary means of production, was owned and controlled by the King (or Queen) and the nobility, a vast array of titled persons who obtained their property and privileged status primarily through inheritance, or, in some instances, directly from the sovereign. Next in the hierarchy of feudalism is the clergy, which Marx dismissed as a parasitical part of the ruling class. Its role was to provide religious rationalization for the privilege and power of the ruling class – the sovereign and nobility. All other persons were relegated to the commons, the lower class of peasants and artisans who did the work in the fields and workshops, providing the real income for the largely self-sufficient estates of the feudal epoch.

What brought about the demise of feudalism was not a revolutionary uprising of the commons – the French Revolution excepted – but the emergence from the growing cities in the medieval era of a new class of merchants, bankers, and traders, who gradually wrested power away from the feudal lords. This new class, loosely described as the *bourgeoisie*, evolved during the industrial revolution into a dominant and powerful class of capitalists, owning and controlling the bulk of the material means of production. As the industrial revolution pushed peasants off the land and craftsmen from their shops into the burgeoning factories, a new class of propertyless, wage-dependent workers emerged – the *proletariat*.

All of history, Marx said, involves changes that come about because of the struggle between classes to own and control the material means of production. He also thought that in this process he had discovered a scientific law that explained history and governed the development of human society. Marx's theory of change he called 'scientific materialism', because of his belief in its scientific character and because it is rooted in the material foundations of production, primarily land and physical capital.

In mid-19th century England, when Marx lived and wrote, the industrial revolution was in full sway. It was a time in which working conditions in the new factories of the emerging capitalistic system were brutal. Twelve to fourteen hour workdays were common, child labour was widespread, and protection for workers against the misfortunes of unemployment, accidental death or injury was non-existent. Workers were simply discarded when, as they aged, they were no longer able to keep pace with industrial production. What drove the system was a relentless scramble by the owners of capital for profit, a competitive scramble so fierce that increasing numbers of capitalists themselves went under, joining the ever-swelling ranks of the proletariat.

While he recognized that capitalism was more productive than any previous economic system, Marx also believed that the progress of the capitalistic system through time was halting and uneven, racked periodically by crises and collapse. 'Boom and bust' has always been characteristic of capitalism, but Marx believed that the severity of the crises would continuously increase, as the capitalist class with its vociferous hunger for profits pushed wages as low as possible. Ownership and control of capital (and land) gave capitalists the power to do this. Thus, the class struggle between a growing mass of workers and a shrinking number of capitalists was the dynamic that drove capitalism inevitably toward a bloody revolution in which the proletariat would seize power and smash the capitalist class.

What came next? In Marx's schema, the revolution led to the 'dictatorship of the proletariat', a transition period which would ultimately usher in a state of pure communism. This Marx saw as a final stage of economic development – in a sense the end of history. Communism would be a classless society in which even the political state itself would 'wither away'. In this Utopian vision all persons would produce voluntarily in accordance with their abilities, receiving a share of output in accordance with their needs. 'From each according to their ability, to each according to their need', became the Marxist slogan.

Marx's *Das Kapital* contains 2500 pages in four volumes, but curiously practically nothing is said about how a classless society of pure communism is to be organized and how it will actually work. Marx apparently assumed that once the final, epochal confrontation between the bourgeoisie and proletariat took place, everything would fall into place following a brief 'dictatorship of the proletariat' transition. In practical terms this meant that when Lenin and his fellow Marxists overthrew the Imperial Russian Government in 1917 they had no blueprint to tell them what to do with the revolution they had made.

MARXISM AND HISTORY

It would be hard to underestimate the enormous political and economic influence Marx had on the development of the modern world. Both the now defunct Soviet Union and contemporary China claim Marxism as the inspiration and ideological foundation for their political, economic and social systems. As a result of the hostility between the West and the East during the 40 years of the Cold War, the ghost of Karl Marx dominated relationships between the world's major powers after the end of the Second World War. Although the Cold War is over and the USSR is now history, China is still *pro forma* a Marxist state, while Marxist ideas remain a major influence in many of the world's under-developed areas. The tragic irony is that Karl Marx, a man who thought he was offering humanity a blueprint for ideal, selfless communities, became in fact the architect of two of the most bloody, totalitarian regimes of the 20th century – Stalin's Soviet Union and Mao Tse-tung's China!

As a prophet of capitalism's future, Marx enjoyed far less success than as the inspiration for the regimes that came to power in Russia and China. Marx thought that communism would come first to the most advanced capitalistic state – Germany was destined for this role – because the more advanced a capitalist society, the more frequent and severe the economic crises that would lead up to revolution and a final collapse. It did not happen this way. Defeat in war brought communism to Russia and China, both relatively underdeveloped, peasant nations at the time. War and its aftermath provided ruthless and deter-mined Marxists like Vladimir Lenin and Mao Tse-tung the opportunity to overthrow and replace existing governments with communist regimes.

Even more important was Marx's failure to understand the emerging strength of democracy in the 19th century, along with the ability of democratic gov-ernments in capitalist societies to tame and soften the worst excesses of the capitalism that shaped Marx's ideas when he was writing *Das Kapital*. Since he saw government as merely an instrument to protect the interests of the capitalist class ('the executive committee of the bourgeoisie'), Marx was necessarily scornful of democracy, which he believed was powerless to do anything but protect the economic interests of the dominant class. Here he was wrong in several respects.

First, slowly and painfully democratic governments in Europe and in the United States began to intervene in the economy to protect and improve the status of workers. Laws regulating child labour, hours of work, conditions of work for women, and even minimum wages were passed by democratic governments in most western nations, including the United States. In the latter, the anti-trust laws of the late 19th century directly challenged a fundamental Marxist principle, namely that inevitably the ferocious competition among capitalists would lead to monopoly control in most industries. American anti-trust laws have not prevented domination of most manufacturing by a handful of firms, but they have prevented the outright growth of naked monopolies.

Second, democratic governments with their growing recognition and support for an array of civil liberties, such as in the American Bill of Rights, have permitted – and even encouraged – the growth of trade unions. While it is true that some trade unions, like the post Second World War Labour Party in Great Britain, or the General Confederation of Labour in France (the CGT) – are Marxist in their basic ideology, trade union action is generally pragmatic. Trade unions, especially in the United States, use their power primarily to improve wages and working conditions for their members. True enough, when the Labour Party came to power after the Second World War, they nationalized a number of major industries – a Marxist-inspired objective – but since then the party and its base in British trade unions moved rightward, becoming more pragmatic and less ideological. This is true of European trade unions generally. America's labour movement never had a strong ideological basis, wedded for the most part to the pragmatic goal of better wages and working conditions.

Finally, and beginning in the late 19th century, democratic governments in the West have moved through legislative action to assume responsibility for protecting the individual and the individual's family from specific kinds of economic misfortune. These have included the loss of income or threats to income from unemployment, industrial accidents and disease, or insufficient income in old age. Germany under Chancellor Bismarck in 1889 pioneered in establishing a system of old age and survivors pensions. Out of this beginning in the late 19th century has come the modern welfare state, which through government protects persons and families from a variety of economic worries, including health care and children's allowances to help with the cost of rearing children. America's more modest welfare state embraces old age and survivors and disability 'insurance' (Social Security), unemployment insurance, medical care for persons over 65 (Medicare), aid to families with dependent children (AFDC), medical care for the poor (Medicaid), foodstamps, help for the working poor (the earned income tax credit) and aged with insufficient income after Social Security (supplementary security income).

The lesson in this is that the system of 'pure' capitalism sketched out by Marx did not evolve as predicted in his theory of 'scientific materialism', but developed into the more pragmatic system of democratic capitalism, now the dominant form of economic and political organization in all of the advanced states of the West. This has not resulted in the abolition of class and conflict between the classes, but has changed in fundamental ways both the nature and struggles within and between classes. Marx's fundamental point was that a system of private ownership of the means of production – capital and land – was so thoroughly flawed that any just distribution of society's output was wholly unattainable. Thus, a complete socialization – or nationalization – of major industries was the absolute prerequisite for a just distribution of income.

Today the question of ownership has largely disappeared from public policy debates. In the United States, the issue of public versus private ownership was never at the forefront of the political agenda, but in Europe it reached a highpoint right after the Second World War when Britain, France and other states nationalized some key industries. Since then the question of ownership has receded in importance. Debate then shifted to the distribution of output, earlier in western Europe, and now in the United States. The expansion of the welfare state attests to this. The modern welfare state is not a product of Marxian class warfare, but it does nonetheless involve class conflict. This is so because conservatives, most of whom are in the upper ranks of income, generally opposed this development. The reason is that the modern welfare state in a rough but imperfect fashion uses government to transfer income from the more affluent members and families of society to those of less affluence.

A recent Bureau of the Census study in the United States found that the distribution of market-based income is much more unequal than the distribution that prevailed after government transfers are taken into account. For example, the study found that without government transfers, the lowest fifth of households received 1.1 per cent of all income, but the highest fifth received 49.2 per cent. After transfers, however, the share of the lowest fifth rose to 4.7 per cent and that of the highest fifth dropped to 45.7 per cent. The same study found that income transfers (both cash and in kind) were much more effective than taxes in raising the incomes of households in the bottom fifth of the population (Government Printing Office (GPO), 1986). The modern welfare state, which reached its peak of development in the 1970s in both Western Europe and the United States, is among the proudest achievements of 20th century liberalism.

MARXISM AND CLASS IN THE UNITED STATES

Marxism and its notions of class and the class struggle never took root in the United States in the same way it did in Europe. There are a number of reasons for this. For one thing, America never experienced the static, hierarchial structure of class that Europe knew under feudalism. First with colonies and later with the union of states, American society was generally more open and with greater mobility than was true of European society. The existence of the vast, western frontier with seemingly unlimited land available to those coura-geous and hardy enough to seize it from the Indians was a reason for this. From its very beginning the federal government encouraged the westward migration of citizens, particularly through the sale of public lands to settlers on relatively easy terms, from the Land Ordinances of 1785 and 1787 to the Homestead Act of 1862.

Until the Civil War, the nation was overwhelmingly rural – in 1860 only 20 per cent of the population lived in urban areas, although by 1910, 55 per cent was urban. More important for the issue of class, and with the partial excep-tion of the South, farms in America were small and family owned. Jefferson's ideal was of a nation of sturdy yeomen (land-owning farmers) who he saw as a strong bulwark against the abuse of power by the federal government, as well as a basis for the expansion of democracy as the nation moved west-ward. The land ordinances of 1785 and 1787 embodied Jefferson's essential ideas.

An exception to foregoing trend was the South, where the institution of slavery gave rise to large estates, worked by slaves, and a land-owning aristocracy, socially and culturally akin to the feudal estates of medieval Europe. Before the Civil War two crucially different and incompatible land systems developed in the United States – that of free land and free labour in the North and the landed aristocracy of the South. Conflict between the two was inevitable, although it would be stretching reality to say that this conflict was Marxian in its essence. The Civil War settled the issue by destruction of slavery, the basis for the South's landed aristocracy (Hughes, 1990, chapter 10).

After the Civil War, there was both a vast expansion of agriculture in lands west of the Mississippi and Missouri rivers, and an explosive growth of big business, manufacturing, and a wage-earning working class as the nation industrialized. These developments led to bitter conflicts, though they were only faintly of a Marxist character. These conflicts did, however, have a powerful effect on the shape of American society in the 20th century.

During the latter half of the 19th century the explosive growth in agricul-tural production and productivity brought declining prices and economic hardship rather than prosperity to many farmers and farm families. Farmers were angered by what they saw as excessively high and unjust freight rates for their produce, and interest rates they believed were exploitative. Farm discontent during these years played a major role in the emergence of 'populism' and the People's Party, formed in 1891. The populist movement, echoes of which were heard in Pat Buchanan's 1996 bid for the Republican presidential nomination, involved a loose coalition of farmers, workers, re- formers, but it also attracted anti-semitic, anti-black, and anti-Catholic zeal- ots, as well as anti-immigration 'nativists'. In spite of its dark, racist underside, the populist movement helped achieve a number of political reforms, includ- ing the direct election of US senators, the secret ballot, and support for women's suffrage. Economically, it was less successful; demands for the abolition of the national banking system, the nationalization of railroads, prohibition of subsidies to corporations, and no alien or corporate ownership of land or natural resources were never attained.

Industrialization not only brought new waves of boom and bust to the American economy – from 1854 through 1913, there were 15 periods of expansion followed by slumps, the longest and most severe of which lasted 65 months – but also the great business giants, and a growing propertyless, wage-earning class, conditions that in some ways bore out the Marxian scenario for capitalism development. But not quite. In spite of extreme hostil- ity by the federal courts to legislative efforts to improve working conditions, including the formation of unions, a labour movement came into existence in the United States between the end of the Civil War and the beginning of the 20th century. There were, first, the unsuccessful National Labor Union (1866– 72) and Knights of Labor (1869–86), followed by the successful American Federation of Labor (AFL), organized by Samuel Gompers in 1886. The secret of Gomper's success was twofold. First, he insisted on the craft as the basis for organization, and, second, he focused on the limited objectives of better wages and working conditions.

Nether the populist movement nor America's early trade unions were Marxist in the European perspective. They were to some extent class-based, but neither was revolutionary in the sense of wanting to overthrow the constitu- tion and America's government. Nor did they want to abolish wholly the private ownership of the means of production. Even more important, they did not challenge the 'free' market as the nation's primary economic institution. Both movements were political, understanding that the federal government was a major source of political power, power that could be used to alter the terms upon which farmers, business, and labour drew their income from private markets. Gomper's pragmatic political programme was to use the voting booth to 'reward labor's friends and punish its enemies'.

If we look at the long span of time from the end of the 19th century through the early 1970s, the economic struggle was roughly between the 'haves', represented by business and its political friends, and the 'have-nots', consisting primarily of labour, farmers, minorities, liberal intellectuals, and some small business people. The lines between these broad groups have always been fluid, never firmly set, rarely explicitly defined in class terms. Nonetheless, the struggle has been real, intense and ofttimes bitter. Though there are many facets to this struggle, a major focus has been control of the federal government and its power through taxes and spending to influence the distribution of income and wealth.

If we make income and wealth distribution the focal point of economic conflict, historical research and available data reveal several clear trends. Among economic historians, there is general agreement that both the First World War and the Second World War tended to make the distribution of income somewhat more equal (Hughes, 1990, chapters 23 and 26). One reason is that during both wars the demand for labour rose sharply, having a highly favourable effect upon wages. This was more pronounced in the Second World War than the earlier war, primarily because of the effectiveness of price controls during the second conflict. A second reason is that high tax rates induced by wartime finance reduced incomes of persons and families at the top of the income ladder much more than those in the lower ranges. In the interim between the two wars, income inequality worsened, primarily because of depression after the First World War, and a sharp reduction in taxes for upper income families during the 1920s.

Since the middle of the 1930s, more precise numbers on the distribution of income have become available. Economists measure inequality by a number called the 'Gini' coefficient, a measurement technique developed shortly before the First World War by Corrado Gini, an Italian economist. A drop in this number means less inequality; an increase more inequality. Reliable figures for American inequality go back to 1936, a span of 60 years. What the 'Gini' number shows is that from 1936 to 1973 (37 years), there was a slow but steady decline in income inequality in the United States. In numbers, the decline was 20.5 per cent. But during the next 23 years (1973 to 1996), income inequality rose by 19.7 per cent, nearly the same by which it dropped from the middle of the Great Depression to the end of the nearly three decades of high prosperity that followed the Second World War! Behind these numbers is the story of an emerging and different form of class warfare in America, to which we now turn (GPO, 1990).

Turning Marx Upside Down

The success of conservatives in using the spectre of class war to derail any serious discussion of the distribution of income and wealth in America obscures an important and ominous development. Since the early 1970s, hard-right conservatives, now dominant in the Republican party, have stood Marx on his head, waging with determination their own version of class war against the poor, the powerless, and even elements in the middle class. Though no blood is flowing in the streets, make no mistake, the struggle is real and will dominate American politics well into the future.

The battlegrounds for class conflict in America are the federal government and the private marketplace, the key institutions which determine the distribution of income and wealth. Political and economic power are the instruments of class warfare, the means to influence and control the way in which government and the marketplace affect the distribution of income and wealth. The story of what has happened to the distribution of income over time is the story of class warfare in America.

Numbers tell this story. Since the mid 1930s the Bureau of the Census has compiled data we have on income distribution. The numbers on income and its distribution show two clear trends. In the 38 years from 1936 to 1973, there was a measurable and significant decline in the extent of inequality in the distribution of family income in the United States. The 'Gini' coefficient measures inequality in the distribution of income and wealth. This measure shows a 20.5 per cent drop in income inequality between 1936 and 1992 (GPO, 1976; Hughes, 1990, p. 502). Families in the lowest quintals (or fifths) increased their share of total income by the largest percentage amounts, while those in the top ranges experienced the sharpest declines in their income shares. After 1973, the picture changed dramatically. In the 19 years from 1974 to 1992 inequality increased. In numbers, using again the 'Gini' technique, the change was 13.2 per cent. The pace at which the nation moved toward greater inequality in income distribution is approximately 28 per cent greater in the latter period than was the pace toward less inequality in the first period (GPO, 1992a, p. B13). In plain English, since 1973 the rich have been getting richer much faster than the poor got less poor after 1936!

It is not too difficult to account for the major developments or factors that played a role in these two trends. Four things are responsible for the downward trend in income inequality from 1936 through 1973. First, there is America's welfare state, begun with Social Security, unemployment insurance, and public assistance during Roosevelt's New Deal, and brought to its present status with the addition of Medicare and Medicaid during the Johnson presidency. Though modest by European standards, it has provided a vital economic safety net for millions of families. Second – unfortunately – there was war, the Second World War, plus the Korean and Vietnam wars. It is generally agreed among economic historians that our wars have made the distribution of income somewhat more equal. In part, this is because in wartime the demand for labour increases – the unemployment rate during the Second World War was less than 2 per cent – with a favourable effect upon wages. In part, too, higher taxes during wartime reduce incomes in the top bracket more than those in the lower ranges.

A third reason is found in the progressive structure of the federal personal income tax. A rough measure of the progressivity of this tax is the marginal rate for persons in the top income bracket. From 1936 through 1973 this rate averaged 81 per cent (GPO, 1991, pp. 55–6). Even if the wartime rates are removed from this statistic, the average is still 80 per cent! In modern times progressive taxes are essential to taming the strong tendency toward income inequality that unfettered markets engender.

Finally, there is economic growth, both a cause and a consequence of the downward trend in income inequality during these years. If the war years are excluded from the picture, growth of output averaged 3.7 per cent, a record that is identical to the nation's long-term growth rate from 1839 to 1960, a span of 121 years (GPO, 1987, p. 247; Peterson, 1996, p. 507). High growth means plentiful jobs at good wages; slow growth means job scarcity and poor wages.

Turning to the other side of the coin – the decline in income equality – what is responsible? At the top of the list are three far-reaching changes in federal taxes. First, between 1973 and 1992 the personal income tax became significantly less progressive – the marginal tax rate for the top income bracket dropped from 70 to 31 per cent (GPO, 1991). Second, the government came to rely increasingly upon regressive payroll taxes (Social Security and Medicare) for its revenue; in 1991, 1992 and 1993 it actually collected a larger share of its revenue from payroll taxes than from the personal income tax (GPO, 1996, p. 373). Third, corporate income taxes declined steadily as a source of federal revenue, from 16.4 per cent in 1973 to 9.8 per cent in 1992 (ibid.). These tax changes skewed the entire federal revenue system heavily toward persons and families at the top of the income ladder.

The tax changes of this period yield a rather clear-cut experiment in the validity of supply-side economics (also known as voodoo economics), the basis tenet of which is that tax cuts – especially tax cuts for the very rich – always stimulate economic growth. This simply did not happen. For the entire period, the economy grew at an annual average rate of 2.7 per cent, and for the Reagan–Bush era (when supply-side was king), the rate was less (2.1 per cent) (ibid., p. 293). In spite of this dismal record Jack Kemp and other supply-siders are still touting tax cuts as a panacea for all our economic ills. Like the Bourbons, they have learned nothing and forgotten nothing.

While tax changes were taking place for the benefit of upper 20 per cent belonging to Galbraith's 'culture of contentment', the real hourly take-home pay for production and non-supervisory employees – who make up 80 per cent of all wage and salary employees – dropped by more than 13 per cent! (ibid., p. 330). Behind this trend, which helped to tilt income distribution toward greater inequality, are two developments. One is the decay of American unions, whose membership dropped from a postwar high of 40 per cent of the labour force to its current 10 per cent. The other is corporate downsizing, which has ruthlessly eliminated jobs – 2.5 million since 1991 alone – in the name of efficiency demanded by global competition.

Economics does not begin to tell the whole story of what has been happening in our nation since the early 1970s. The Institute for Innovation in Social Policy at Fordham University constructs and publishes an Index of Social Health which monitors the nation's social well-being. It does this by tracking 16 different measures of social problems, ranging from infant mortality, child abuse, teenage suicide, health insurance coverage, drug abuse, alcohol related traffic deaths, homicides, poverty among children and the aged, and others. These are the problems that beset many families and often lie behind the 'breakdown' in moral values that hard right conservatives see as the root of all our problems.

Since the Fordham Institute began compiling and tracking this index in 1970, it has declined from a peak of 77.5 in 1973 to a low of 38.1 in 1991, a drop of 50.1 per cent! (Fordham Institute for Innovation in Social Policy, 1995, p. 4). What is paradoxical is that during these same years – 1970 to 1991 – the economy as measured by its real GDP grew by 56 per cent! If economic growth is such a great thing, why is the social health of the nation getting so much worse? There really isn't any great mystery. It is no accident that the deterioration in social health parallels quite precisely the worsening distribution of income in our nation, as well as a 30.6 per cent increase in the poverty index since 1973 (GPO, 1992b, p. xvi).

This, of course, is not the story being told. What the conservatives of the hard right have done – and done very cleverly – is shift the argument over the cause of the social problems that are the source of so much national anxiety from economics to culture. Their basic message is that of a cultural crisis involving a breakdown in the nation's traditional moral values. The cause of this crisis? It was spawned by the permissiveness of the 1960s, which in turn was a progeny of the 'liberal and educated elite' that created the social welfare state. Thus, if the anger and worry over serious social problems cannot be directed against the victims themselves, as with single parents on welfare, then the hard right's target is an allegedly over-blown and out-of-control federal government. Except for some atypical fingerpointing at corporations by Pat Buchanan, hard right conservatives believe uncritically in the 'magic of the marketplace'. Even the religious right isn't much concerned with the entrepreneurs of market-capitalism who create and sell the violence, profanity, and sex found on TV and in films. When it comes to big business and tobacco, a product that has brought death to millions, there is only silence.

The Distribution of Wealth

The story on the distribution of wealth is the same as on the distribution of income, except that the degree of inequality in wealth ownership is even more extreme than is inequality in the receipt of income. Information on the ownership and distribution of wealth is much more sketchy than information on the distribution of income. There is no government agency like the Census Bureau responsible for the collection and periodic publication of data on the ownership and distribution of wealth by American families. What we do know comes from a handful of classic academic studies and occasional reports from the Federal Reserve System based upon periodic surveys of consumer finances.

One of the most recent of the surveys by the Federal Reserve showed that between 1983 and 1989 the share of net household wealth owned by the top 1 per cent of households climbed from 31.5 per cent to 37.0 per cent, a 17.5 per cent gain in the relative position of families at the very top of the wealth-income pyramid! (Kennicksell and Woodburn, 1992). The 37.0 per cent figure (the latest for which data are available) was a 67-year high for wealth inequality in the United States. What is especially alarming is that in 1929 – the eve of the Great Depression – the top 1 per cent of households owned a slightly smaller share of the nation's wealth – 36.3 per cent (GPO, 1992c, pp. 1562–77).

After the Great Crash of 1929, the share of wealth owned by the top 1 per cent of American families declined to 20.8 per cent by 1949, primarily because of the impact of New Deal legislation and wartime tax rates. But by 1949, the share of net wealth owned by the top 1 per cent of families had climbed back to the levels of the 1920s. In the aftermath of the 1929 crash, Marriner Eccles, chairman of the Federal Reserve during most of the New Deal era, speculated that the depression may have been caused by the 'giant suction pump' of maldistribution, the result of policies that pulled more and more income and wealth into fewer hands (Greider, 1987, p. 38). It is not unreasonable to ask: is such a 'suction pump' at work today.

The Gini coefficient on the distribution of both income and wealth is instructive. Since the early 1980s, the Gini coefficient for both income and wealth has been rising – an increase in this coefficient indicates an increase in inequality – but what is even more significant is the much greater size for the Gini coefficient for wealth distribution as compared to income distribution. In 1989, the Gini coefficient for income distribution was 0.428, but the number for wealth distribution was 0.793, indicating that inequality in the distribution of wealth is nearly twice as extreme as in this distribution of income! (GPO, 1990, p. 202).

As is to be expected, inequality in the distribution of income and wealth move together, as greater inequality in income distribution works to increase inequality in the distribution of wealth. Once the ownership of wealth reaches a kind of 'critical mass' – the level at which the income generated by wealth begins to exceed what any single person or family can consume or use – the 'magic' of compound interest ensures the accumulation of wealth practically without limit.

So where do we stand now? The boldest assault to date on America's welfare state – and, of course, the distribution of income – has been Newt Gingrich's 'Contract With America', or as some would prefer, 'Contract on America'. Ronald Reagan talked a good game about cutting Washington down to size, but in the end did nothing – when he left office the federal government as measured by its spending as a percentage of GDP was nearly the same as when he became president – 22.4 versus 21.9 (GPO, 1996, pp. 280, 373).

The first round in this challenge went to the right, when President Clinton signed into law the 'welfare reform' bill that through block grants turned 'welfare as we have known it' back to the states. This means that the United States – the wealthiest nation in history and first among the wealthy and developed nations of the West – has turned its back upon the weakest and most vulnerable people in society – children!

Step one in finally ending the New Deal is history. Next will be proposals for the privatization of Social Security, attractively packaged to appeal to a Baby-Boomer generation nourished by the anti-government pabulum of the Reagan–Bush years. And then there is the flat tax, vigorously pushed by House Majority Leader Dick Armey, whose proposal is blatantly designed to exempt income from capital from practically all taxation. This, too, will be packaged and sold as needed tax reform.

What Is To Be Done?

William Greider says that the distribution of income and wealth – the fundamental question of who gets what and why – is the 'buried fault line of American politics' (Greider, 1987, p. 37). He is right. To confront this fact and help the public become aware of what is involved is the first order of business for progressives. There is hope that this issue can become a part of the political agenda, for even the major news and business magazines have run in-depth articles on the subject, something unheard of only a few years ago. It won't be easy, but until this is done, our most serious economic and social problems will linger on, eating away at the foundations of our society.

How is this to be done? There is no easy answer to this question, but if anything is to be done by economists, it will have to be done by members of the heterodox groups. It is scandalous but true, as Robert Heilbroner pointed out recently, that mainstream economics has concluded that no public policy has any value whatsoever – that our political system cannot affect the economy in any way, other than to allow the market full sway (Heilbroner and Milberg, 1995, p. 94). This, Heilbroner says, is an abdication of moral responsibility by a profession that would have no '...raison d'etre if social malfunctions did not exist in the portion of society we call "the economy"' (ibid.).

What these ideas suggest is that the first task we face involves the problem of government. Conservatives, with ample help from mainstream economics, have achieved two cherished goals with respect to government. First, they have persuaded significant segments of the public that government's role in the economy is essentially negative, that government cannot do anything to improve the nation's well-being. Second, they have also persuaded substantial numbers that governments do not create any economic value – that all economic value originates through private transactions in the market place.

Value in an economic sense – what it is and how it comes into existence – is the bedrock upon which much economic analysis exists. Thus, it is entirely appropriate that heterodox economists make the analysis of collective or social value a matter of utmost priority. This analysis must also seek to persuade the public of the economic worth of government and its activities. Unless and until this is done, not much else will happen. This is so simply because without constructive and creative action at the governmental level, little can be done about the critical problems facing the nation.

It is not hard to sketch out the essentials of an economic programme, one to blunt and reverse the conservatives's war against the poor, the defenceless, and major portions of the middle class. We need a massive programme of public/private investment, one that will revitalize productivity growth. We need a comprehensive system of health care, one that will bring the best of American health care to all our citizens. We need a thorough overhaul of the federal tax system, one that will be simple, progressive, and purged of the vast array of loopholes – tax expenditures as they are technically known – that are skewed primarily toward large corporations and families at the top of the income pyramid. We need to dismantle the military–industrial–educational complex, using at least $100 billion annually of the resources now tied up in military outlays for some of the constructive objectives just sketched out. The labour movement must be revitalized, as well as the regulatory role of government, both seriously weakened and undercut during the Reagan–Bush years.

Market capitalism at its best is – and has been – an enormously productive economic system, capable of generating wealth and economic well-being on a scale never attained by any other social or economic system. But this does not happen just through the institutions of the market, but it also needs the institution of a democratic, imaginative, creative, and compassionate government. Without the latter, there is no vision, and where there is no vision, the people perish.

REFERENCES

Fordham Institute for Innovation in Social Policy (FIISP) (1995), *Index of Social Health: Monitoring the Social Well-Being of the Nation*, Tarreytown, NY: Fordham Graduate Center.

Government Printing Office (GPO) (1976), 'Historical Statistics of the United States', *Bureau of the Census*, Washington, DC.

Government Printing Office (GPO) (1986), 'Measuring the Effect of Benefits and Taxes on Income and Poverty', *Bureau of the Census, Current Population Reports*, Series P-60, No.164, Washington, DC.

Government Printing Office (GPO) (1987), *Economic Report of the President*, Washington, DC.

Government Printing Office (GPO) (1990), 'Money Income of Households, Families, and Persons in The United States', *Bureau of the Census, Current Population Reports*, Series P-60, No.174, Washington, DC.

Government Printing Office (GPO) (1991), 'Overview of the Federal Tax System', *Committee on Ways and Means*, Washington, DC.

Government Printing Office (GPO) (1992a), 'Money Income of Households, Families, and Persons in The United States', *Bureau of the Census, Current Population Reports*, Series P-60, No. 184, Washington, DC.

Government Printing Office (GPO) (1992b), 'Poverty in the United States: 1992', *Bureau of the Census, Current Population Reports*, Series P-60, No.185, Washington, DC.

Government Printing Office (GPO) (1992c), *1992 Green Book*, Committee on Ways and Means, US House of Representatives, Washington, DC.

Government Printing Office (GPO) (1996), *Economic Report of the President*, Washington, DC.

Greider, W. (1987), *Secrets of the Temple*, New York: Simon and Schuster.

Heilbroner, R. and Milberg, W. (1995), *The Crisis of Vision in Modern Economic Thought*, Cambridge: Cambridge University Press.

Hughes, J. (1990), *American Economic History*, Glenview, Ill.: Scott Foresman/Little Brown Higher Education.

Kennicksell, A.B. and Woodburn, R.L. (1992), 'Estimates of Household Net Worth Using Model-based and Design-based Weights: Evidence from the 1989 Survey of consumer Finance', unpublished manuscript from the *Board of Governors, Federal Reserve System*, Washington, DC, April.

Keynes, J.M. (1936), *The General Theory of Employment, Interest and Money*, New York: Harcourt Brace and World.

Peterson, Wallace C. (1996), *Income, Employment and Economic Growth*, 8th ed., New York: W.W. Norton & Company.

7. Why wage and price flexibility is destabilizing

Basil Moore

INTRODUCTION

Macroeconomics began with Keynes as the study of large-scale economic pathologies; mass unemployment, prolonged depression, persistent inflation, and of the appropriate policy response. So, Keynes (1936) argued that 'The effect of an expectation that wages are going to sag by say 2 percent in the coming year will be roughly equivalent to the effect of a rise of 2 percent in the amount of interest payable for the same period' (p. 265). More recently, Davidson (1994) argued that 'Despite the bravado claim that their "rigour" and "statistical techniques" permit New Keynesians to be in a "better position than Keynes to figure out how the economy works", the record of recent years does not support the idea that today's mainstream economists have any idea of how a monetary, entrepreneurial economy operates' (p. 2). This chapter is an attempt to document this claim with respect to the 'stabilizing' effects of wage and price flexibility.

Much contemporary new Keynesian and new classical macroeconomics has acquired a Panglossian character, with a policy propensity to 'leave it to the market'. Unemployment problems are viewed as nested directly in market supply side imperfections which prevent less than instantaneous price flexibility. 'Real market imperfections ... are crucial for understanding economic fluctuations ... imperfect competition, imperfect information, and rigidity in relative prices [are] central to the theory' (Mankiw and Romer, 1991, p. 2).

Hahn and Solow have recently expressed their 'profound disagreement with the main trend of macroeconomic theory in the early 1980's', as well as their 'desire to create some sort of respectable theoretical resistance to it' (1995, p. 1). Currently whole schools of economists fully share both sentiments. The unresolved questions are: 'How best to express this disagreement?' and, 'How best to formulate an alternative?'.

The simplification of the macroeconomic coordination problem to sticky wages and prices is at the root of the decline of relevance of both new classical and new Keynesian macroeconomics.[1] 'Any supply failure that produces a wage and/or price inflexibility – whether ephemeral or not – is not the essence of Keynes's analysis of unemployment' (Davidson, 1994, p. 10).

This reduction and distortion of the coordination problem is widely attributed to the immense logical appeal of the Walrasian association of perfect price flexibility with perfect coordination (Howitt, 1990; Hahn and Solow, 1995). As Tobin has recently noted, the 'neoclassical synthesis' invited disbelief in the possibility of involuntary unemployment among, 'Students and teachers dazzled by the general-equilibrium paradigm ... made rigorous by Arrow and Debreu ... Panglossian conclusions were inevitable. ... To many of the most powerful intellects in the profession ... that logic was more persuasive than realism' (Tobin, 1996, p. 18).

The Walrasian general equilibrium model is immensely compelling in its simplicity. Assuming all markets are perfectly competitive, all prices perfectly flexible, all markets clear, a complete set of Arrow–Debreu markets all open at time zero, and the presence of a Walrasian auctioneer to assure that no trading takes place at 'false' (disequilibrium) prices, the system can be shown to reach a general equilibrium configuration, which is unique, stable, and satisfies all the well-known Pareto-optimality conditions.

In the Walrasian paradigm, in every market, if there is excess supply, the price will fall, and if there is excess demand, the price will rise. Full coordination is achieved by giving all buyers and sellers full information, in the form of the set of relative prices for each commodity. Depending on the speed at which prices adjust, a comparative static general equilibrium will be attained where all markets clear. As a result greater price flexibility has increasingly come to be regarded as desirable.

The main drawbacks to the Walrasian vision are twofold:

1. The timeless nature of the equilibrium. All markets clear at the initial moment. Expectations are frozen. There is no continuous trading (Hahn, 1984).
2. The lack of any significant role for money. Money acts only as a numeraire, with the implied well-known property of monetary neutrality (Hahn, 1984).

When the Walrasian paradigm is applied to labour markets, it is typically illustrated with a diagram like Figure 7.1. The neoclassical explanations for the *existence* of unemployment: that real wages $(W/P)_1$ are 'too high' relative to their equilibrium market-clearing levels $(W/P)_E$, and for the *persistence* of unemployment: that wages are sticky downwards, become immediately self-evident, and appear logically irrefutable.

Neither rational workers nor employers should be subject to 'money illusion'. It therefore appears plausible that both the supply and the demand for

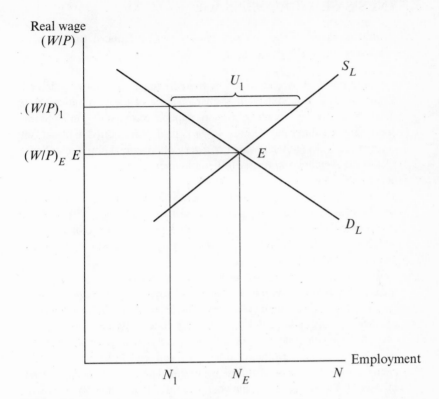

Figure 7.1

labour be in terms of the real wage. The supply of labour will be upward-sloping, due to the increasing disutility of additional work. The demand for labour will be downward-sloping, due to the law of diminishing returns.

To the student in the classroom, and to the man on the street, the neoclassical conclusion that persistent unemployment is due to the existence of downward wage inflexibility appears to be logically unassailable. A reduction in real wages appears necessarily to result in an increase in employment. Greater wage flexibility appears unequivocally to be a good thing. This is the vision that lies behind the customary pro-market policy recommendations of many contemporary financial advisors, business men, politicians, editors, and, sad to say, even economists.

KEYNES'S CENTRAL MESSAGE

The central message of the *General Theory* can be reduced to four main components (Howitt, 1990):   •

1. Something is very wrong with how markets function to coordinate economic activity. The 'outstanding characteristic of the economic system in which we live' ... (is that) 'it seems capable of remaining in a chronic condition of subnormal activity for a considerable period without any marked tendency either towards recovery or towards complete collapse ... full, or even approximately full employment is of rare and short-lived occurrence' (Keynes, 1936, pp. 249–50).
2. The existence of persistent and pervasive unemployment is not, as the neoclassical view maintains, attributable to sticky wages. 'To suppose that a flexible wage policy is a right and proper adjunct of a system which on the whole is one of *laisser faire* is the opposite of the truth' (Keynes, 1936, p. 269).
3. Investment is the component of aggregate demand that is the source of the coordination problem, and so of unemployment and excess capacity. This is due to the presence in the real world, but not in Walrasian general equilibrium, of fundamental (nonergodic) uncertainty and missing markets. As a result, due to 'the extreme precariousness of the basis of knowledge in which estimates of the prospective yield have to be made', changes in expectations of future events 'renders the marginal efficiency of capital subject to the somewhat violent fluctuations which are the explanation of the Trade Cycle' (Keynes, 1936, pp. 149, 144).
4. The main policy inference, as drawn in the final chapter, 'Concluding Notes on the Social Philosophy Towards Which the General Theory Might Lead', is that central banks should reduce interest rates down to the level where aggregate demand is consistent with full employment output:

Interest today rewards no genuine sacrifice, any more than does the rent of land. The owner of capital can obtain interest because capital is scarce, just as the owner of land can obtain rent because land is scarce. But whilst there may be intrinsic reasons for the scarcity of land, there are no intrinsic reasons for the scarcity of capital. ...

I see, therefore, the rentier aspect of capitalism as a transitional phase which will disappear when it has done its work. ...

Thus we might aim in practice (there being nothing in this which is unobtainable) at an increase in the volume of capital until it ceases to be scarce, so that the functionless investor will no longer receive a bonus. (Keynes, 1936, p. 376)

Keynes concluded these 'Notes' with the question, 'Is the fulfilment of these ideas a visionary hope?'. He answered powerfully in the negative. Academics should surely applaud his famous response: 'soon or late, it is ideas, not vested interests, which are dangerous for good or evil' (Keynes, 1936, pp. 383–4).

'CHANGES IN MONEY WAGES'

In many areas Keynes was undoubtedly a great success. His theory of effective demand carried the day in both theory and practice. It resulted in a fundamental reorientation of governments' fiscal and monetary policy throughout the world. This lasted throughout the so-called 'Golden Age' of growth, from the end of the Second World War until the breakdown of the Keynesian consensus, during the historically unprecedented stagflation of the 1970's.

However, in one of his main objectives: freeing the theoretical explanation of unemployment from depending on sticky wages, Keynes must be judged a failure. He failed to propose any compelling coherent alternative to the classical explanation of unemployment.

Keynes's analysis, 'Changes in Money Wages', chapter 19 of the *General Theory*, was not compelling. This was in part because he offered only a verbal analysis of a complicated and incompletely specified dynamical system (Howitt, 1990). It was also in part because in the *General Theory* Keynes unfortunately reverted to the neoclassical view that the money supply could be treated as an exogenous variable, controlled by the central bank (Moore, 1988).

As a result Keynes never succeeded in producing a rigorous logical argument why downward wage flexibility would *necessarily* be destabilizing and deviation-amplifying. He argued that the impact of money wage reductions on employment in essence depended on their net effect on entrepreneurs' expectations of the marginal efficiency of capital. He was able only rather weakly to conclude that, although general wage cuts might increase employment, they need not: 'The consequences of a change in money-wages are complicated' (Keynes, 1936, p. 257).

Keynes strongly insisted that the classical argument of the automatic self-equilibrating effect of flexible money wages was logically incorrect. In Keynes's opinion it reflected a simple fallacy of composition: 'In its crudest form, this is tantamount to assuming that the reduction in money wages will leave demand unaffected' (Keynes, 1936, p. 258). He did successfully demonstrate that there was no *direct* tendency for a reduction in money wages to increase employment:

For we have shown that the volume of employment is uniquely correlated with the volume of effective demand measured in wage units, and that the effective demand, being the sum of the expected consumption and the expected investment, cannot change if the propensity to consume, the schedule of marginal efficiency of capital and the rate of interest are all unchanged... There is no method of analyzing the effect of a reduction in money-wages, except by following up its possible effects on these three factors. (Keynes, 1936, pp. 260–2)

Most simply, Keynes demonstrated that in market economies the economy-wide supply and demand for labour were *interdependent*, and not independent as the simple neoclassical (partial equilibrium) presentation presumes. The demand for labour was derived from the demand for the goods that labour produces. As a result a *general* change in the level of money wages, by directly affecting wage incomes, must *necessarily* affect costs, prices, and aggregate demand, and therefore the demand for labour.

In chapter 19 Keynes went on to list seven distinct channels whereby a fall in wages conceivably could *indirectly* result in a stimulation of effective demand:

1. A reduction in money wages will presumably somewhat reduce prices, and will therefore involve some redistribution of real income to other factors whose remuneration has not been reduced, in particular rentiers. 'What the net result will be on a balance of considerations we can only guess. Probably it is more likely to be adverse than favourable' (Keynes, 1936, p. 262).
2. If the reduction in money wages is 'a reduction relative to money wages abroad, it will tend to increase the balance of trade', and so stimulate net investment (Keynes, 1936, pp. 262–3).
3. If the reduction in money wages 'is likely to worsen the terms of trade... there will be a reduction in real incomes, ... which may tend to increase the propensity to consume' (Keynes, 1936, p. 263).
4. If the reduction in money wages 'is expected to be a *reduction relative to money-wages in the future*, the change will be favourable to investment', but if it 'leads to the expectation ... of a further wage reduction in prospect, it will have precisely the opposite effect', and 'will lead to the postponement both of investment and consumption' (Keynes, 1936, p. 263).
5. The reduction in the wages bill 'will diminish the need for cash for income and business purposes', and by reducing the schedule of liquidity preference, 'will reduce the rate of interest and thus prove favourable to investment' (Keynes, 1936, p. 263). But if the reduction in wages 'disturbs political confidence', the resulting increase in liquidity preference may cause interest rates to rise (Keynes, 1936, p. 264).

6. 'Since a special reduction of money-wages is always advantageous to an individual entrepreneur or industry, a general reduction ... may also produce an optimistic tone in the minds of entrepreneurs', which may break through the pessimistic expectations of the marginal efficiency of capital 'and set things moving again' (Keynes, 1936, p. 264). But, 'since there is no means of securing a simultaneous and equal reduction of money-wages in all industries', and, 'it is in the interests of all workers to resist a movement in their own particular case', it may lead to labour troubles and offset this favourable factor (Keynes, 1936, p. 264).

7. 'The depressing influence on entrepreneurs of their greater burden of debt may partly offset any cheerful reactions from the reduction of wages.' If the fall of wages and prices goes too far, the heavily indebted entrepreneurs, 'may soon reach the point of insolvency, - with severely adverse effects on investment' (Keynes, 1936, p. 264).

Keynes summed up his discussion as follows: 'If, therefore we restrict our argument to the case of a closed system, ... we must base any hopes of favourable results to employment from a reduction in money-wages mainly on an improvement in investment' ... to either 'an increased marginal efficiency of capital under (4), or, a decreased rate of interest under (5)' (Keynes, 1936, pp. 264–5).

Keynes argued the most favourable contingency would be if 'money-wages are believed to have touched bottom, so that further changes are expected to be in the upward direction' (Keynes, 1936, p. 265). In contrast the most unfavourable contingency is that in which 'money-wages are slowly sagging downwards and each reduction in money-wages serves to diminish confidence in the prospective maintenance of wages' (Keynes, 1936, p. 265).

Keynes concluded his discussion of wage flexibility as follows: 'it would be much better that wages should be rigidly fixed and deemed incapable of material changes, than that depressions should be accompanied by a gradual downward tendency of money-wages, a further moderate wage reduction being expected to signalise each increase of, say, 1 percent in the amount of unemployment' (Keynes, 1936, p. 265).

He then threw out the following brilliant insight: 'For example, the effect of an expectation that wages are going to sag by, say, 2 per cent. in the coming year will be roughly equivalent to the effect of a rise of 2 per cent. in the amount of interest payable for the same period' (Keynes, 1936, p. 265).

Unfortunately, Keynes never developed this insight. In fact he obscured and confused it on the very next page: 'It is therefore, on the effect of a falling wage- and price-level on the demand for money that those who believe in the self-adjusting quality of the economic system must rest the weight of their argument.' He went on to argue, 'if the quantity of money is virtually fixed, ... its quantity in terms of wage-units can be indefinitely increased by a sufficient reduction in money-wages' (Keynes, 1936, p. 266).

This led him to conclude, 'we can, therefore, ... produce precisely the same effects on the rate of interest by reducing wages whilst leaving the quantity of money unchanged, that we can produce by increasing the quantity of money whilst leaving the level of wages unchanged' (Keynes, 1936, p. 266). Note that wage reductions now are viewed as *raising* the real money supply and so *reducing* the rate of interest, and therefore have become *expansionary* in their effects. They have in fact become the key to the homeostatic property of the economic system. He has forgotten his brilliant insight.

Keynes continued:

> wage reductions, as a method of securing full employment, are also subject to the same limitations as the method of increasing the quantity of money. Just as a moderate increase in the quantity of money may exert an inadequate influence over the long-term rate of interest, whilst an immoderate increase may offset its other advantages by its disturbing effect on confidence; so a moderate reduction in money-wages may prove inadequate, whilst an immoderate reduction might shatter confidence even if it were practicable. (Keynes, 1936, pp. 266–7)

However one might evaluate this inadequate-immoderate argument, the key point is that wage reductions, by increasing the quantity of money in wage units, and thereby reducing the rate of interest (the 'Keynes Effect'), are now regarded as having an *expansionary* macroeconomic effect (Keynes, 1936, pp. 267–9). Keynes appears to have temporarily forgotten his insight on page 265 that expected reductions in money wages were broadly equivalent to a comparable *rise* in the rate of interest!

A *lower* price level implies a larger aggregate demand, while a *falling* price level tends to reduce aggregate demand. Alternatively expressed, an aggregate demand depends *negatively* on the price level, but *positively* on the rate of change of prices. The expansionary effect of wage reductions follows from a comparative static equilibrium argument. It completely hides the forces that occur out of equilibrium during the adjustment process. The contractionary effect of wage reductions is a dynamic argument. It is concerned solely with the sequence of events during the disequilibrium process while prices are changing.

ENDOGENOUS CREDIT MONEY: COMPARATIVE STATIC ANALYSIS

Hahn and Solow have recently criticized the Walrasian analysis of wage flexibility by a process they call 'boring from within' (Hahn and Solow,

1995). By changing two fundamental assumptions: replacing the immortal 'representative agent' by an overlapping generations model, and by introducing private debt and having savers allocate their wealth between holding money and bonds, they show that a model with perfectly flexible wages yields badly behaved dynamics with distinctly anti-Panglossian implications.

Hahn and Solow construe perfect wage flexibility to guarantee continual full employment market-clearing in the face of insufficient aggregate demand. When the model is disturbed by an unanticipated permanent increase in the supply of labour, perfect wage flexibility leads to cumulative wage and price deflation. As a result even though agents are otherwise assumed to have perfect foresight, because of the unanticipated fall in wages intergenerational disruptions occur. The economy once disturbed may never return to the steady state, but go off on an unstable path (Hahn and Solow, 1995, chapter 2). 'A return to steady state cannot be guaranteed if the economy is left to itself' (Hahn and Solow, 1995, p. 43).

These conclusions are impressive. But as the authors themselves acknowledge, their model is awkward and unrealistic in its treatment of money and finance. They first state that the outside money they introduce 'might as well be currency' (Hahn and Solow, 1995, p. 12). Its quantity is assumed exogenous, to which the endogenous real income and expenditure variables must adjust. (Hahn and Solow, 1995, pp. 13, 20).

Hahn and Solow then introduce 'banks', but in a decidedly unsatisfactory manner. 'Banks' are not allowed to create deposits, but instead lend currency to firms (interest free) to finance their working capital needs. These 'banks' are assumed to be (somehow) endowed with the entire initial stock of money, which limits the total amount they can lend. They also introduce 'bonds', which yield a real rate of return equal to the marginal product on capital (Hahn and Solow, 1995, pp. 17–18).

As the return on money is defined as equal to the inverse of the inflation rate, they must somehow motivate holding money in times of price stability. They do this by assuming that agents are either subject to a Clower 'cash in advance' liquidity constraint, or can be characterized by portfolio indifference when the return on bonds equals the return on money (Hahn and Solow, 1995, pp. 19–26).

Most of the above unsatisfactory assumptions were logically forced on the authors, due to their seemingly innocuous assumption that the money supply is exogenous. In *The General Theory* Keynes assumed that the money supply could be treated as given and under the control of the central bank. As a result he left himself open to Pigou's criticism that a deflationary wage-price spiral must necessarily, after some finite period of time, raise the real value of the money stock to a sufficiently high level to engender full employment aggregate demand.

With endogenous money, as Keynes recognized, there is 'nothing to hope in this direction' (Keynes, 1936, p. 266). In a system with endogenous credit money, even perfectly flexible wages will not be stabilizing.

Keynes's argument in *The General Theory* was fatally conscribed, because he here treated the money supply as one of his three 'ultimate independent variables'. Its quantity was 'determined by the action of the central bank' (Keynes, 1936, p. 247). 'A change in the quantity of money...is already within the power of most governments by open-market policy or analogous measures' (Keynes, 1936, pp. 267–8).

Keynes may not have been totally comfortable with his *General Theory* assumption that the money supply was exogenously controlled by the central bank. After all in the *Treatise* he had given detailed considered reasons why the money supply in contemporary economies in practice varied endogenously with the demand for credit. He had even formally modeled the nominal money supply as varying directly with the wage bill during the expansion phase of the trade cycle (Keynes, 1930, p. 275; Moore, 1984; Moore, 1988, chapter 8). It is perhaps for these reasons that in *The General Theory* Keynes stated: 'If the quantity of money is itself a function of the wage- and price-level, there is indeed, nothing to hope in this direction' (Keynes, 1936, p. 266).

His argument in chapter 19 may be simply summarized as follows: In the presence of insufficient aggregate demand, downward wage and price flexibility would result in a deflationary wage–price spiral. Other than the 'Keynes Effect', which was subject to the 'inadequate-immoderate' objection limiting the effectiveness of expansionary monetary policy in times of depression, there were no *automatic* mechanisms whereby wage cuts stimulate aggregate demand to enable the system to reach full employment.

As is well known, Keynes's argument was analytically 'trumped' by the 'Pigou Effect' (Pigou, 1943, 1947). But with endogenous money there is no Pigou, Real Balance, or Wealth effect. The supply of money is not exogenously set by the central bank, but is determined by system demand for bank credit (Moore, 1988). As such it varies pari pasu with the wage bill.

The Post Keynesian view is that *the supply of credit money is endogenously credit-driven* (Moore, 1988, part 1). Rather than controlling the quantity of money, the monetary authorities administer the nominal level of short term interest rates as their chief exogenous policy instrument (Moore, 1988, part 2). The adoption of this monetary endogeneity position enables Keynes's central vision, that income and output are determined by the level of effective demand, independently of the unit in which wages are measured, to be simply and clearly presented.

Production takes time. Business firms must pay for factor services *before* they have received the sales proceeds from their production. The wages and materials bills constitute the most important component of business working (circulating) capital needs. Short-term bank loans are dominated by business demand for working capital. Business firms maintain large unutilized credit commitments. As a result, loans create deposits (Moore, 1988, chapters 3–5).

A reduction in money wages or a decline in employment reduces the demand for working capital. Business firms will then use current income to repay their existing bank loans. As a result aggregate demand for goods and services, and the supply of credit money, will fall. Changes in the money supply are empirically well-explained by changes in bank loans, and changes in bank loans are well-explained by changes in money wages and employment (Moore, 1988, chapters 6–9).

Similarly with endogenous money there is no 'Keynes Effect'. Short-term interest rates are *exogenously* administered by the central bank, depending on its policy reaction function. Changes in interest rates are the monetary authorities' chief instrument to achieve its policy objectives. Long-term rates are determined by capital market expectations of future short-term rates, that is of future central bank behaviour (Moore, 1988, chapters 10–11). The monetary authorities will be able to reduce long-term rates only if they can persuade the capital markets that they intend to maintain short-term rates at low levels over the relevant future horizon. Central bank credibility is central to the success of this exercise.

A lower level of wages and prices would be associated with a lower wage bill, a lower demand for working capital, lower bank loans, and a lower money supply. The nominal money supply would move proportionately with the wage and price level. Real money balances thus become invariant to the wage level, no matter how flexibly wages change in response to unemployment.

As a result with endogenous money the Aggregate Demand (AD) curve, as a stylized fact, becomes *vertical in* price-output space (Moore, 1988, chapter 12). As shown in Figure 7.2 this provides a simple representation of Keynes's central insight: even perfect downward wage and price flexibility (were it to exist, which it emphatically does not) would not be automatically stabilizing.[2]

The position of the AD curve (Keynes's effective demand) determines the level of money income. Tautologically, AD may be expressed either as the sum of consumption, investment, and government spending, or as the money supply times the income velocity of money. To the extent investment and consumption expenditure are interest elastic, both the money supply and the income velocity of money vary with the level of interest rates set by the central bank. Given the state of expectations (animal spirits), there is thus a whole family of aggregate demand curves, one for each level of interest rates set by the central bank (Moore, 1988, chapters 13–14).

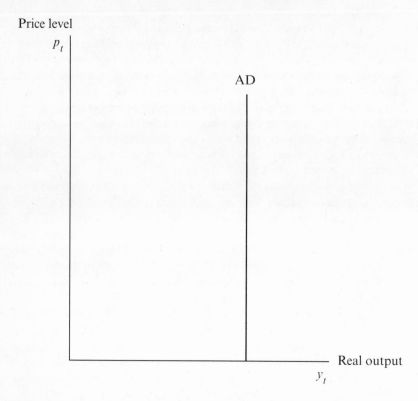

Figure 7.2

The vertical AD curve in price-output space represents a diagrammatic formulation incorporating endogenous credit money of Keynes's central argument in chapter 19: a reduction in money wages will not automatically increase effective demand.

ENDOGENOUS CREDIT MONEY: DYNAMIC ANALYSIS

It is now possible to demonstrate the negative relationship between wage *changes* and interest rates, which Keynes recognized but failed to develop in chapter 19. *Ceteris paribus* the expectation of future price inflation ($\dot{p}$) *reduces* the anticipated real return paid or received on financial assets denominated in fixed money units. If R_c represents the nominal cost of bank credit, and R_m represents the nominal pecuniary and non-pecuniary (services-in-kind) return on holding bank deposits, the real *ex ante* costs and returns may be represented:

$$r_c = R_c - \dot{p}, \, r_m = R_m - \dot{p}.$$

The inflation-induced reduction in the real cost of credit will increase the demand for bank loans, and so, depending on the interest-elasticity of demand for credit, increase the rate of growth of the money supply and aggregate demand. The reduction in the real return on money will also induce wealth-owners to seek to reduce their holdings of money balances relative to their income, and so increase the income velocity of money and aggregate demand. As a result aggregate demand will rise without limit as the inflation rate increases. The AD curve will be upward-sloping in inflation-change in output ($\dot{p}/\dot{y}$) space. [Note: ($\dot{}$) denotes percentage change]

Rather than vertical, as shown in Figure 7.3 the AD curve is *positively sloped* in ($\dot{p}/\dot{y}$) space. In a credit money economy, wage and price inflation will cause AD to increase without limit. The higher the rate of wage inflation, the greater the demand for working capital, the lower the (negative) real cost

Inflation rate
(Percentage change in price)

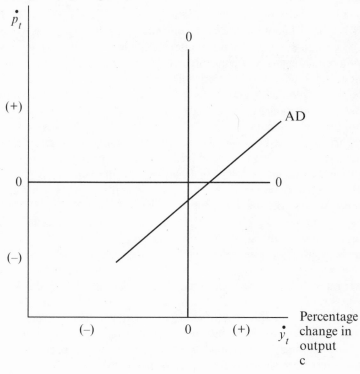

Figure 7.3

of credit, and the higher the rate of growth of the money supply. At the same time the negative return on holding money balances (the inflation tax) will induce wealth-owners to economize on their holdings of money balances, thus raising the income-velocity of money.

As a result AD will rise explosively with the inflation rate. This is due to the double effect of both the money supply and the income velocity of money increasing without bound: $(DY \equiv DM.V + DV.M)$. Since expectations of inflation can easily become self-fulfilling, this is one reason why inflation, once started, is so difficult to stop.

The argument holds in reverse for the case of wage reductions. As the rate of deflation increases, the anticipated real cost of borrowing and the real return on holding money both rise without limit. Borrowers, in response to the increase in the *ex ante* cost of borrowing, will strive to repay their existing loans. By devoting current income to debt repayment, they will reduce both the money supply and aggregate demand. Depositors, by raising their desired money/income ratios in response to the increased *ex ante* real return expected on money balances, will reduce the income velocity of money balances and aggregate demand.

As a result AD will implode as the deflation rate rises: $(-DY = -DM.V - DV.M)$. With deflation measured downwards from the origin, the AD curve will be upward-sloping. Wage and price flexibility thus does not merely not provide an automatic self-adjusting homeostatic mechanism to ensure full employment. Rather, wage and price flexibility is actively *destabilizing*.

During inflation the reduction in the real cost of credit and the real return on deposits inflation can be offset by appropriate monetary policy. If the central bank is committed to its goal of price stability, by raising nominal rates *pari pasu* with the inflation rate, it can maintain the real rate of interest at some target level. In this case the real cost of credit, and the real return on holding money balances, will remain invariant to the inflation rate. The AD curve will again be vertical, and the economy will be largely unaffected by the inflation rate.[3] (Figure 7.4)

However in the case of deflation the central bank will be unable to maintain a real interest rate target. So long as the nominal pecuniary return on fiat money (currency) has a zero floor, and its nonpecuniary liquidity services-in-kind return is positive, the central bank will be unable to reduce nominal market rates on bills, or administered rates on deposits, below this positive floor. Asset holders always are free to transfer their credit money deposits into currency, whose *ex ante* real return in deflationary circumstances would be high. As a result the positive non-pecuniary services-in-kind on money balances impose a lower bound to the nominal rate of pecuniary return required for both financial and real investment.

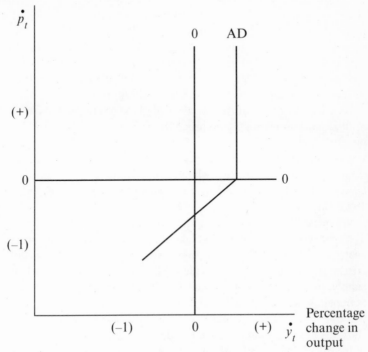

Figure 7.4

As shown in Figure 7.4, the AD curve may be viewed as kinked at zero inflation. If the central bank targets the real short term interest rate, so that the expected real cost of credit and real return on holding deposits remains constant, the AD curve would be vertical and invariant to inflation for all positive rates of inflation (AD′). But so long as fiat money circulates to ensure the acceptability and liquidity of credit money, and offers a non-negative pecuniary return, and a positive non-pecuniary return, it will be impossible for the monetary authorities to lower nominal interest rates on financial assets below zero. The AD curve therefore remains positively sloped in deflation space.

POST KEYNESIAN AD/AS ANALYSIS

Most firms in modern economies have market power, and may realistically be regarded as price-setters rather than price-takers. Since in a non-ergodic world firms cannot precisely estimate their future demand curves, they are unable to calculate their marginal revenue curves. As a result they are forced to follow more simple rules-of-thumb than MC=MR. As a stylized fact, prices may be viewed as set at some stable mark-up over average variable costs (Kalecki, 1969; Okun, 1981; Lavoie, 1992).

In the process firms build-in excess capacity, to be able to meet unantici-pated surges in demand. Excess capacity also serves as an entry deterrent to potential competitors. As a result the volume of sales, in most periods, is demand- rather than quantity-constrained (Kaldor, 1975).

As a stylized fact Post Keynesians regard the Aggregate Supply (AS) curve as *horizontal* in price-output space. The price level is essentially cost-deter-mined, while output is demand-determined. This is consistent with Keynes's vision that real world economies are demand-constrained. Changes in costs determine changes in prices, while changes in aggregate demand determine changes in output and employment (Kaldor, 1975; Moore, 1988; Lavoie, 1992; Davidson, 1994).

Whenever average money wages increase more rapidly than the increase in average labour productivity, unit labour costs and so prices will rise. This will cause the AS curve to shift upward. An increase in money wages also in-creases firms' demand for circulating capital, bank loans, and the money supply. In consequence the AD curve will concurrently shift to the right. The nominal aggregate demand (AD) and aggregate supply (AS) relationships are therefore interdependent, and so useless for analysis, since when both curves shift, the new $p - y$ combination is indeterminate.

In order to make the AD and AS curves independent, we must follow Keynes's lead in the *General Theory*. Both demand and supply must be measured in wage units. In this case, assuming mark-ups and average labour productivity remain constant, an increase in money wages will raise prices, the nominal money supply and nominal money income proportionally. But the real money supply (M_w), real aggregate demand (AD_w), and real output (AS_w), measured in wage units, will be left unaffected.

Where AD_w^t and AS_w^t intersect does not represent any *ex ante* equilibrium configuration. It merely denotes the inflation rate ($\dot{p}^t$) and change in real output ($\dot{y}^t$) over a particular period in time (t). Net surplus or deficit spending on goods and services by firms and households will cause AD_w^t in the next period to shift, for example to AD_w^{t+1}.[4]

From the quantity identity, the change in nominal aggregate demand and GDP over any period from t to $t+1$ (DY^{t+1}) is identically equal to the change in the money supply times velocity, plus the change in velocity times the money supply: $DY^{t+1} \equiv DM^{t+1}.V^t + DV^{t+1}.M^t$. This identity shows how posi-tive net deficit spending was financed: either out of *new* money creation by

Inflation rate
(change in price level)

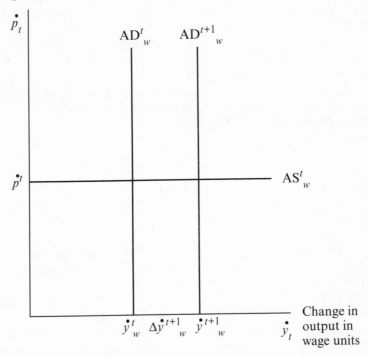

Figure 7.5

net bank borrowing (DM^{t+1}), or from reducing the ratio of *previously existing* money balances relative to money income (DV^{t+1}).

Aggregate demand may increase due to deficit spending financed out of *previously existing* money balances. However, current deficit-spending by some groups out of previously existing money balances will be largely offset by surplus-spending and accumulation of money balances by other groups. Aggregate demand will only increase if the average money/income ratio of economic units falls, so that the income-velocity of the existing money supply increases. Ordinarily money/income ratios do not fall cumulatively over time, nor does income-velocity rise secularly. Changes in income velocity due to deficit-spending financed out of previously-existing money balances normally account for the 'noise' in the fundamental relationship linking changes in the money supply to changes in money income.

As a stylized fact, the AS curve may be represented as a horizontal line in $\dot{p}/\dot{y}$ space. The rate of (core) inflation ($\dot{p}$) will be equal to the excess of the rate of money wage increase ($\dot{w}$) over the average labour productivity growth rate ($\dot{y}/L$): $\dot{p} = \dot{w} - (\dot{y}/L)$. In the case of wage inflation, $\dot{p}$ will be positive, in the case of wage deflation, $\dot{p}$ will be negative.

A reduction in interest rates by the central bank *ceteris paribus* shifts the AD_w curve to the right, to the extent it induces a net increase in the demand for bank credit to finance increases in investment or consumption spending (DM_{t+1}), and/or a reduction in average existing money balances (DV_{t+1}). An increase in interest rates will have the opposite effects.

Endogenous money serves to vindicate Keynes's position that perfect wage flexibility is destabilizing. So long as price and wage flexibility is not instantaneous (another way of getting rid of time[5]), but occurs over some finite time period, the more rapid the rate of adjustment of money wages to excess supply or demand, the greater will be the change in anticipated real returns, and the more destabilizing would be the outcome.

CONCLUSIONS

Post Keynesian theory offers an explanation of the monetary transmission mechanism that is simple, intuitively clear, and direct. Increases in the money supply provide the finance for increases in deficit spending by firms and households on investment or consumption goods. Net deficit spending by economic units out of *newly created* money balances is the central event that causes aggregate demand to increase. Monetary change may thus be seen to be explicitly and powerfully non-neutral. *Monetary change directly causes (finances, enables, permits) permanent increases in the level of aggregate demand.*

Walrasian General Equilibrium theory cannot incorporate historical time, fundamental uncertainty, or money in any significant way. In consequence it offers a seriously misleading model with which to explain and understand real world macroeconomic activity. The Walrasian model must be completely rejected as a macroeconomic guide to a nonergodic world, especially one characterized by imperfect competition and increasing returns.

In a credit money world with aggregate demand deficiency, perfectly flexible wages cannot maintain the system at full employment. Instead they would have precisely the opposite effects. In Keynes's words, perfect wage flexibility would result in 'great instability of prices, so violent perhaps as to make business calculations futile' (Keynes, 1936, p. 269).

Monetary policy may be able to offset the inflationary instability created by upward wage flexibility by the appropriate monetary policy: targeting real interest rates at some positive level. But in the case for which the classical solution was recommended, the presence of unemployment and demand deficiency, downward wage flexibility would initiate an implosive deflationary contraction, which central banks would be impotent to alleviate.

In the presence of nonergodic uncertainty, imperfect competition and increasing returns, intuition based upon a Walrasian representation is likely to point in the completely wrong direction. One example is the widespread belief that the cure for employment lies with more flexible money wages. Even on a purely micro level, if the short-run labour supply were inelastic wage flexibility would lead to violent shifts in wage differentials among occupations and industries, which would severely impede rational calculations, allocations, and coordination.

In contrast to Walras, wage flexibility is not unequivocally a good thing. It is rather, from a macroeconomic point of view, *unequivocally bad*. With endogenous money, perfect wage flexibility is destabilizing, and sluggish wage adjustment stabilizing. Social institutions and practices that make for wage stickiness should be viewed *not as imperfections and obstacles to a frictionless economy, but as adaptive mechanisms that have evolved to reduce economic uncertainty and increase stability of output*.

Macroeconomically, sticky wages are a good thing. Many different levels of employment and unemployment are consistent with the same real wage. A wider range of employment levels compatible with a stable level of money and real wages is a huge advantage for activist demand management policy. In the presence of imperfect competition and increasing returns, very simple models directly yield multiple steady-state equilibria. This generates considerable doubt as to the unique coordinating power of markets.

Largely as a result of the Walrasian diagram, it is widely believed that the economy-wide demand for labour is inversely related to the real wage. However to the extent the economy is characterized by constant or increasing returns, increases in employment do *not* come about by raising prices relative to money wages. Employment gains may even result in lower prices, so that real wages may *rise* with increases in aggregate demand.

Keynes argued that wage bargains are always in nominal terms, since labour lacked the means of determining its real wage. But this of course does not exclude the likelihood that nominal wage increases are causally related to past and expected future price increases.

Real wages appear empirically to be mildly procyclical. But even if it could be conclusively shown that real wages and employment were significantly negatively or positively interrelated, this relationship cannot be given a causal interpretation. Both the real wage and the level of employment, like the money supply, are endogenous variables.

The fact that higher employment may be associated with higher wages does not imply that high wages 'cause' employment. It makes no more sense to attribute the cause of unemployment to 'real wages being too high' than to 'real wages being too low'. Real wages are what firms facing given money wages make them. One cannot conclude that a reduction, or an increase, in real wages 'causes' employment to rise.

Similarly the quantity equation is widely misinterpreted and given causal interpretation, for example an increase in the money supply *causes* prices to rise. Both the money supply and the price level are endogenous. A higher money supply is neither necessary nor sufficient for higher prices. Compared to real wages, employment, output, and the money supply, money wages are more accurately characterized as exogenous. Money wages do not directly adjust to clear labour markets, but are influenced by many noneconomic factors. It is therefore valid to conclude that a higher level of money wages wil *cause* both prices and the money supply to rise.

The level of employment varies positively with the quantity of money expressed in terms of wage units, while the real wage may be invariant to employment. Multiple unemployment equilibria are perfectly consistent with rational agents, in the sense that no agent has an incentive to change the adopted action. There is no 'natural' unemployment rate.

If the economy is imperfectly competitive, 'lack of demand' means that for many firms, the demand curve is too low, compared to their potential output. Many different levels of aggregate demand may be compatible with equilibria in the labour market, in the sense of no tendency for the real wage to change. The 'lack of effective demand' is the underlying cause for the low level of output, and perhaps the low level of real wages, that the market itself can do nothing to escape from.

All agents, private and public, lack precise information on the future consequences of their present actions. Providing the government has well-defined and well-formulated policy objectives, the government does not need to be fully informed, nor even better informed than the private sector. Government policy, like private, is impossible to get perfect. But the proper *direction* of policy, whether it is appropriate to expand or contract aggregate demand, will usually be clearly visible,

Imperfect information is not an argument for inaction. If a policy of aggregate demand expansion has inflationary potential, supply-side policies to make wages more sticky are called for. As labour militancy shifts the rising labour supply boundary to the left, incomes policies such as TIP shift the supply boundary to the right.

If one is intent on blaming unemployment on workers or unions, it is not because they demand 'too high' a level of money wages. It is rather because their expected future behaviour, for example to *raise* wage demands when unemployment falls, or when employment rises, make a central bank policy to reduce interest rates impossible, given the central bank's commitment to fight inflation.

When there is no incomes policy in place, it may be impossible for central banks to reduce interest rates in order to increase the real money supply in wage units. It may be a sad commentary on democracy, but central bankers have increasingly become the main government official with the responsibility for, and strong commitment to, price stability.

NOTES

1. The irony of this situation is of course that one of Keynes's main purposes in writing *The General Theory* was to refute the idea that unemployment was attributable to downward wage inflexibility: 'a decline in employment ... is not necessarily due to labour's *demanding* a larger quantity of wage goods; and a willingness on the part of labour to accept lower money-wages is not necessarily a remedy for unemployment' (Keynes, 1936, p. 18).
2. Perfect wage flexibility could be construed as *instantaneous*, in order to guarantee continual full employment market-clearing in the face of insufficient aggregate demand, at all dates. However, Hahn has stated that 'the view that with "flexible" money wages there would be no unemployment has no convincing argument to recommend it. ... Even in a pure tâtonnement in traditional models convergence to equilibrium cannot be generally proved' (Hahn, 1977, p. 37).
3. The crucial importance of monetary policy for the effects on inflation on aggregate demand may explain in part why inflation rates are so variable internationally, and why with cross-section data such a huge scatter is observed between counties' growth rates and inflation rates.
4. Changes in GDP do not seem to be systematically related to the level of GDP. Empirical time-series evidence suggests that GDP has a unit root. This implies that the effects of transient demand shocks are permanent. Real world economies do not follow any stable trend growth path.
5. This serves to confirm Tobin's position that in theory any degree of stickiness which prevents instantaneous wage adjustment is the only necessary condition to explain unemployment (Tobin, 1993). Hahn and Solow's demonstration that the adjustment dynamics of a Walrasian system with perfectly flexible wages may be badly behaved, so that once disturbed it may go off on an unstable path, reinforces Keynes's insight that even perfectly flexible wages will not lead automatically to a full employment equilibrium, but are likely to be destabilizing (Hahn and Solow, 1995).

REFERENCES

Davidson, P. (1994), *Post Keynesian Macroeconomic Theory*, Aldershot, Hants: Edward Elgar.

Hahn, F.H. (1977), 'Keynesian Economics and General Equilibrium Theory', in *The Microfoundations of Macroeconomics*, edited by G.C. Harcourt, London: Macmillan.

Hahn, F.H. (1984), *Equilibrium and Macroeconomics*, Oxford: Blackwell.

Hahn, F.H. and Solow, R. (1995), *A Critical Essay on Modern Macroeconomic Theory*, Cambridge, Mass.: MIT Press.

Howitt, P. (1990), *The Keynesian Recovery and Other Essays*, Ann Arbor: University of Michigan Press.

Kaldor, N. (1975), *Economics Without Equilibrium*, Armonk, NY: M. Sharpe.

Kalecki, M. (1969), *Studies in the Theory of Business Cycles 1933–1939*, Oxford: Blackwell.

Keynes, J.M. (1930), *The Collected Writings of John Maynard Keynes*, volume 5, *A Treatise on Money*, Part 1, *The Pure Theory of Money*, London: Macmillan, 1971.

Keynes, J.M. (1936), *The Collected Writings of John Maynard Keynes*, volume 7, *The General Theory of Employment, Interest and Money*, London: Macmillan, 1971.

Lavoie, M. (1992), *Foundations of Post Keynesian Economics*, Aldershot, Hants: Edward Elgar.

Mankiw, G. and Romer, D. (1991), 'Introduction', *New Keynesian Economics*, Cambridge, Mass.: MIT Press.

Moore, B.J. (1984), 'Keynes and the Endogeneity of Money', *Studi Economici*, **22**, 23–69.

Moore, B.J. (1988), *Horizontalists and Verticalists*, London: Cambridge University Press.

Okun, A. (1980), *Prices and Quantities*, Washington, DC: Brookings Institution.

Pigou, A.C. (1943), 'The Classical Stationary State', *Economic Journal*, **53** (4), 343–51.

Pigou, A.C. (1947), 'Economic Progress in a Stable Environment', *Economica*, **14**, 180–8.

Tobin, J. (1993), 'Price Flexibility and Output Stability, An Old Keynesian View', *Journal of Economic Perspectives*, **7**.

Tobin, J. (1996), 'An Overview of the General Theory', in *The General Theory "Second Edition"*, edited by G.C. Harcourt and P. Riach, London: Macmillan.

8. On sticky prices: A post Keynesian perspective*

Roy J. Rotheim

INTRODUCTION

The neoclassical theory of pricing both at the level of the firm *and for industry as a whole* conceptualizes upward sloping supply and downward sloping demand curves indicating a short run procyclical movement between demand and nominal price. The neoclassical Keynesian perspective (new Keynesian economics) retains this traditional framework while recognizing that prices tend to be relatively sticky, especially when demand has fallen, for a variety of reasons (see Akerlof and Yellin, 1985a,b; Mankiw, 1985, 1993; Gordon, 1990).

As it thinks in terms of market metaphors at both the level of the firm and for industry as a whole, neoclassical theory considers the issue of sticky prices to be relevant in terms of their impact in inhibiting *market clearing* for the economy as a whole. With an exogenous fall in demand, equilibrium in every market is restored to the extent that relative prices are free to adjust. The final impact on aggregate demand (and presumably on supply and employment) is perceived to be less than the initial fall because some of the reduced demand has been redressed by an increased quantity demanded brought about by the lower prices.[1] While understood to be based on rational (or near-rational) behaviour, such reluctance to adjust price, especially when demand falls, indicates a short run *aberration* from what would otherwise be a longer run competitive outcome. Recent empirical studies (Ball, Mankiw and Romer, 1988; Blinder, 1992) allege the verification of such explanations. Money neutrality is thus believed to be operant in the long run, as prices eventually adjust to their equilibrium (market clearing) levels. Consequently this adherence to the eventual attainment of conditions characterized by the classical dichotomy leads to a continuation of mind frames that separate real from nominal phenomena, once the long run has been reached. Thus, price setting at the level of the firm establishes *relative* prices reflecting relative positions of scarcity. And inflation continues to be explained by an increase in nominal prices brought about by a money stock growing faster than some scarcity based trend rate of growth of real output.

As is well known, Keynes considered such theoretical devices to be premised on profoundly illogical structures. One could not think in terms of individual market phenomena and then take those constructs – which, he believed, relied on aggregate output and employment remaining constant – and apply them to macrophenomena where the nature of such enquiries was to assess the causes and consequences of changes in aggregate output and employment. To do so would indicate the fallacy of *ignoratio elenchi*: the inappropriate use of one logical structure to explain another. As a result of this theoretical observation, Keynes was confident in saying that the (neo)classical theory had no basis upon which to base its macroeconomic conclusions. An aggregate *market* in output, employment, or capital simply made no sense from an operational perspective (see Keynes, 1936; *Rotheim, 1988; Davidson, 1997*). As such, Keynes's accusation would vitiate the neoclassical obsession with thinking about cyclical fluctuations in terms of sticky prices at the level of the individual firm. It is not that prices may or may not be sticky, but rather such observations give us little if no insights into the causes, consequences, and remedies of and for changes in aggregate economic activity.

Post Keynesians have also been concerned with the pricing decision of firms, and the conditions underlying price stickiness, *although not as a theory explaining economic fluctuations*. Like new Keynesians, they also envision such questions as emanating from an *institutional* perspective recognizing that conditions on the supply side might warrant prices to be relatively insensitive to fluctuations in demand. However, unlike the strictly static neoclassical approach of the new Keynesians, many post Keynesian theories understand the pricing process to be but one element in a more dynamic context of firm and economy-wide growth. Here price setting behaviour is not only concerned with net revenue generation to maximize current profits for given plant and equipment, but it can take on the added role of strategic mechanism for generating additional revenue to underwrite financial exigencies of all sorts including (but not limited to) capital accumulation (see Çapoglu (1991, p. 84), who refers to such pricing strategies as 'profit-targeting behaviour').

Moreover – and this is an extremely critical distinction from the new Keynesian view – post Keynesian theories of price contribute to an understanding of movements in the *general* price level. In this regard, the typical line of reasoning does not accept the dichotomy of price/quantity (in either direction) nor does it proceed from questions of the effects of price on quantity – either directly through market effects or indirectly through real balance effects. Rather, product prices are but one element in a more general theory of effective demand, whereby conditions of aggregate supply and demand both affect and are effected by movements in flows of income, out, and spending. Here there is no sense of an enquiry about the output inhibiting effects of sticky prices. In fact, post Keynesians recognize that price *inflexibility* is a prerequisite for economic growth.[2,3]

In this post Keynesian tradition, there has been a resurgence of theories of the firm that are at variance with the neoclassical approach [cf. Davidson, 1972; Eichner, 1973, 1976; Kregel, 1973; Minsky, 1975, 1986; Wood, 1975; Harcourt and Kenyon, 1976; Sylos-Labini, 1979; Sawyer, 1983; Çapoglu, 1991; Arestis, 1992].[4] It is the intention of this chapter to elaborate on this post Keynesian tradition by showing how it can help explain macroeconomic phenomena involving changes in employment, interest rates and prices, where the latter two concepts are liable to move in the opposite direction of the level of employment or to be somewhat insensitive to such changes in employment. Sticky prices will take on a new and profoundly different role in this post Keynesian view of the pricing process. Paul Davidson has in fact written extensively on this aspect, and it would become apparent in what follows the relationship between the essence of this chapter with his work in the area.

The model to be developed is an extension of that originally put forth by Eichner (1973, 1976). The first section of this chapter will briefly consider Eichner's basic model whereby the firm may choose to employ its mark-up over unit cost as a strategic variable in providing internal finance for capital accumulation needs. Eichner's assumption that firms face a perfectly elastic supply of external finance then will be relaxed in favour of an external finance function that is positively related to the firm's demand for additional finance. Such a modification is consistent with more recent work by both new and post Keynesians on the effect of the credit channel on the path of economic activity. This generalized model will then be employed to assess some implications that interdependencies of real and monetary phenomena manifested by the pricing decision of firms expounded in this chapter might have on macroeconomic processes.

What the model in this paper emphasizes is the extent to which non-competitive firms may use their mark-up in a strategic fashion as a factor in the financing of the capital accumulation process, specifically, and in the acquisition of finance for any other purposes, in general. From a post Keynesian perspective, one is interested not only in the pricing behaviour of firms but also changes in aggregate prices, emanating from the same processes. In the tradition of Keynes, what is apparent is that the extent to which interest rates and prices, at both the level of the firm and for industry as a whole, are seen to be sensitive to fluctuations in economic activity (although, as we shall see, in a way that is contrary to orthodox wisdom) depending in large measure on the policies pursued by the financial community: by the banks and other financial institutions in their portfolio decisions and by the central bank in the policies it chooses for the conduct of monetary policy.

A POST KEYNESIAN MODEL OF PRICE CHANGE

It will be assumed that a firm pays for capital accumulation in one of three ways: by retained earnings; externally, by the sale of new issues on financial markets, *and* by increasing mark-ups over unit cost in order to provide a source of additional *internal* finance. In his original formulation, Eichner sought to develop a model that could explain the proposition that 'because of its market power, [the megacorp] can increase the margin above costs in order to obtain more internally generated funds, that is, a larger "cash flow", to finance its intended investment expenditures' (Eichner, 1973, p. 1130). He accomplishes this by the derivation of a schedule similar to the one illustrated in Figure 8.1.[5] For a given demand for additional investment funds (schedule D_{fI} or D_{fII}) the firm's decision to finance this growth internally or externally will depend upon the relationship between two rates of interest: an *implicit* rate of interest (R) and a market rate of interest (i).

The implicit rate of interest reflects the potential costs of financing additional investment internally via increases in the mark-up over per unit cost, n.[6] These potential costs of financing may be derived from 'the possible subsequent decline in revenue from increasing the margin above costs in order to augment the current cash-flow – i.e., the effects of elastic demand in the medium and long run' (Eichner, 1973, p. 1190).[7]

Possible causes of declining sales resulting from an increase in the mark-up are threefold: (a) a substitution effect; (b) an entry factor; and (c) meaningful government intervention (ibid.). The first will be relevant when the firm believes that it will lose its sales to competitors, reducing its long-run market share, as a result of raising its mark-up. The entry factor relates to the firm's belief that by raising its mark-up:

> new firms will find it easier to overcome the barriers that inhibit their entry into the industry; and that if a new firm of a certain size relative to total industry demand should gain entry, every established firm in the industry can expect its own sales to decline by that same percentage. (Eichner, 1973, pp. 1190–1)

Governmental intervention always stands as a potential threat to oligopolistic firms, causing such firms to believe that inordinate increases in their mark-ups might call forth some inquiry into their pricing policies.

Combining these three factors, Eichner identifies what he calls an implicit rate of interest, R, as the ratio of the additional finance provided in the present by increasing the mark-up to the discounted sum of future cash flow expected

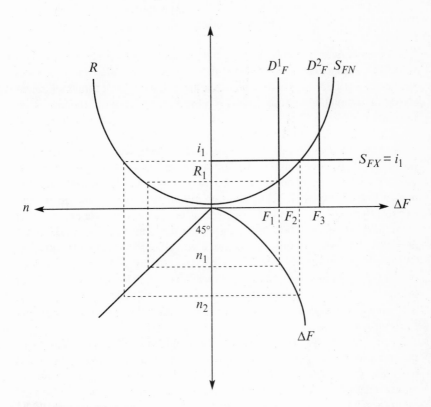

Figure 8.1

to be lost on account of the higher mark-up. This is shown in quadrant IV of Figure 8.1, where the implicit rate of interest, R, is plotted on the ordinate and increases in the mark-up, n, are plotted on the abscissa. By increasing the mark-up, the flow of additional funds per planning period, ΔF, will also increase.

This relationship is shown in quadrant II of Figure 10.1. The flow of additional funds per period schedule, ΔF, is drawn under the same assumption as in the R schedule, that is that the possibilities of substitution and/or entry increase as the mark-up is increased. These two schedules, the implicit rate of interest function and the additional flow of funds per period function, can be combined to derive a schedule which Eichner defines as 'a supply curve for additional internal finance (S_{FN}) indicating how the implicit interest rate, R, on those funds varies as the amount of additional funds obtained per planning period, ΔF, varies' (ibid., p. 1193, with modifications of symbols). This supply of additional internal funds schedule is drawn in quadrant I of Figure 8.1.

Additional funds per period can also be obtained from external sources, as well. The *composite* rate reflecting these sources is called by Eichner a market rate of interest, i, where he explicitly assumes that a firm 'can obtain all the additional investment funds it wishes from external sources at an interest rate, $i...$' (p. 1193). This assumption is represented by the horizontal schedule S_{FX} in quadrant I of Figure 8.1.

Suppose that the firm plans an investment scheme that requires an additional flow of finance equal in amount to $0F_1$ in Figure 8.1. At this required flow of finance, the expected implicit rate of interest, R_1, is less than the market rate of interest, I_1. Thus the firm will attempt to generate the amount $0F_1$ strictly from internal sources by increasing its mark-up over per unit cost by an amount equal to $0n_1$. Instead, suppose the firm requires an additional flow of finance equal to $0F_3$. In this case it will attempt to finance the quantity $0F_2$ internally by raising its mark-up by $0n_2$, obtaining the remainder F_2F_3 externally by selling new issues on financial markets. This strategy is rational for the firm since after the quantity $0F_2$ the perceived implicit rate of interest will exceed the market rate of interest, signalling the firm not to raise its mark-up beyond $0n_2$.

In the above model, Eichner makes the simplifying assumption that firms face a perfectly elastic supply of external finance function, although he did recognize that it could only be justified 'as long as the amounts required remain relatively small'. As external financial requirements increased, interest rates would be higher and the supply curve for external finance would be upward sloping (see Eichner, 1976, pp. 86–7). However, Eichner did not integrate this assumption into his model. This I shall try to remedy in the next section by developing an external finance function the slope and position of which depend upon the relationships between increased firm indebtedness and the rates they face for the acquisition of the requisite external funding. Given the recent work done on the *credit channel* of monetary policy (see Bernanke and Gertler, 1995) and credit crunches (Greenwald and Stiglitz, 1993; Federal Reserve Bank of New York, 1993; Dow, 1996), it seems appropriate to recognize the role played by credit in the extent to which firms, both in particular and in general, are affected by the institutional constraints administered under differing credit configurations. Once this relationship is specified, it can be added to the D_F and S_{FN} schedules constituting a model better capable of explaining the interactions of the decisions of firms' growth and the consequent effects on financial markets in particular as well as on the economy as a whole.

EXTERNAL FINANCE, CREDIT RISK AND THE RATE OF INTEREST

Unlike the horizontal S_{FX} schedule developed in Figure 8.1, it is posited here that the supply of external funds schedule is capable of possessing an upward slope. This result follows from the fact that for a given flow of investment, the higher are the firm's gearing ratios, that is, the higher are their ratios of external debt to the current realizable value of their assets, the greater the risks lenders feel they must take in providing this additional finance (see Marris, 1964). This *lender's risk* is defined by Adrian Wood as the risk that, in the event of the company going bankrupt, lenders may not get their principal back because the salable assets of the company are insufficient to cover its liabilities (1975, p. 28; see also Keynes, 1936, Kalecki, 1937). Furthermore, '[T]o attract loans, a company must pay a higher interest rate the higher its gearing ratio' (Wood, 1975). Therefore, to the extent that this is the case, then as a firm expands its capital stock, its gearing ratio will also increase, implying that the rate of interest on external finance that it faces will in all likelihood be higher. Consequently, the supply of external finance schedule, S_{FX} should be drawn as upward sloping as gearing ratios continue to rise with greater indebtedness (see Dow 1989, 1996; Wray, 1990). This modification is realized in Figure 8.2.

Figure 8.2 illustrates that for a given flow of additional net investment and therefore a given demand for additional finance, D_F, the firm will choose to finance this net investment from internal or external sources depending upon the relationship between the S_{FX} curve and the S_{FN} curve. Consistent with the model, above, firms will seek to obtain additional finance entirely from expected ploughed back profits, by increasing their mark-up over per unit cost, so long as if $R \leq i$. Alternatively, a proportion of the additional investment will be financed externally if $R > i$.

Thus, consider an increased demand for capital by a firm that requires an additional quantity of finance equal to D_F^1. In this case, R_1 is less than i_1 for the entire region of the increase in the demand for finance and consequently the whole amount of additional finance will be obtained internally by the firm's expanding its mark-up over per unit cost by the amount $0n_1$.[8]

Assume, alternatively, that the firm intends to deepen its capital stock by an amount which requires D_f^2 in additional finance. Here it is observed that R is less than i only up to point a. After that point, however, the situation is

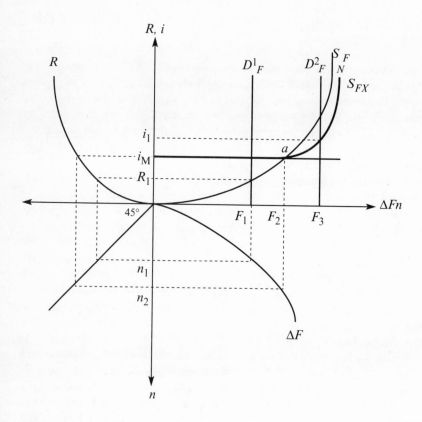

Figure 8.2

reversed, inducing the firm to externally finance an amount equal to F_2F_3. In this case, the firm will attempt to secure the remainder of the required additional finance, $0F_1$, by increasing its mark-up by the amount $0N_2$.[9] The interest rate paid by the firm would now be i_1, a rate greater than the general market rate of interest i_M, to the extent that this increased indebtedness causes lenders to be more wary of the firm's ability to repay its debt, thus adding a risk premium to the cost of the loan. In Figure 8.2 the supply of external finance schedule is assumed to begin rising only after the point at which borrowing occurs.

MORE ON THE SUPPLY OF EXTERNAL FINANCE SCHEDULE

Using four quadrant schedules can be cumbersome, although their explicitness more than compensates for some of their shortcomings. One such difficulty is attempting to make inference when the variables themselves embody notions of change. As such, it will occur that the supply of external finance schedule will shift position as firms continue to demand more finance. Take, for example, the following situation described in Figure 8.3.

At time period t_1 the firm desires an additional quantity of finance, D_F^1, in order to implement a specific increase in net investment. Given the supply schedules for additional internal and external finance, S_{FN} and S_{FX}^1, the firm will borrow an amount F_1F_2 while financing the remainder, $0F_1$, by increasing its mark-up over per unit cost by an amount $0n_1$. Suppose that in time period t_2 the firm again desires to finance an equivalent amount of additional net investment such that D_F^1 equals D_F^2. In addition to raising its mark-up, the firm must once again go to securities markets to provide the necessary external finance.[10] Now, it was stated above that as firms borrow to a greater extent, lenders may perceive this as increasing the uncertainty of the borrower's ability to repay its total debt. Therefore, the interest rate that firms face may be expected to rise as their total outstanding debt increases. However, the impression given by the intersection of D_F^2 with S_{FX}^1 is that the rate of interest on external finance is unchanged. If the above mentioned effect is to be accounted for, then it will be necessary that the supply curve for external funds shifts upward and to the left at every level of additional finance. This is indicated by the movement of the S_{FX} curve from S_{FX}^1 to S_{FX}^2 in Figure 8.3.

The operant rate of interest for the firm, at the end of the first scenario, was i_1. Any additional finance obtained on capital markets may need to be sold at yet higher rates of interest. Faced with these circumstances, the firm must now revise its desired financial mix. Given the higher interest rate schedule, the firm will borrow fewer additional funds in time period t_2 (F_2F_3) than in time period t_1 (F_1F_2) while it will be forced to seek a greater quantity of funds internally in period t_2 ($0F_3$) than in period t_1. Such an outcome would require that the increase in the mark-up in period t_2 ($0n_2$) exceed the increase in the mark-up in period t_1 ($0n_1$).

Thus, over time, when all other things remain the same (including actions of other firms, financial institutions, and the central bank), one would expect that rising demands for finance would be followed by increases in interest rates and in the rate of increase in the price level. However, once these static assumptions are relaxed, there are additional observations that need to be addressed in the context of the role played by the conditions underlying the supply of external finance. One has to do with the influence and effects

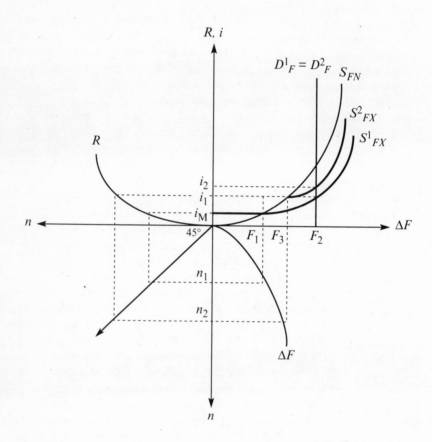

Figure 8.3

played by the general state of liquidity preference; the other focuses on the posture taken by the central bank.

The analysis underlying Figure 8.3 depended upon the relationship between a specific firm and a specific source of finance. An additional explanation for shifts in the supply of external funds schedule would also depend upon the state of liquidity *in the system as a whole*. It is not, however, only the supply of liquidity which is relevant to shifts in the S_{FX} schedule but also the state of liquidity preference borne by the financial community as a whole at any moment in time (see Wray, 1990; Dow, 1996). In other words, interest rates on borrowed funds will not only be affected by the perception held by lenders of the individual firm's current and prospective balance sheet, but will also be affected by perceptions of broader factors characterizing prospective yields in the market in general. Interest rates on new issues can be expected to rise or fall if economic conditions in general are perceived to become less or more sanguine, and if financial markets (secondary markets) become more or less bearish in response to these and other perceived data.

When the future environment is perceived to be conducive to economic growth, then even a firm with higher leverage and with less confidence of the prospective yield on new assets (irrespective of any concept of asymmetric information) will be able to benefit from a lower yield curve on financial assets. Here the S_{FX} schedule they face and the cost of such funds will, *pari passu*, be lower than might be warranted by the state of their own gearing ratio.

Alternatively, when circumstances are such that economic conditions worsen, one might expect an initial rise in the yield curve in financial assets for at least two reasons. First, to the extent that contracts are fixed in money terms, firms' contractual obligations (labour, resources, and finance) will not fall to the same extent that their current and near term sources of revenue are falling. As such, firms, as a whole, may be forced to maintain their financial requirements by increasing their demand for finance, that is keeping the D_F schedule in the first quadrant, even though the demand for new capital assets may have been curtailed. The effect of this continued demand for finance as downturns ensue is that interest rates on new issues can be expected *not* to fall, and in fact, may even rise if any liquidity crisis exhibits profound secondary effects (see Greenwald and Stiglitz, 1993, p. 29).

Such a scenario was envisioned by Keynes when in response to the conventional wisdom that increased savings would *lower* interest rates thereby increasing the incentives to investment, he asserted:

> I have argued in my *Treatise* [*on Money*] that causes which determine the increment of capital wealth are only contingently and indirectly connected with those which determine the amounts of individual savings. If an increment of saving by an individual is *not* accompanied by an increment of new investment – and, in the absence of deliberate management by the central bank or the government, it will be nothing but a lucky accident if it is – then it *necessarily* causes diminished receipts, disappointment and losses to some other party, and *the outlet for the savings of A will be found in financing the losses of B*. (Cannan, *et al.*, 1932, p. 14)

Moreover, in the context of this section, this changed motivation for borrowing funds internally may very well have the effect of increasing the degree of lenders' risk perceived by banks and other lending institutions. Even if they did find themselves with rising free reserves as borrowing for productive purposes waned, the rising demands for money to re-finance existing debt positions might cause interest rates not to fall (despite the increase in free reserves) and might even cause them to rise as financial institutions preferred to increase their liquidity positions in light of the changed nature of indebtedness and the uncertainty over prospective yields in the future (see Dow, 1996). Here we might find S_{FX} remaining stable and even shifting upward as economic conditions actually worsened, *again independent of the nature of financial requirements of any individual firm.*

The final concern with regard to the position of the S_{FX} schedule can be observed in terms of the central bank's conduct of its monetary policies. Over the last 25 years, central banks have taken on different perceptions of their role in the overall economic process: sometimes seeing themselves as the institution which provides for order in financial markets (including a lender of last resort) so that private and public debt can be responsibly marketed; othertimes seeing themselves as the guardian of the price level. These goals have been translated into policies that roughly resemble either the intermediate targeting of some money market rate of interest (usually on interbank funds) or on the targeting of some measure of reserves (high powered money, as they like to call it), respectively.[11]

If the monetary policy (either explicit or *de facto*) of the central bank is to provide for stability in money market conditions (resulting in a totally endogenous money stock), then some of the pressures put on the costs of external funds as a result of the above name cases, may be smoothed to some degree. This theme will be elaborated below. On the other hand, when long-run monetary aggregates are targeted, changes in the demand for external finance falling out of the central bank's normal range will *not* be accommodated, resulting in the full burden being placed on the portfolios of lending institutions: reserve positions will rise or fall in direct response to changes in the demand for finance as well as the institution's changed preference for liquidity.[12] The cost of external funds would rise and fall in direct proportion to changes in the demand for such funds, and changes in liquidity preference of lending institutions (primary assets) and in financial markets (secondary markets whose prices may under such extreme circumstances create the benchmark to which primary market assets must fall in line).

We are now in a position to take this post Keynesian model and address the issue of price stickiness when economies turn down. The focus, however, will not be from a new Keynesian viewpoint in which nominal prices do or do not fall in response to an exogenous nominal shock. Rather, the post Keynesian vision considers the rate of increase in prices as the cycle turns down. Prices are always assumed to rise; the question for post Keynesians is how sticky will this rate be under conditions of economic slowdown.

EMPLOYMENT, INTEREST RATES AND PRICES: PRELIMINARY OBSERVATIONS

A new Keynesian macroeconomic analysis of slowdowns in economic activity looks at the paths that prices and outputs take in the course of the restoration of equilibrium. In such circumstances, as was noted above, individual prices will fall allowing quantity demanded to be partially increased, with the remainder of the restoration being achieved by the effect such price deflation has on real balances and aggregate spending behaviour. The idea of falling prices follows from the idea that a lower demand causes producers to sell at any price that will clear their markets. The belief that relative prices will be restored to their original position as a reflection of relative scarcities implies that no theory of price inflation or deflation can be found occurring because of such cyclical activity. Instead, inflation is perceived, in the traditional sense, as a long run relationship between rates of growth of full employment output and rates of growth of the money supply. The former refers to discrete changes in prices that assist in the process of restoring equilibrium; the latter reflects rates of change in prices of goods and services along their equilibrium growth path.

Post Keynesians do not accept such a classical dichotomy. For them, the rate of growth of output and employment are considered to be path dependent (not independent of the fluctuations about that path) such that the price/quantity dual has little, if any, exegetical relevance. As such, they envision the rate of change of the price level as emanating from pricing decisions made at the level of the firm, where such price changes are strategic variables in the course of assessing the level of revenue required to maintain the continued solvency of those firms. This assertion has been the basis of the model presented above, and will constitute the focus as we assess a post Keynesian perspective on the role of prices, interest rates, and employment, in this case as an economy declines. In this regard, such a view appears to be more consistent with the historical evidence that path dependent economies experience continual price increases, to the extent that prices stand as strategic variables linked to the maintenance of internal finance. Neoclassical theories posit a dual between price stability (zero inflation) and deviations from that level – whatever may be the source of that deviation. A post Keynesian theory moves beyond such a dualism (see Dow, 1991), so that the relevant question focuses, instead, on the circumstances and multitude of factors which cause the rate of inflation to be increasing, decreasing, or stable. Moreover, as we shall see, the rate of growth of the money stock (depending upon the policies chosen by the central bank) can have an effect on changes in prices and interest rates, but in the context of a model in which employment, output, and pricing decisions are organically bound. Here inflation is in no way a *monetary phenomenon* although the model presented clearly indicates that *money matters* in a profoundly richer way than what exists in neoclassical models.

And finally, by way of introduction, post Keynesians make an important distinction between prices of existing goods and assets and those of goods and assets that are yet to be produced (see Keynes, 1930a; Weintraub, 1958; Davidson, 1972). One might expect the prices of stocks of goods and assets to fluctuate in direct proportion to changes in demand, consistent with the neoclassical view. However, reproducible goods and assets (those things that are relevant to individuals' abilities to make purchases in the future) will find their prices responding more likely to conditions of production and changes in the relative powers of those who compete for the surplus (that is, relative changes in profit margins). In the short run, one would expect that constant returns and other factors (such as explicit contracts among firms) would cause product prices to remain *relatively* constant in the short run. This proposition plays an important role in post Keynesian literature, signifying that changes in short-run demand are primarily dealt with among firms by a lengthening and shortening of the queue for delivery rather than by fluctuations in prices (see Davidson, 1972). These conjectures have been borne out by a recent study at the Bank of England (1996) which observed industrial prices to be relatively inflexible in the short run reflecting these traditionally post Keynesian factors, rather than because of menu-costs as are believed to exist by new Keynesian economists.

Such observations regarding sticky prices do not, however, undermine the post Keynesian assertion that firms use their mark-up over unit costs as a strategic variable in its overall decision making process. In terms of a theory of inflation (as was the motivation of the original Eichner model), this perspective recognizes that prices do not rise and fall in direct response to changes in demand conditions, but that prices continually rise; it is only the extent to which they rise that becomes an interesting question for post Keynesian theorists. And what will be seen in the next two sections is that one of the factors contributing to an explanation of such changes in prices will be the extent to which banks and other financial institutions, as well as central bank policy makers, are responsive to the requirements of firms to finance a portion of their economic growth with external sources of funds. Such an approach can explain why prices may not fall (and may even rise) when economies turn down, and why prices may not appreciably rise when economies expand.

THE INDIVIDUAL FIRM

Methodologically, post Keynesian analysis follows directly from Keynes's belief that questions relating to the classical dichotomy between real and nominal sectors are inapplicable to an ongoing economic system. In this regard he said:

> The division of Economics between the theory of Value on the one hand and the Theory of Money on the other hand is, I think a false division. The right dichotomy is, I suggest, between the theory of the Individual Industry or Firm and of the rewards and the distribution between different uses of a *given* quantity of resources on the one hand, and the Theory of Output and Employment *as a whole* on the other hand. (1936, p. 293)

Suppose, then, that a firm requires F_1 additional finance based on its predictions of the state of long term expectations of prospective yields on its capital assets. This situation is depicted in Figure 8.4. At the given term structure of interest rates and its perception of its implicit rate of interest, the firm will choose to increase its mark-up by $0n_1$ (expecting an increase in revenue equal to $0F^e$) and then borrow an amount equal to F_1F^e on financial markets at a rate of interest i_1. Now let the firm experience a fall in sales revenue (the reason being immaterial) such that the actual revenue received through market sales, given the above strategy, turns out to be $F^a < F^e$.[13] If the firm were to lower its price to clear the market, as new Keynesians would suggest, then it is conceivable that it might not take in sufficient gross receipts to repay contractual commitments incurred during the previous expansionary period. Should sales receipts fall, firms would still be liable for their contractual obligations. It is in cases such as these the value of firms' assets puts a constraint on future production and consumption decisions (Clower, 1965).[14]

Rather, in a post Keynesian model it is assumed that physical resources, debt obligations, as well as labour have been contracted for prior to the receipt of revenues out of which these commitments must be paid. In addition, it must be assumed that these contractual commitments were tendered in fixed money terms (to the extent that they were debt rather than equity financed) so that if production has taken place, the factors *must* be paid regardless of the state of business conditions. Therefore, the demand for finance (that is, *liquidity*) will continue to be a relevant factor in subsequent periods so that these fixed commitments can be met. Thus, in Figure 8.4, it might be expected that the D_F schedule will continue to exist in the positive (first) quadrant. For ease of exposition, assume that the demand for finance in period t_2 (which represents periods subsequent to t_1) also equals D_F^1. The unexpected fall in sales revenue is depicted as the new curve S_{FN}^a, where actual revenue brought about by any prior increase in mark-ups is lower than previously expected. Here the increased demand for liquidity is not occurring for reasons of purchasing more goods and services, but rather as means of *payment* on past contractual obligations (see Minsky, 1965; Rotheim, 1991). How will these funds be obtained by the firm?

Any unexpected shortfall in revenue will result in an unanticipated increase in inventories of finished goods. As the costs of these goods have been laid out prior to their sale, firms may be forced to cover those outlays by selling those products at spot at whatever price the market will provide (assuming that such a market exists and that the spot price does not fall so low as to make it unattractive for firms to sell at spot, see Davidson, 1972). The neoclassical (new Keynesian) theory of the firm does not distinguish between spot and flow supply prices under such circumstances so that their programme focuses solely on the extent to which spot prices do or do not fall to clear the goods, labour, capital markets, and so on. But in a post Keynesian theory, the distinction between the price of existing goods and the price of newly produced goods is fundamental to any theory of pricing and inflation behaviour (see Davidson, 1972, p. 340).

As the conditions of production are such that unit costs do not fall appreciably as a firm scales back its production, it is rather unlikely to expect that firms, especially those who are heavily leveraged, would be posting lower supply prices of their output with such reductions in demand for their product.

Beyond any added funds that may be obtained by selling off inventories at spot (and, of course by any subsequent reductions in labour and other resource demands), firms may be able to secure needed funds by selling additional financial assets on securities markets (including at banks). Gearing ratios will increase because such money is demanded as means of payment (financing finance) rather than as means of purchase (financing real assets). As such, given the arguments made above, it can be expected that firms who require more finance for these circumstances will be met by a financial community expecting a risk premium to be built into the returns paid by these firms: these assets will by necessity be sold at a greater discount, that is, at a higher effective rate of interest. This likelihood is depicted in Figure 8.4 as the rotation of the supply of external finance function from S^1_{FX} to S^2_{FX}.

Given the revised perceived implicit and explicit costs of obtaining finance, the firm will increase its mark-up, again, this time by $0n_2 > 0n_1$ to obtain added revenue equal to $0F_2$, with the remainder of the finance ($F_2F_1 > F^e_NF_1$) coming from the sale of assets at a rate of interest, i_2. All other things remaining unchanged, we can be assured that i_2 will always be greater than i_1 because the further increased sale of assets will again increase the firm's gearing ratio and thus a greater discount will be required by lenders if they are to purchase these assets. How much the firm must increase its prices and

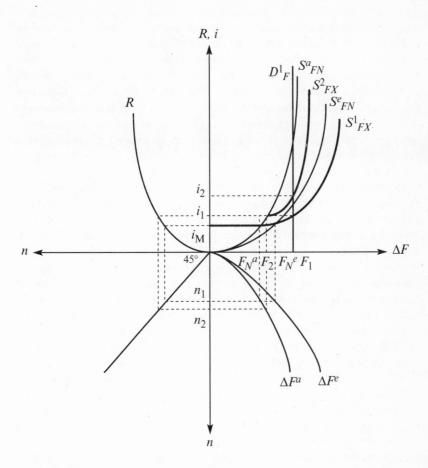

Figure 8.4

pay higher rates on the new issues will be determined by the magnitude of their increased financial needs as well as their perception of the costs of obtaining funds via external sources.

Downturns in economic activity do not impact on only one firm, however, but rather spread their effects over industry as a whole. When considering the possible impacts of cyclical downturns on pricing, interest rates, and output, it is therefore necessary to understand both the economy-wide implications of the model being presented, as well as the integral role played by varying monetary policies in the determination of such outcomes.

INDUSTRY AS A WHOLE

In a new Keynesian environment, activity occurring at the level of the firm provides sufficient knowledge to predict outcomes occurring at the level of industry as a whole. For Keynes and post Keynesian analysis, knowledge of firm activity, while necessary to an understanding of economy-wide behaviour, is certainly insufficient to capture the openness and organically interdependent nature of collective economic behaviour.[15] Thus, when proceeding from the effects of revenue shortfalls at the level of the firm to the economy-wide impact any pervasive shortfalls might have, we need to recognise two additional components to the problem, one of a systemic nature, the other reflecting matters of public policy. The first will be discussed in this section; the second will be analysed in the subsequent section.

Consider, once more, our representative firm, here depicted in Figure 8.5. Assume that, for whatever reason, there occurs an economy-wide slowdown in sales revenue. Initially, for all of the reasons enumerated in the previous section, the continued need to service debt fixed in money terms will, again, keep a positive demand for money, despite any fall off in production costs as a result of the decline in sales. What is true for all firms, even though no one firm is capable of such an impact, is that there will be an increased demand for money as a whole, resulting in increased sales of new issues. The effect of such a pervasive increase in money demand will be a depressing of asset prices on primary markets.[16] Moreover, to the extent that a heightened lenders' risk is perceived by lending institutions, it could happen that any subsequent credit rationing would force greater discounts among new issues.

Taking both effects into account there would occur an increase in the yield curve faced by *all* firms regardless of their individual state of solvency and demand for money. Thus, every firm will experience an upward shift in its S_{FX} curve (depicted here as a movement from S^1_{FX} to S^2_{FX}).

It is here that the post Keynesian model yields interesting results. For if firms find that the continued increased demand for money, even with a downturn, will cause an *increase* in the cost of external finance, then it will be forced to resort to a course of action not anticipated by a traditional new Keynesian model. For the new Keynesian model predicts that a fall in sales will cause firms to *lower* their prices in ideal circumstances, the extent to which this does not occur being explained by menu-costs and efficiency wage theories. But from a post Keynesian perspective, the pervasive increase in the demand for money and the subsequent increase in interest rates will force firms to *increase* their mark-ups over unit costs. This occurrence is clearly indicated in Figure 8.5. Empirical confirmations of rising mark-ups during recessions have been found by Chevalier and Scharfstein (1995, 1996).[17]

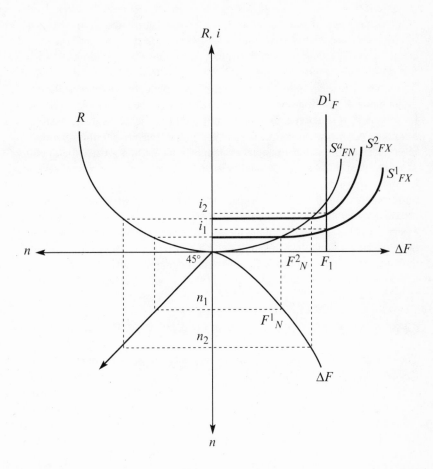

Figure 8.5

The extent to which such increases in prices will occur depends on many factors both internal and external to firms and to industry as a whole. Among those are firms' ability to reduce expenditures on variable costs (cutbacks in labour usage, lower expenditures on overtime pay, and so on), as well as their individual abilities to access finance in light of a *general* increase in the demand for money in the economy. In fact, the rate of interest paid by firms will be higher than was the case in Figure 8.4 to the extent that there is an economy-wide increase in the demand for money as means of payment, affecting all potential borrowers regardless of their individual financial exigencies.

From a post Keynesian perspective, the idea of sticky prices translates into the extent to which prices rise with a downturn in economic activity. To this point it has been shown that this rate will be determined partly by firms' abilities to raise prices under such circumstances, but in addition on the extent to which their financial structure requires them to seek additional finance and the response to financial institutions to those increased demands for money. The picture, however, is not yet complete, because the willingness of financial institutions to provide that finance, given their perceptions of lenders' risk, is also dependent upon the quantity of reserves in the system as a whole. All other things remaining the same, the greater the quantity of reserves available to the financial system as a whole, the greater the quantity of money that will be lent out and at interest rates lower than if total reserves in the system remained the same or even fell. Correspondingly, the rate on borrowing externally will determine the rate by which firms must raise their prices in order to obtain the revenue that would be too costly if borrowed externally. Thus, to complete the picture as to the possible rate of increase in prices during a downturn, we must see how different monetary regimes have their effects on the ability/willingness of financial institutions to meet the demands for money at different rates of interest on borrowed funds.

CENTRAL BANK POLICY AND STICKY PRICES

The role played by monetary policy differs between new Keynesian and post Keynesian models. As Mankiw has clearly indicated, new Keynesians tend to be monetarists but with an explanation (1994). In the short run, their heuristical perspective compels them to inquire as to the extent to which money is neutral in the economy. Beginning at a point of general equilibrium, new Keynesians query as to how a nominal shock to the system (a change in the stock of money) does or does not affect the real sector. Their conclusion is that real output may be affected by a monetary shock because of stickiness in prices, wages, and rates of interest. These apparent violations of the classical dichotomy are melded over in the long run as flexible prices cause a restoration in the real sector equilibrium so that changes in absolute prices move directly with changes in the stock of money.

A post Keynesian view does not begin in equilibrium but rather accepts the fact that an economy is evolving in a cumulative fashion, sometimes expanding, othertimes declining, where the paths marked out by these movements are not independent of the movements themselves. As a result of this perspective, post Keynesians tend to view the money stock as an endogenous element, driven by the demand for money in the economy relative to the banking system's ability and willingness to lend out funds in response to that demand.

As such, we see new Keynesians to be prescribing long run targeting of an exogenous money stock achieved through some form of long run targeting of high powered money to the banking system. Post Keynesians, on the other hand, recognize that the principal responsibility of an economy's central bank is to provide for money market stability, the result being that an endogenous money stock policy will attempt to regulate bank reserves in response to changes in the demand for money in the economy. When superimposed with the model presented in this essay, each policy will lead to drastic differences in the effects it will have on interest rates and the rate of increase in the level of prices.

Figure 8.6 is an elaboration on Figure 8.5 where now the supply of external finance schedules shift position depending upon the monetary regime chosen by the central bank. Following from the scenario presented above, assume that output has fallen, there continues to be a demand for money to finance committed positions, and that financial institutions raise the structure in interest rates in the economy forcing mark-ups to rise by an amount $0n_2 > 0n_1$. In other words, left to its own accord we can expect that a downturn will exhibit increased demands for money, reticence on the part of financial institutions to lend out money (magnified by bearish behaviours in secondary markets), higher rates of interest on external finance, and consequently the necessity of increasing prices by *greater* amounts – prices increasing at an increasing rate. Should a central bank pursue a long-run policy prescribed by new Keynesians, then the relatively slow rate of growth in the money stock will, in fact, lead to greater increases in prices.[18] The lower reserve ratios of the banking system caused by an increased demand for money relative to an increase in reserves that is not growing as fast as the demand for money (tempered by increased liquidity preference by banks) and the increased demands for interbank loans of reserves and subsequent increases in the rates of interest on those loans, will receive a cold shoulder from the central bank. The higher rates on the cost of funds to banks will force them to push up the structure of their lending rates. And, as we have seen in such cases, the higher rates of borrowing externally force cash starved firms to push up their mark-ups in an attempt to gain the needed money at a perceived cost which is less than the cost of obtaining the funds externally.

However, to what extent are these results affected by a post Keynesian monetary policy? Under these circumstances we see that the commitment to maintain stability in financial markets will mean that the central bank will respond to increases in the rate of interest on interbank lending of reserves so as to satisfy those demands with greater infusion of reserves in the banking system. With appropriate compensations for the effects of increased lenders' risks, such a central bank policy will result in relatively *stable* interest rates rather than the rising rates that were experienced with a monetarist policy.

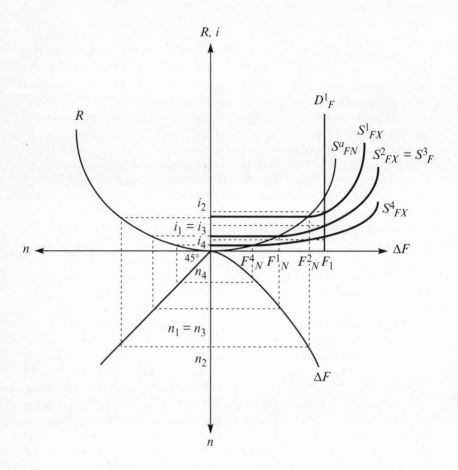

Figure 8.6

Such a policy is translated into Figure 8.6 by stable interest rates, $i_2 = i_1$. And with the cost of borrowing funds externally now relatively stable because of an accommodating monetary policy, firms will be able to increase their mark-ups by the same rate as in the previous period, $0n_2 = 0n_1$. Here it is evident that a post Keynesian monetary policy will result in a relatively stable rate of inflation, rather than the accelerating rate experienced by a monetarist policy.

And finally, the normal expectation is that the rate of price inflation will ease (the rate will lessen, although prices will not fall) as the economy continues to slow down. The traditional explanation is that lower demand will eventually slow down increases in prices. However, as was shown above, such a perspective diverges from realism in that to understand pricing policies of firms a distinction must be made between prices of inventories which can be sold at spot for whatever the market will bear and flow supply prices of newly produced commodities, which rely more on costs of production and long-run financial requirements. Even when demand has fallen, constant costs and long-run financing needs will indicate that flow supply prices will not fall. What the model in the essay would indicate is that the extent to which price inflation slows during prolonged downturns is also the result of the chosen monetary policy.

Suppose, then, that the central bank recognizes its role as one of increasing the rate of growth of bank reserves in order to provide greater quantities of loanable funds hopefully offered at lower rates of interest. Such a policy is observed in Figure 8.6 where an expansionary monetary policy will cause an outward shift in the cost curve for external funds faced by firms to S_{FX}^4. Now with the lower rate of interest, firms will be able to borrow more funds on financial markets ($F_1 F_N^4$) at lower rates (i_4) enabling them to borrow fewer funds internally ($0 F_N^4$) with smaller increases in the mark-up ($0 n_4 < 0 n_3$). What we see, then, is that it is not conditions of demand that cause a slow-down in the rate of price increases during a recession. Instead, all other things taken into account, the rate of increase in prices during a recession, what one might call the post Keynesian interpretation of how sticky are prices, will be determined on the responsiveness and aggressiveness of monetary policy when such a recession occurs.

CONCLUDING REMARKS

This essay has presented a post Keynesian model of pricing behaviour within a dynamic framework which has led to an alternative explanation for the relative sluggishness of price inflation during downturns in economic activity. The model indicates that contracts being fixed in money terms cause the continued need to pay off debts even when sales revenue falls. It outlines the extent to which firms will seek finance from internal versus external sources based on their estimates of the cost financing by raising the mark-up relative to the cost of obtaining funds from external sources. What is indicated is that slow rates of increase in prices during recessions may be the result of post Keynesian monetary policies which attempt to provide stability in money market conditions. As such, any increased demand for money as means of payment when normal sales recede would be readily met by a central bank policy which monetized any increased demand for reserves in light of the increased demand for external funds on financial markets.

An interesting investigation would be to use this same model to explain why price inflation does not increase at a rapid pace as is believed by neoclassical theory. Again, what needs to be understood in this case is the extent to which constant costs and explicit contracts prevent firms from normally raising prices when demand conditions rise. In addition, prices would be relatively stable to the extent that the central bank pursues a Post Keynesian monetary policy so that the increased demand for money to finance capital accumulation can be met by normal retained earnings plus external finance the price of which is relatively constant.[19] As such, there would not be the necessity for firms to raise their mark-ups at an increasing rate to finance those investment requirements. But these ideas cannot be developed in this essay.

NOTES

*   Some of the ideas in this chapter were extracted from my doctoral dissertation written under the supervision of Professor Paul Davidson at Rutgers University. I am extremely grateful to Victoria Chick, Paul Davidson, the late Alfred S. Eichner, and G.C. Harcourt for their comments on earlier versions of this paper. None of them is responsible, however, for the final product.
1. Or if there is a fall in nominal demand, then the reduced price level would create a real balance effect restoring the original level of aggregate demand (see Mankiw, 1994).
2. Although it should not be assumed that such sticky prices are mere *imperfections* in an otherwise perfectly functioning economic system (see Davidson, 1972; Rotheim, 1993).
3. Greenwald and Stiglitz (1993) now also contend that sticky prices might be more conducive to economic stability than when prices are flexible. However, the logic they use to arrive at such conclusions emanates from the type of sticky-price logic that Keynes found erroneous.
4. The roots of this tradition can be seen in Keynes's *Treatise on Money,* and in the works of Kaldor and Pasinetti.
5. The most significant difference between the model as presented in Figure 8.1 and Eichner's is that Eichner assumed that the demand schedule for funds represented a demand for investment that was sensitive to changes in interest rates. In both his *Economic Journal* article (1973) and his book (1976) Eichner assumes that this schedule is nothing more than a marginal efficiency of investment function: the locus of equilibrium points of the schedule of the marginal efficiency of capital and the market rate of interest equated with the flow of investment. Thus, if the schedule for additional investment funds is allowed to be downward sloping, then a higher market rate of interest, *ceteris paribus*, will reduce the quantity demanded for additional investment funds. Rather than add this element of orthodox Keynesianism to the model, I have assumed that there is a zero interest elasticity of demand for finance to underwrite capital expenditures. Thus all demands for finance will be perfectly vertical in interest rate/additional finance space. Relaxing this assumption only complicates the analysis without changing its fundamental results.
6. It is essential to note that the symbol n represents not the absolute mark-up over per unit cost, but rather *changes* in this mark-up.
7. Deprez (1994) has recently stated some strong objections to Eichner's implicit rate of interest function.
8. Edward Nell has argued that such a scenario suffers from a fundamental 'internal inconsistency'. He observes an interdependency between financial requirements satisfied by increases in the mark-up and subsequent reductions in capacity requirements and therefore investment and finance demands by the firm. Such an interdependency would imply

that any increase in the demand for finance would be self-defeating, in the limit. While an interesting addition to the overall structure of the Eichner model, Nell's observation may not have the pervasive negative impact that he anticipates. The reason for this is that the Eichner model does not have to be seen in terms of a static situation whereby the firm attempts to grow *independent* of industry as a whole. Certainly one could consider a *closed* environment where an individual firm would attempt to grow with nothing occurring in any other sectors of the economy. Then, Nell's criticism could be considered with some sense of logical importance. However, if we consider an *open* system, then capacity requirements for firms would be increasing despite relative problems with corporate levies caused by firms using the mark-up as a strategic variable to provide additional internal funding.

9. The supply of external finance schedule is assumed to be horizontal up to the point where the firm commences its borrowing from external sources, in this case point a. Obviously a firm would not face higher rates, *ceteris paribus*, if it did not increase its borrowing from external sources.

10. Any subsequent increase in the mark-up will be partially tempered by any additional flows of retained earnings accruing to the firm from previous returns to capital expenditures. Changes in these flows will affect the degree but not the nature of the process described in the current model.

11. Occasionally central banks have stated that they were following one goal but choosing an intermediate target that supported the other goal, as was the case of the FED from 1970 to 1979.

12. During its New Operating Procedure in 1979, the FED changed its acceptable range for the federal funds rate from less than one percentage point to over five, which, for all intents and purposes, caused it to ignore any changes in the short-run demand for money except for extreme circumstance where its lender of last resort function was required.

13. Although not depicted in Figure 8.4, actual *total* sales could be so much less than expected *total* sales that the additional total revenue obtained by the expansion of firms could be negative.

14. Real balance and real wealth effects are ruled out as theoretically incapable of restoring market equilibrium (as well as being empirically non-existent). As Keynes pointed out (1930), a fall in money prices would increase the real value of a firm's debt causing bankruptcies that would more than offset any equilibrating effects that might occur as a result of the effect lower prices would have on nominal wealth.

15. Recent new Keynesian literature, initiated by Cooper and John (1988), emphasize the types of spillover and complementary effects characteristic of a Keynes/post Keynesian perspective. However, such initiatives will not bear fruit so long as they insist on emanating from the more traditional new Keynesian sticky price models. On this see Rotheim (1996).

16. The effect on the secondary market will be uncertain. Holders of previously issued assets may sell off in response to the increased sales on primary markets as asset prices fall. A countervailing force, tending to assuage any bearish tendencies among bondholders, is the extent to which they anticipate central bank intervention in response to any fall in asset prices and/or an overt interventionist policy.

17. The models employed by Chevalier tend to be more traditional rather than conforming to a post Keynesian perspective. In fact, their explanations of the results tend to be less realistic and more *ad hoc* than those provided in a post Keynesian model.

18. Such a view was taken by Gardner Means in his appendix on monetary policy to the famous 1933 report done on administered prices for the US Department of Agriculture. See Means (1933).

19. Moreover, one would expect that costs would not increase with increases in demand, to the extent that capital accumulation would have the effect of keeping constant or perhaps raising labour productivity.

REFERENCES

Akerlof, G. and Yellen, J. (1985a), 'A Near Rational Model of the Business Cycle, with Wage and Price Inertia', *Quarterly Journal of Economics*, Supplement, 823–38.

Akerlof, G. and Yellen, J. (1985b), 'Can Small Deviations From Rationality Make Significant Differences To Economic Equilibria?', *American Economic Review*, September, 708–21.

Arestis, Philip (1988), 'Post Keynesian Theory of Money, Credit and Finance' in *Post Keynesian Monetary Economics*, edited by P. Arestis, Aldershot, Hants: Edward Elgar.

Arestis, Philip (1992), *The Post Keynesian Approach to Economics*, Aldershot, Hants: Edward Elgar.

Arestis, Philip (1996), 'Post Keynesian Economics', *Cambridge Journal of Economics*, **20** (1), January, 111–36.

Ball L., Mankiw, N.G. and Romer, D. (1988), 'The New Keynesian Economics and the Output–Inflation Tradeoff', *Brookings Papers on Economic Activity*, **1**, 1–65.

Bernanke, Benjamin and Gertler, Mark (1995), 'Inside the Black Box: The Credit Channel of Monetary Policy Transmission', *Journal of Economic Perspectives*, Fall, 49–72.

Blinder, Alan (1992), 'Why Are Prices Sticky? Preliminary Results from an Interview Study', *American Economic Review*, June, 334–48.

Cannan, E. et al. (1932), 'Symposium on Usury', *Economic Journal*.

Çapoglu, Gökhan (1991), *Prices, Profits, and Financial Structures*, Aldershot, Hants: Edward Elgar.

Chevalier, Judith and Scharfstein, David (1995), 'Liquidity Constraints and the Cyclical Behavior of Markups', *American Economic Review*, May, 390–5.

Chevalier, Judith and Scharfstein, David (1996), 'Capital Market Imperfections and the Countercyclical Markups: Theory and Evidence', *American Economic Review*, September, 703–25.

Chick, Victoria (1983), *Macroeconomics After Keynes*, Cambridge, Mass.: MIT.

Clower, Robert (1965), 'The Keynesian Counterrevolution: A Theoretical Appraisal' in *The Theory of Interest Rates*, edited by F. Hahn and F. Brechling, London, pp. 103–25.

Cooper, R. and John, A. (1988), 'Coordinating Coordination Failures in Keynesian Models', *Quarterly Journal of Economics*, **103**, 441–63.

Davidson, Paul (1972), *Money and the Real World*, 1st edn, London.

Davidson, P. (1997), 'Setting the Record Straight', in *New Keynesian Economics/Post Keynesian Alternatives*, edited by R.J. Rotheim, London: Routledge.

Deprez, Johan (1994), 'The Macroeconomics of the Megacorp's Determination of the Markup' in Milberg (1994), pp. 169–83.

Dow, Sheila C. (1989), 'Endogenous Money Creation and Idle Balances' *New Directions in Post-Keynesian Economics*, edited by J. Pheby, Aldershot, Hants: Edward Elgar, pp. 147–64.

Dow, Sheila C. (1991), 'Beyond Dualism', *Cambridge Journal of Economics*, **15** (5).

Dow, Sheila C. (1996), 'Horizontalism: A Critique', *Cambridge Journal of Economics*, July, 497–508.

Eichner, A.S. (1973), 'A Theory of the Determination of the Mark-Up under Oligopoly', *Economic Journal*, **33**, 1184–200.

Eichner, A.S. (1976), *The Megacorp and Oligopoly: Micro Foundations of Macro-Dynamics,* Cambridge: Cambridge University Press.

Federal Reserve Bank of New York (1993), *Quarterly Review,* issue on 'The Credit Slowdown', Spring.

Gordon, R.J. (1990), 'What is New Keynesian Economics?', *Journal of Economic Literature,* **28,** 1115–71.

Greenwald, Bruce and Stiglitz, Joseph (1993), 'New and Old Keynesians', *Journal of Economic Perspectives,* Winter, 23–44.

Harcourt, Geoff C. and Kenyon, Peter (1976), 'Pricing and Investment Decisions', *Kyklos,* **29,** fasc. 3.

Kalecki, Michel (1937), 'The Principle of Increasing Risk', *Economica,* **3,** 440–54.

Kalecki, Michel (1954), *Theory of Economic Dynamics,* London: Allen and Unwin.

Keynes, J.M. (1930a), A *Treatise on Money,* 2 Volumes, London: Macmillan.

Keynes, J.M. (1931), *Essays in Persuasion,* reprinted as *Collected Writing of J.M. Keynes,* vol. IX.

Keynes, J.M. (1932), 'Saving and Investment' in Cannan *et al.,* 'Symposium on Hoarding' in *Economic Journal.*

Keynes, J.M. (1936), *The General Theory of Employment, Interest, and Money,* London.

Kregel, J.A. (1973), *A Reconstruction of Political Economy: An Introduction to Post Keynesian Economics,* London.

Mankiw, N.G. (1985), 'Small Menu Costs and Large Business Cycles: A Macroeconomic Model of Monopoly', *Quarterly Journal of Economics,* May, 529–37.

Mankiw, N.G. (1992), *Macroeconomics,* New York: Worth.

Marris, Robin (1964), *The Economic Theory of Managerial Capitalism,* London.

Means, Gardner (1933), 'Report on Pricing', US Department of Agriculture.

Minsky, Hyman (1965), *John Maynard Keynes,* New York: Columbia University Press.

Minsky, Hyman (1986), *Stabilizing an Unstable Economy,* New Haven, Conn.: Yale University Press.

Nell, Edward J. (1994), 'Demand, Pricing, and Investment' in Milberg (1994), pp. 27–57.

Rotheim, R.J. (1988), 'Keynes and the Language of Probability and Uncertainty', *Journal of Post Keynesian Economics,* Fall, 82–99.

Rotheim, Roy J. (1991), 'Marx, Keynes, and the Monetary Theory of Production' in *Marx and Modern Economics,* Volume II, edited by G. Caravale, Aldershot, Hants: Edward Elgar.

Rotheim, Roy J. (1993), 'On the Indeterminacy of Keynes's Monetary Theory of Value', *Review of Political Economy,* April, 197–216.

Rotheim, Roy J. (1996), 'New Keynesian Macroeconomics and Markets' in *New Keynesian Economics/Post Keynesian Alternatives,* edited by R.J. Rotheim, Routledge (forthcoming).

Sawyer, Malcolm (1983), *Business Pricing and Inflation,* London: Macmillan.

Sylos-Labini, Paolo (1979), 'Industrial Pricing in the United Kingdom', *Cambridge Journal of Economics,* September.

Weintraub, S. (1958), *An Approach to the Theory of Income Distribution,* Philadelphia: Chilton.

Wood, A. (1975), *A Theory of Profits,* Cambridge: Cambridge University Press.

Wray, L. Randall (1990), *Money and Credit in Capitalist Economies,* Aldershot, Hants: Edward Elgar.

Wray, L. Randall (1993), 'Money, Interest Rates, and Monetarist Policy', *Journal of Post Keynesian Economics*, Summer, 541–69.

9. Some considerations on the economics and politics of the EU and the Maastricht Treaty

Kurt W. Rothschild

Perhaps before starting my chapter properly I should explain why something meant as a tribute in honour of an outstanding *American* economist deals with the comments of an 'angry' *European* economist dealing with a predominantly *European* problem. This can be excused by the fact that the chapter, though not referring to any special contribution by Davidson, is inspired by Davidson's general approach mirrored in all his writings: stressing the importance of relevance and realism, looking beyond the narrow limits of economic theory, and the attempt to develop and extend Keynesian thinking without falling into dogmatic traps. In all these respects I had always admired his work and I hope that the following considerations fall into this tradition. Davidson (1996, p. 92) argues that:

> Mainstream economic theory has become very anti-Keynes in the past 20 years. People in political authority are, to paraphrase Keynes, distilling their frenzy against expansionary demand influences from the academic mainstream scribblers. The conventional wisdom now is that Keynesian demand influencing policies are neither effective nor needed.

Part of the argument of this chapter is to show that Keynesian policies should be used in the 'real world', in perfect agreement with Davidson's argument.

It is no secret that economists, like other social scientists, differ in their general approaches, their theories and in the forecasts and prescriptions flowing from them. The social and economic environment is too complex and changeable, human motives and actions are too volatile, to permit the construction of one accepted theoretical framework covering all possible situations and problems. Taking into account that in addition ideologies and interests enter when questions and outlooks are chosen it is no wonder that competing theories co-exist side by side, partly overlapping, partly in contradiction to each other.

Among the multitude of approaches and theories two important dividing lines can be distinguished. The first points to the fact that we have a number of different approaches dealing with the 'mechanics' of contemporary economic interactions. These theories can be roughly divided into two groups. On the one hand we have the mainstream neoclassical tradition with its highly sophisticated model based on a strictly axiomatic approach borrowed from mechanical physics. It studies the intricacies of the interrelations between competitive markets and aims at exact 'rational' equilibrium solutions. It is particularly suited for insights into questions of resource allocation and the interdependencies of markets and prices. On the other hand we have a bunch of several theoretical approaches, with Keynesianism and post Keynesianism as the most developed representatives (to which have to be added institutional, evolutionary, radical economics, and so on), which have in common that they are non-neoclassical in the sense that they do not feel bound by the neoclassical axioms and equilibrium orientation. They start off from the fact that real market economies are unstable and 'disturbance-prone'. This involves a renunciation of 'nice' and exact structures and results, but permits a more realistic and flexible approach to a variety of real world economic and social problems.

Added to this 'horizontal' division between neoclassical and non-neoclassical theories dealing with the 'mechanics' of the current economic process, we have a 'vertical' division that separates these theories from approaches which attempt to analyse the emergence of and the changes in the *framework* within which current events take place. Such 'visions' of fundamental long-term changes, exemplified in classical and Marxist theory but also in the writings of Schumpeter and Galbraith, are of course necessarily even more speculative than the narrower 'pure' economics; but they certainly address important questions which deserve not to be neglected. By being forced to include history (regarded by Schumpeter as being of equal importance for a 'good' economist as economic theory and statistics) in its analysis this branch also leads to an interdisciplinary approach which is so universally regarded as desirable but so difficult to realize in practice.

The two divisions just mentioned, the 'horizontal' and the 'vertical' one, can be seen as relevant when we now turn to a critical evaluation of some of the major aspects of the EU and the Maastricht Treaty. I want to deal with two questions:

1. What are the reasons that after the mid-1980s the former European Economic Community (EEC) could suddenly acquire such a rapid dynamism from a comparatively loose customs union towards a political and economic union with the special characteristics of Brussels and Maastricht?

2.   What are the economic arguments behind the present programme and
     what are its probable consequences?

It is obvious that the first question, to which I shall turn presently, lies
more in the political–economic 'visionary' tradition, while the second question has more to do with the horizontal division between neoclassics and
Keynesianism (for short) and the interests connected with these theories.

UNITED EUROPE

The idea of a politically and economically united 'Europe' (not always defined
in the same way) is by no means a new one. Proposals in this direction by
'visionaries' and statesmen reach far back in history (Machlup, 1977, chapters 6 and 7). In the interwar period the 'Pan-European Movement' founded
by Count Coudenhove-Kalergi in 1923 found a considerable echo. In 1925 28
states participated in the first Pan-European Congress and statesmen like
Stresemann from Germany and Briand from France advocated the formation
of a United States of Europe. Economic arguments were put forward but the
main force behind this and similar proposals was a desire to build a strong
bloc against the Soviet Union and the spread of communism. But the proposals remained pure rhetoric and with the onslaught of the great depression and
the revival of nationalism and chauvinism it lost what little ideological
influence it may have achieved.

During and after the Second World War and under its influence vague ideas
of a World Government and more down-to-earth ideas of a united Europe
made again an appearance, as before based on political (peace) and economic
(free trade) arguments. When in 1952 the European Coal and Steel Community was established at the initiative of the French Foreign Minister Robert
Schuman a first concrete step in the direction of a 'European' development
was taken. Though it represented only a cartel-like arrangement with free-
trade elements among the few members it was from the very beginning
regarded – at least by the French – as a stepping stone to a wider economic
integration leading ultimately to European Federation (Meade, Liesner and
Wells, 1962, p. 197). A decisive move in this direction seemed to be achieved
when in 1957 the foundation was laid for the EEC, the European Economic
Community. But while this was without doubt an important event in the
commercial history of Europe, it did not by itself constitute a clear element
for building a 'European house'. Rather it was an intensive customs union for
one-half of developed Western Europe (the other half being organized in
EFTA), and its activities – just like those of EFTA – were in line with and
part of the worldwide trend towards liberalizing foreign trade from its

inter-war protectionist heritage. EEC and EFTA were means of intensifying and accelerating this process on a regional basis.

The *aim* of a closer economic and political union on a European level remained on the agenda of the EEC, but for about a quarter of a century – from the beginning of the 1960s till about the mid-1980s – there was hardly any progress beyond the complete abolition of tariffs (outside the agricultural sector) and the establishment of a common tariff *vis-à-vis* third countries. An attempt to enter on a gradual realization of an 'Economic and Monetary Union' based on the so-called 'Werner Plan', which was agreed upon in 1971, oozed away and was finally given up. With the oil crisis, declining growth, and increasing unemployment the 1970s almost brought a reversal of the integration process through non-tariff barriers of one sort or another.

And then, almost suddenly (at least on an historic scale), the advance towards a more closely knit European Union took off after all these years and decades of empty declarations. In 1984, in the so-called declaration of Luxemburg, a decision was taken to extend and deepen the Free Trade Agreement with the EFTA countries and beyond them. In the following year, with Spain and Portugal entering the Community, the Commission issued a White Book which laid down the path for finalizing the steps for the completion of a free internal market by 1992. In order to ease the way towards this target and to open a wider field for the political and economic activities of the Community (foreign policy, social policy, research and development, and above all a fuller economic and monetary union) the 'Single European Act' was enacted in 1987, which changed the European Economic Community (EEC) into a European Union (EU) with a larger programme and the permission for majority decisions in place of the former principle which insisted on unanimity in all cases.

The way was now open for a speedy adjustment to the legal, administrative, and institutional preconditions for a 'fuller' Single Market with its 'four freedoms' for goods, services, capital, and labour. The new opportunities were to a large extent used and the Single Market could be declared as completed by the end of 1992. In the same year the Maastricht Treaty was adopted with an elaborated timetable for the next steps towards a fuller and wider Economic and Monetary Union (EMU) with 1999 as the (latest) target date for the establishment of a common currency in at least some of the member states (to be extended later to all members[1] including the prospective additional members from Eastern Europe).

ECONOMIC AND POLITICAL EUROPEAN UNION

We can now turn to the first of the two questions raised earlier. What was it that so suddenly set into motion a process of semi-European economic unification (with the Eastern half of Europe still excluded) which had been propagated for so many years without any noticeable progress? When one tries to answer this question one has first of all to deal with the age-old 'puzzle' whether men make history or history makes men. The truth certainly lies in the combination of these 'either-or' statements: individuals with different capacities and backgrounds have different visions and motives, and history creates varying situations. When strong individuals happen to meet a favourable historic situation both the person *and* history get a chance for quick and spectacular action.

This was – so it seems to me – typically the case for the recent dynamism in the EU-development. People who adhere to a 'personalistic' interpretation of historic development tend to stress the efficiency and continuous engagement of Jacques Delors as the driving force which opened a new chapter for European economic unification. There is no need to deny the role and assiduity of Delors' activities as president of the EU when one says that these activities cannot be the whole story. People like Coudenhove-Kalergi, Briand, Schuman and others were probably as much attracted by the idea of a united Europe as Delors and not less efficient, but their historic chance had not arrived. But when Delors entered the stage fundamental shifts in the economic scene had taken and were taking place which created the opportunities for progress in the European programme.

The shifts I am referring to are connected with the dramatic rise in the number and size of transnational companies, mergers, and cooperations,[2] which evolved together with the tremendous technological innovations occurring in the fields of communication and information. This development which sneaked in almost uncommented at first has, within a short time, revolutionized the international economic environment. Speaking of the developed capitalist world only, one is probably justified to distinguish three significant stages in its historical development: *Competitive Capitalism* in the 19th century which changed into *Monopoly Capitalism* towards the end of the century with national monopolies and oligopolies expanding in line with the advance of mass production methods, which in turn changed a hundred years later (in the last quarter of the twentieth century) into *Transnational Capitalism* with trans- and multinational firms and conglomerates spreading quickly over wide regions and the world as a whole accompanied by new information technologies and the decentralization possibilities opened up by them.

This shift from national to transnational concerns as a dominant feature in economic and political affairs has important effects, particularly in connection with the question we are dealing with here. The big semi-monopolistic firms of the late 19th century – like Ford in the US, Krupp in Germany, ICI in Britain and so forth – were mainly interested in and obtained their main strength from a protected home market where they produced their output and found their main (private and public) clientele. On the basis of this stronghold they could then attempt to conquer foreign markets. Their main objective had to be to foster a strong industry-oriented state and a sufficient degree of protectionism (tariffs and other barriers) in order to maintain their basis of strength.

The interests and aims of the transnational concerns are quite different. With their places of production, their suppliers of inputs, and their customers spread over several countries – about one-third of international trade nowadays consists of intra-firm deliveries – tariffs, national differences in laws and regulations, variations in exchange rates, and so on are a nuisance, creating complications for international dispositions and causing 'unnecessary' costs. With the growing strength of this sector and its formation into a powerful lobby (in Brussels and nationally) the idea of a European Union freed from tariffs and other barriers, with 'weak' governments which cannot interfere in a union-wide framework, and – last not least – with a common currency to get rid of exchange rate risks had found a societal force to back it up: the completion of the EU had become the 'logical' outcome of the changed economic background and the power relations connected with it.

The fact that the 'logic' of the transnational firms was an important, if not *the* driving force behind the European development left a strong imprint on the actual forms which this development takes. 'Europe', after all, is a very vague programme, though with strong emotional overtones. Quite apart from the changing and opportunistic delineations of the 'Europe' one wishes to choose, there can obviously be many different kinds of European agendas. First of all there was always the idea of achieving economic *and* political union for Europe. Probably a more useful arrangement would have been to achieve first a certain degree of political cohesion in order to arrive at a more consensual democratic and better enforceable economic framework. But as the realistic motive force came above all from the business world the opposite route was taken. The desired economic changes took the lead leaving behind the uncertain hope that a more or less close political unification will follow from them. But the influence and parentage of transnational business does not only show up in this preference for the economic aspects of European collaboration; it is also visible in the actual economic programme outlined for the EU. And this brings us to the second question, namely the question about the contents of this programme and the ideas behind it.

When one looks at the main props of the EU's economic policy programme, neglecting the voluminous rules, regulations, and deregulations dealing with competition, R&D, regional cohesion, agricultural policy and so on, one thing sticks out rather distinctly (though it is rarely commented upon in the political debates of the EU countries). It is the implicit stream-lined adherence to a dogmatic neoclassical policy and ideology which leaves practically no room for even thinking of, let alone bringing about modifications or alternative approaches. Such a situation has, of course, been well-known for some time in various countries. Thatcher or Reagan are telling examples. But when one considers that the EU is a collection of a group of economically and politically rather heterogeneous nations with different traditions, institutions, and histories, *within which* the choice of this or that economic policy mix, this or that target combination, are central aspects of the political discussions and the political process, it is amazing how little – or rather nothing – of this appears in the deliberations and decisions emanating from Brussels which find their way into the EU 'constitution' and the Maastricht Treaty. The dominating influence of current conservative thinking and of the transnational lobby is clearly visible: there is a lot of Kohl's Germany but nothing of Palme's Sweden.

ECONOMIC CONSEQUENCES OF THE MAASTRICHT PROGRAMME

What then are the main characteristics of the actual and intended EU economic programme and the 'philosophy' behind it? In this chapter we must restrict ourselves to the core of this programme. It is expressed in the 'four freedoms' of the EU already mentioned and more or less already in force, and the planned transition to the fuller Economic and Monetary Union (EMU) laid down in the Maastricht Treaty. Not much needs to be said about the 'four freedoms'. They only present a particularly extensive sample of the neoliberal tendency which is – at least with regard to the 'freedom' for goods and capital movements – characteristic of the world as a whole (GATT, WTO, OECD, IMF, and so on).

The most problematic aspect here is of course the complete liberalization of capital movements (which would however become partly 'endogenous' once a common currency comes into existence) with their destabilizing effects on exchange rates and monetary policy. More important perhaps is the political aspect. By threatening the transfer of real capital (and production) to another country (which in the case of transnational firms often only involves a move to an already existing branch in that country) pressure can be (and is) exerted on governments and trade unions in order to obtain concessions of various sorts (subsidies, legal changes, wage concessions, and so on). This increase in bargaining power is not counter-balanced by the freedom for labour granted to EU citizens throughout the Union. Quite apart from the fundamental difference between the 'freedoms' for capital and labour – the first can be moved without having to learn a language and without leaving behind friends and a familiar environment – labour even when organized in a union cannot threaten to transfer as a body to another firm or country. The freedom of labour does not present a countervailing power to the bargaining power obtained by business through the complete liberalization of capital movements. On the contrary; that bargaining power is additionally strengthened by the uninhibited possibility of attracting workers from low-wage EU countries.

But as was said before, this question is – at least as far as trade and capital liberalization are concerned – not a special EU phenomenon though there it is more complete than in other parts of the world. The *special* traits of the EU strategy become more prominent when we turn to the Maastricht Treaty and its provisions for the establishment of EMU. Its hard core – the concrete basic orientation – became contained in the timetable for the move towards a common currency (to be called EURO) and in the so-called convergence criteria which have to be met by each member state in order to be admitted to full membership (that is, including the common currency). On these aspects we shall concentrate in the following considerations.[3]

The main provisions in this field as laid down in 1992 can be summarized quickly. The advance to the establishment of the common currency was divided into three stages. Stage one expected that right from the beginning all EU states should be members of the already existing EMS (European Monetary System) which aimed at a close alignment of exchange rates with fluctuations remaining within a band of (+ or –) 2.25 per cent around fixed central parities. As we know today this requirement broke down shortly after it was adopted when divergent developments in some countries, intensified by currency speculation, forced them to devaluate beyond the band limits (Britain, Italy, Spain, Portugal). This could have been a warning that things might not be developing as smoothly as originally planned. But rather than considering the emerging problems this expansion of the fluctuations (a widening of the band) was simply acknowledged without any changes in stages two and three.

Stage two provided for the creation of the European Monetary Institute (EMI) which became established in 1995. It is managed by a council consisting of a president (with Alexander Lamfalussy as the first occupant of this position) and the governors of the national central banks. Its main tasks are to foster convergence by strengthening the coordination of national monetary policies, to supervise the working of the EMS, and – most importantly – to prepare all the procedures and mechanisms of control which would be needed when the third (final) stage of monetary union comes into existence.

This third stage represents the 'meat' of the whole undertaking: the birth of a common currency, the EURO, which should be reached – at least for some countries – before the end of this century. The steps to be taken started in 1996 with a report by the EMI showing how far the different member states have managed to achieve the five Maastricht criteria (to be discussed presently) necessary for admittance to the 'inner circle' of EURO-countries. On the basis of this report the Council of Ministers of the EU had to decide (1) whether a majority of states fulfilled the necessary conditions; (2) whether it was appropriate to enter the final stage; and (3) assuming that it was appropriate at what date the common currency should become a reality. 1997 would thus have been the earliest year for the transition to the new currency. Already before the end of 1996 it was, however, clear that only a few, certainly not a majority of countries would be able to reach all the convergence targets. For this case the Maastricht Treaty stipulates that the final transition should take place at the beginning of 1999 irrespective of the question how many of the members can enter the currency union at that time. 1997 thus vanished as a possible beginning rather early while 1999 became the practically accepted date still in line with the provisions of the Maastricht Treaty.

At the time of writing this it is still uncertain whether this target can be fully maintained considering the small number of countries which can achieve the convergence criteria before that date without running into serious economic, social, and political difficulties. Deliberations about possible revisions of the EU-agenda and the Maastricht Treaty which started in spring 1996 and which will run well over one year might lead to a postponement of the creation of the EURO (its *practical* introduction into everyday transactions has already been postponed until 2002) or to a softening of the conditions for entering the inner circle. But even if this retardation should take place the following considerations remain valid, because such possible revisions (postponement and/or softening) are only consequences of bad planning and unforseen economic developments; they do not indicate any change in the underlying strategy and 'philosophy' of the Maastricht programme.

Before we try to evaluate this programme the five convergence criteria for 'full' membership have still to be enumerated. Here they are:

1. In the year prior to the examination whether a country is 'fit' for joining the currency union an inflation rate no more than 1.5 percentage points above the average of the three EC states with the lowest price rises.
2. In the same year a long-term rate of interest within two percentage points of the average of the three members with the lowest rate of inflation.
3. A national budget deficit (covering national, federal, and local governments) less than 3 per cent of GDP.

4.   A public debt ratio which does not exceed 60 per cent of GDP.
5.   A currency for two years within the normal band of the EMS which has
      not been devalued.

When one looks at these five criteria it becomes immediately obvious that they
are exclusively concerned with monetary matters and the monetary framework:
inflation, interest rates, public debt and deficits, exchange rates. In other words
they deal only with *instruments* affecting the monetary environment but have
nothing at all to say about the *real outcomes* of the economic process, such as
economic growth, employment, productivity, development, income distribution, in short about the things that really matter for the welfare of nations and
people. These aspects are of course not completely overlooked and the *desire* to
achieve results in this respect – not least as an outcome of the EU/Maastricht
programme! – is stressed again and again in the EU-rhetoric and in its reports
and plans such as the early and soon outdated Cecchini-Report (1988), the
Delors-White Book on employment (1993) and the declarations at the Amsterdam Conference of June 1997. But the fact remains that the only hard and fast
criteria refer to the monetary and fiscal targets mentioned above which means
that in the systemic and interdependent network of monetary and real developments all adjustments to disturbances have to be absorbed by changes in the
real sector (Heylen, Van Poeck and Van Gompel, 1995).

One can easily see that an EU would have to follow a very different path if
instead of setting *absolute* limits to inflation, public debts and deficits with
'freedom' for unemployment levels, and so on, admission to the inner circle
would require the realization of an unemployment rate no more than, say,
three percentage points above the average of the three countries with the best
employment performance while permitting some 'floating' for deficits and
debts. But such a course was not only not considered (though advocated by
some people), even the mere idea of finding a balance between monetary and
real targets was shelved by stressing the absolute priority of the monetary
programme. This is further cemented in the planned constitution of the European Central Bank (managing the common currency and monetary policy)
which is to be completely independent and has to follow one target and one
target only: price stability. Other targets like employment, growth, and so on
can also be considered, but only if the price stability target is not endangered.
The same one-sidedness is also shown by the fact that in contrast to the
definite monetary regulations the EU has so far not been able to come to an
agreement about a Social Charter which would lay down common rules for
'real' welfare conditions.

Before commenting on the 'sense' or 'nonsense' of the Maastricht criteria
and their possible consequences it should be stressed that their basic quality
is that they fit perfectly into the picture of the 'transnational business logic'

mentioned earlier. By concentrating on a common currency with 'guaranteed' stability the financial basis for unhindered financial dispositions over the entire EU is obtained and this is combined with the freedom of capital and labour movements (with, for instance, Portuguese building contractors moving with their work force to offer building contracts in Germany). At the same time the monopoly of a conservative European Central Bank over monetary policy and the strict rules for national fiscal policies (deficits and debts) create 'lean' states with very little power to run their own economic policies which might disturb private cross-country transactions. The restrictive bias of the Maastricht criteria which provide no binding obligations with regard to social and employment targets creates also a climate which favours the conservative aim of 'cutting back' the Welfare State and which gives up 'full employment' as an explicit goal competing with or even overriding the price stability target. Kalecki's prophetic vision, expressed more than 50 years ago (Kalecki, 1943) that business circles may lose interest in full employment policies because of their political effects (like strengthening trade union bargaining power) has obviously come true.

The EU and Maastricht provisions are of course not presented in this way showing clearly the sectoral interests behind them. In a union of democratic states public support must be obtained for such a far-reaching integration policy. This has not been easy. Where public referenda regarding membership in the EU (as against the narrower free trade agreements which cover all Western European countries) were carried out they showed that in spite of considerable government pro-EU propaganda the populations were almost everywhere approximately equally divided between pros and cons, with Switzerland and Norway coming out on the negative side, and Austria, Denmark, France, Finland, and Sweden on the positive side (in all cases – except Austria – with very narrow majorities).

The arguments for the Maastricht strategies were supported in various ways. First of all in many countries there were some good and generally acceptable reasons to introduce some restrictive measures in the fields of monetary and fiscal policy because in the course of recessionary tendencies governments had run into considerable debt and got used to continued deficit spending even in (the few) good years. As a consequence of this and a policy of high interest rates (to contain inflation) interest payments began to become a serious burden on government budgets. This gave some obvious support for the concern with deficits and debts, but cannot by itself explain that a *single* rule with regard to the extent and timing of counteracting measures should apply to all countries for all times irrespective of their special conditions and irrespective of effects on other economic and social fields.

To bolster up the economic argument, particularly after a certain disappointment had set in because unemployment continued to rise after the EU was adopted, one often escaped into political arguments. The EU, so it is said, has to be accepted because it offers an *entrée* to a peaceful united Europe. This argument has a strong attraction since political unity could be a positive peace factor and could also provide the basis for a truly *democratic* European economic policy (which at present is missing). But the obvious way of advancing *first* towards a certain degree of political union (which earlier on had been discussed as an alternative) had been given up because of its difficulties. An economic union with a strictly circumscribed economic programme can thus not be justified merely by offering a hope that it *might* lead to a political union and even less so when one does not know what sort of economic aims and strategies such a United Europe would want to adopt.

But by far the strongest support for the Maastricht programme is 'rationally' provided by using and misusing mainstream economic theory both for explaining and legitimizing the planned strategies. It is not the first time that neoclassical theory and its forerunners are used both as a guide and as a legitimizer for extreme liberal and neoliberal economic policies. But in the Maastricht case we find a particularly strong use of the equilibrium arguments of the neoclassical model contained in the belief and promise that 'free' markets and the provision of a stable monetary framework will bring about almost automatically economic growth and full employment and even something like an 'equitable' or at least Pareto-optimal income distribution. This basic belief is preached and propagated as if Keynes (and other theories which have similarly recognized the inherent instabilities of real unregulated market economies) whom one tries to kill were really dead, as if there were not any amount of opposing historical examples from the days of Manchester liberalism up to the monetary policies of Mrs Thatcher, and as if the continuous rise of unemployment caused by and accompanying the deflationary activities of the EU countries in line with the Maastricht imperatives did not exist. Indeed, the public anxiety which these new unemployment records have raised in most countries have led some leading politicians to demand a greater consideration for the employment question in the EU; but so far no definite steps have been taken and there is an absolute opposition in Brussels and elsewhere to accept any clearly defined commitment in this respect comparable to the strict monetary and fiscal targets.

But while neoclassical theory has been borrowed and is used for justifying and adding prestige to the 'grand design' of the Maastricht strategies, it is neglected or by-passed where it throws up doubts or does not fit into the desired path. A few hints should suffice to illustrate this point. The classical and neoclassical Free Market optimism which had been developed on the assumptions of atomistic competition between economically and politically powerless firms is transferred to a world of oligopolies and mammoth concerns without any intensive questioning what role the state and regulations do or should play in such an environment. Although the EU consists of a rather heterogeneous group of countries with great differences in wealth and development reaching from some of the richest countries of the world like Sweden, Germany etc. to rather poor countries like Greece and Portugal and with even poorer Eastern European countries standing before the door no or little thought is given to the arguments about the need for special industrial policies and developmental protection for the establishment of modern competitive industries (Amin and Tomaney, 1995). Similarly, the long theoretical debate about an optimum currency area should have created a more guarded and less jubilant attitude to the common currency programme (De Grauwe, 1996). It is also worth noting that historically currency unions which were not based on political union or soon followed by one all broke down. The negative attitude to special protective treatment for poorer regions and their development is the more astonishing in view of the fact that the EU is not opening its own economic frontiers world-wide (as pure free trade theory would suggest) on the ground that it must try to become more competitive *vis-à-vis* the US and the Far East.

A few further remarks are in place when we climb down from the 'grand design' of the EU, which we saw to be inspired by neoclassical theory adapted to the main interests involved, and turn to the details of the convergence criteria. As far as the rules referring to exchange rate stability and low inflation and interest rates are concerned no special comment is necessary. They are a clear foundation for the desired common currency with price stability as its prominent target. Far less obvious are the two fiscal criteria which demand limits of 3 per cent of GDP for deficits and 60 per cent of public debt, and this not only as an entry condition to the common currency but also for all time to come.

Reasons for the 3 and 60 per cent limits are not given and are difficult to find (Buiter, Corsetti and Roubini, 1993), particularly when one considers that they are applied indiscriminately to countries which diverge widely in these matters and in the stabilization needs and opportunities before them. Though there is a vague provision that some leeway may be allowed if there is an obvious and fast movement towards the prescribed targets they remain nevertheless as an astonishingly rigid condition considering that they were adopted under the fairly prosperous economic conditions of 1992 without provision for cyclical and regional influences which could call for deviations in *both* directions (higher or lower limits). The strictness of the five criteria means that at the time of writing this paper only Luxemburg can meet them all. Even if they were relaxed a bit they mean that for a long time to come the 'united' Europe will remain a Europe with two types of members: 'full' members with a common currency and the others who are outside this circle, with all the conflicts and pressures that may arise therefrom.

CONCLUDING COMMENTS

The critical note of this paper stems from the author's 'value'-system that social and welfare targets are important and from his economic and social understanding that unregulated free markets can lead to lasting unemployment and severe social conflicts which in turn can become a threat to democracy. While it is dangerous to point to historical analogies – history never repeats itself! – it is nevertheless not quite absurd to remember that it was the persistent endeavour to maintain a given monetary standard (the gold standard) at all costs which contributed to the depth and duration of the inter-war depression with its catastrophic political consequences leading to fascist dictatorships supported by big business in Germany and elsewhere. One does not have to be 'left' to see such problems. After all it was the conservative Bismarck who introduced a public system of social security in Germany because he wanted to suppress the social unrest arising from the growing labour movement.

One problem is that the political and economic interests behind the present EU development (supported by dogmatic neoclassical economists[4]) have in their popular propaganda managed to equate 'Maastricht-Europe' with the old dream of a peaceful, politically united Europe which would prosper economically because of its size and the opportunities it would be able to offer. To criticize the EU is branded as an anti-European attitude pure and simple. But this is nonsense. One has to distinguish between Maastricht and Europe. Criticizing the Maastricht programme can mean that one is in favour of a Europe that will be politically *and* economically safe as far as possible, interpreting 'economically safe' as an area where the fight against unemployment and poverty and for greater regional equality takes high priority. This requires the renouncement of dogmatic neoclassical positions and a return to the 'magic polygons' of the 1960s when economic policy was aware that – difficult as it may be – a balance has to be found for the delicately interlinked targets of price stability, employment, balance of payments equilibrium, growth, and income distribution. Neoclassical theory can be a help in this, but it cannot be the solution. There are no easy prescriptions like 'deregulation', 'privatization', 'supply side policy', and so on. It is a difficult task for which all that economic theory as a whole and economic insight have to offer has to be mobilized in order to find strategies which are adapted to the conditions of the outgoing twentieth century or else to show ways how to change these conditions in order to open a path towards a better realization of a democratically chosen combination of targets.

NOTES

1. Great Britain and Denmark preserved the option to remain outside the common currency system.
2. According to the UNCTAD World Investment Report of 1994 (*Transnational Corporations, Employment and the Workplace*) 'Multinationals employ directly about 73 million people, representing 10 per cent of paid non-farm jobs worldwide and close to 20 per cent in the industrialized countries' (quoted from Williams, 1994). The figures do not include the important employment of the subcontractors working for the multinationals.
3. For a fuller treatment of these aspects than given here see Swann (1996, chapter 7).
4. It is interesting to note that neoclassical economists in the US and other countries outside Europe are far more able to look at the EU in a more detached and differentiated way than the majority of neoclassical EU economists who are biased towards a political trend which seems to be so much in line with their basic philosophy and which makes so ample use of their popularized tenets.

REFERENCES

Amin, A. and Tomaney, J. (1995), *Behind the Myth of European Union: Prospects for Cohesion*, London and New York: Routledge.

Buiter, W., Corsetti, G. and Roubini, N. (1993), 'Excessive Deficits: Sense and Nonsense in the Treaty of Maastricht', *Economic Policy: A European Forum*, 8(16), 57–100.

Davidson, P. (1996), 'The viability of Keynesian Demand Management in an Open Economy Context', *International Review of Applied Economics*, 10(1), 91–105.

De Grauwe, P (1996), 'The Economics of Convergence: Towards Monetary Union in Europe', *Weltwirtschaftliches Archiv*, 132(1), 1–27.

Heylen, F., Van Poeck, A. and Van Gompel, J. (1995), 'Real Versus Nominal Convergence: National Labour Markets and the European Integration Process', *Labour*, 9(1), 97–119.

Kalecki, M. (1943), 'Political Aspects of Full Employment', *Political Quarterly*, 14(4), 322–31.

Machlup, F. (1977), *A History of Thought on Economic Integration*, New York: Columbia University Press.

Meade, J.E., Liesner, H.H. and Wells, S.J. (1962), *Case Studies in European Economic Union: The Mechanics of Integration*, London: Oxford University Press.

Swann, D. (1996), *European Economic Integration: The Common Market, European Union and Beyond*, Aldershot, Hants: Edward Elgar.

Williams, F. (1994), 'Global Business a Fact of Life – Unctad's World Investment Report Assesses Role of Multinationals', *Financial Times*, 31 August, 4.

10. The international oil market: Structural changes and stabilization policies

Alessandro Roncaglia

THE ANALYTICAL BACKGROUND[1]

During the industrialization process, the energy of machinery progressively substituted human energy. Thus energy sources – particularly oil, over the past 50 years at least – came to play a central role in our economies. Correspondingly, energy economics became a crucial area for theoretical and policy debate.

As Davidson (1978, p. 151) remarks, 'Post-Keynesian theorists view the economic problems surrounding ... natural resources in a very different light from orthodox neoclassical economic theorists.' As oil is a non-renewable, and hence ultimately scarce, natural resource, it might seem that the marginalist ('scarcity') approach should be better able to deal with it than the contending post Keynesian or classical ('reproducibility') approaches. However, as both Davidson (1963, 1978) and myself (Roncaglia, 1985) maintained, precisely the opposite is true. Though geopolitical factors are crucial in the oil sector, due to the unequal distribution of oil reserves, worldwide ultimate scarcity is too far off in the future for it to have any effect on current prices, investment and production decisions. These should rather be explained, in the international oil market, by looking at oil as a reproducible commodity, though with its own peculiarities.

Marginalist theorizing in the field of non-renewable natural resources mainly consists in variations on the Hotelling theorem (Hotelling, 1931). According to it, the equilibrium price of the scarce resource net of extraction costs (that is, the rent accruing to its owners) rises over time at a rate which is equal, year after year, to the rate of interest. Over time, this induces substitution of the scarce resource with other factors of production, through changes in both production technologies and the structure of consumption. Continuously decreasing returns for each factor of production are assumed, ensuring a smooth transition and that the demand for the natural resource will become nil simultaneously with its supply.

In its simplest formulation, this approach requires not only convex preference and production sets but also a world of perfect certainty and perfect
competition. In such a world, the ultimately available amount of the scarce
natural resource is finite and known to all agents, and they know not only
today's technologies but also the way in which production functions will
change over time. Under perfect competition, when the ultimate exhaustion
of the resource is estimated to be far away in the future, Hotelling-based
analysis indicates that crude oil prices should be nearly equal to production
costs (Dasgupta and Heal, 1979, p. 172). When some of the assumptions are
relaxed and unforeseen changes in the estimated parameters are admitted, the
'generalized' model becomes empty because everything becomes possible.[2]

On the opposite side, Davidson (1963) stresses the role of expectations on
an uncertain future in determining events in the oil sector. While long-term
expectations determine decisions on investment (that is, exploration and development of new fields), short-term expectations on price changes are incor-
porated in 'user costs' influencing current production levels. Together with
other experts of the oil industry,[3] Davidson (1979a, b) stresses that current
prices and production decisions in the oil sector have nothing to do with the
ultimate scarcity of this natural resource. Malthusian fears of an impending
exhaustion of oil reserves (as in Meadows, 1972) are due to a gross statistical
mistake, the confusion between 'proven reserves' and ultimately available
oil. Proven reserves correspond to a sort of shelf-inventory for oil companies;
their location, size and characteristics (quality of crude, depth and pressure of
the field) are already known, and on the basis of such data it has been
confidently decided that they are economically recoverable with known technology at prevailing price-costs relationships. Thus proven reserves can be
produced through exploration, as well as through research on new technology
reducing extraction costs and increasing the percentage of oil-in-place recoverable for any given field.[4] As a matter of fact, 'world proven crude oil
reserves grew from 76 billion barrels in 1950 to 997 billion barrels in 1994 (a
13-fold increase) despite the world producing nearly 700 billion barrels over
this period' (Streifel, 1995, p. 23).

Though not determined by a Hotelling-type mechanism, crude oil prices
are clearly much higher than average unit costs, including exploration and
development costs.[5] Since the difference between prices and costs is not due
to a Hotelling-type scarcity mechanism, the reason for it must be found in
market power. The issue of the prevailing market form thus arises.

The role attributed to this element is a characteristic of part at least of the
post Keynesian literature (Sylos Labini, 1962; Eichner, 1976). Monopoly and
competition are considered as limit cases – absolute or zero barriers to entry
– of the general case where entry in an industry is difficult and costly, though
not impossible. Barriers to entry due to economies of scale (concentrated

oligopoly) or to product differentiation and market segmentation (differentiated oligopoly) allow existing firms to set prices higher than the competitive
level. The difference between the oligopolistic price and the competitive
('natural', in the terminology of classical economists) benchmark level depends on the size of the barriers to entry, which is often difficult to evaluate
and which changes over time because of changes in the elements characterizing the market structure.

Davidson's user cost mechanism (Davidson, 1963) is usefully comple-
mented, in my opinion, by an analysis of the prevailing market form, and its
evolution, in the international oil sector. Without it, user cost analysis only
provides a 'bootstrap theory' of oil prices.

According to my own interpretation (Roncaglia, 1985), the international
oil market can be considered a case of trilateral oligopoly. There are three
groups of agents: oil companies, oil-exporting countries and oil-consuming
countries. Each group includes many individual agents; a few of them, by
virtue of their size, have a direct significant influence on events, while the
others can only do so by jointly entering or leaving the market. Price levels
respond over time to the changes in market structure, which in turn depend
on the strategic choices of the main protagonists and on the responses of the
multiplicity of minor agents. Policy choices of main producing and consuming countries thus play a crucial role, together with the strategic choices of
the main companies.

The arguments for the 'trilateral oligopoly' interpretation are illustrated in
Roncaglia (1985). They range from the technical characteristics of oil and the
world distribution of oil reserves, to the high ratio between fixed and constant
costs in the different stages of the oil industry with the ensuing importance of
economies of scale. These elements are used both for interpreting past events,
and for evaluating the perspectives. My 'most likely scenario' foresaw at the
time 'a future course of oil prices in real terms lower than those prevailing at
the beginning of the 1980s'.[6] This view was a minority one, as the huge
majority of marginalist economists relied on Hotelling-type analysis for pro-
jecting oil price increases in real terms over the medium–long range; these
latter forecasts were commonly accepted in official publications such as
those of the EEC, the IEA, or the Italian state company ENI.[7] Happily,
theories are not evaluated by a majority vote; over time the course of events
showed the greater usefulness of the 'trilateral oligopoly' interpretation compared to the standard marginalist Hotelling-type one. In fact, the latter fared
systematically worse even compared to the null hypothesis of prices stable at
the level reached at any given moment in time.

In what follows, I will briefly apply the 'trilateral oligopoly' interpretation
in surveying the main stages through which the international oil market
underwent over time: (1) the stage up to the early 1970s, dominated by a few

multinational vertically integrated oil companies (the 'majors', or the 'Seven Sisters'); (2) the golden period of OPEC, until the 'countershock' of 1985–86; (3) the present stage of highly volatile prices, determined on relatively small spot markets. This kind of historical sketch helps in locating the factors affecting barriers to entry and the market structure of the international oil sector. In conclusion, since the instability of the oil market is a source of worldwide upheaval, we will briefly discuss possible stabilization policies.

THE RISE OF THE OLIGOPOLISTIC STRUCTURE

The history of the oil industry[8] goes back to the second half of the nineteenth century: a process for refining kerosene and lighting gas is patented in 1854, and the first oil well is drilled in Pennsylvania in 1859. Rockefeller's Standard Oil Company is born in 1870, and already in 1879, exploiting economies of scale in the transport and refining stages, it controls 90 per cent of US refining capacity. Its power is then attacked by a strong popular anti-monopolistic movement; following the 1890 Sherman Act, in 1911 the Supreme Court decrees the dismemberment of the Standard Oil Trust into 34 separate companies.[9] Among these, we find Exxon, Mobil, Standard Oil of California: namely three of the seven oil 'majors' (together with Shell, British Petroleum, Gulf and Texaco) known as the 'seven sisters', which dominate the oil sector for most of this century.

In the nineteenth century, oil is mainly used for oil lamps. The big leap of the oil sector takes place with the spread of the gasoline car: the famous Ford T model dates to 1912, but already in 1911 for the first time gasoline sales surpass kerosene sales in the US. In the same period Great Britain converts its navy from coal to oil. New oil provinces are discovered, as in Kirkuk in Iraq in 1926, and oil consumption extends into new areas, but in 1929 the world crisis provokes a drastic fall in demand. This is preceded, in 1927–28, by a price war between Exxon and Shell springing from the availability of low price Russian crude; the price war is at first limited to the Indian market, but soon extends to the rest of the world.

This is a period of instability, with oil markets oscillating between near-monopoly and sudden competitive outbursts. Such oscillations are typical of sectors with a high ratio of fixed to variable costs, where the entry-preventing price is much higher than the short-period elimination price, since the latter corresponds to average variable costs while the former also includes average fixed costs.[10] This period ends when the international oil market arrives at an oligopolistic structure based on four main pillars: the prorationing system and oil import quotas within the US, and two cartel agreements among major oil companies for operation outside the US.

Prorationing consists in limiting exploitation of oil wells to a few days per month. This system is adopted in the US in order to avoid excess supply and falling prices after the discovery of low-cost Texan fields. With the Connally Hot Oil Act in 1935, prorationing is legalized and a public body, the Texas Railroad Commission, takes care of its administration. Also intended to limit competition from low-cost sources of crude are the quotas to oil imports into the US. These too become compulsory (from 1959 up to 1973), after an initial period of voluntary restraints.

Prorationing and import quotas need be administered by public bodies within the US in order to escape antitrust laws. Outside the US, major companies feel free to enter directly into two cartel agreements, both stipulated in 1928. The 'red line agreement' establishes that within the boundaries of the ex-Ottoman empire (including Turkey, Iraq and Saudi Arabia, and later extended to cover Iran and Kuwait) the oil companies in the agreement (BP, Shell, Exxon, Mobil and the Compagnie Française des Pétroles) should operate only jointly, through consortia, for exploration and production of crude oil. Complex and detailed operating rules for these consortia involve a pluriannual planning of liftings of crude for each company in the consortium. Thus any company willing to expand its market share at the expense of the others has to give advance notice for its increased liftings, which also have to be paid at a premium.

This mechanism is not sufficient to forestall competition from new oil provinces outside Middle East. Thus the 'As is' agreement calls for cooperation in maintaining the then prevailing market shares in oil product markets (hence for preserving the situation 'as it is' at the time of the agreement). The 'majors' should thus expand only in proportion to overall market growth, or possibly at the expense of minor companies outside the agreement. Here too the rules are complex: country by country, market by market, coordinating committees are created and specific rules are established with particular attention to bids for supplying public bodies. The agreement remains secret up to 1952, when it is unveiled following US enquiries on the 'oil cartel'.[11]

The 'As Is' agreement also favours a pricing mechanism (the so-called 'Gulf Plus System') whereby in each market, independently from the origin of the crude, 'posted prices' (that is, those prices at which the companies declare to be willing to sell crude to anyone willing to buy) are linked to those prevailing in the Texan harbours of the Mexican Gulf, plus transport costs computed on the basis of a tariff system built on purpose (called AFRA: cf. Adelman, 1972). The 'base point' mechanism requires an elaborate system of price differentials in order to keep into account quality differences between different crudes (such as those due to density and sulphur content).

After the Second World War a new 'base point' (Ras Tanura in the Arabic Gulf) is added, possibly as a consequence of the Marshall Plan Commission pressing for a reduction in the prices of oil supplies to Western Europe, where the after-war reconstruction of industrial plants is the occasion for the shift from coal to oil as the main energy source. Though remaining much higher than production cost, the prices of Arabic crude gradually decline relatively to Mexican Gulf prices, while the area supplied from Middle East oilfields expands.

Most of crude oil in this period moves within the major vertically integrated companies,[12] utilizing posted prices as accounting prices for the deals between production and refining subsidiaries. However, according to a well-known dictum, 'only fools and affiliates pay posted prices': in crude oil deals between 'crude-long' and 'crude-short' majors (that is, between companies whose share in crude oil production is greater than the share in refined products sales, and those in the opposite condition), long-term agreements are stipulated at prices well below posted prices.

The eight major companies (the Seven Sisters plus the French CFP) control in 1950 99.4 per cent of crude oil produced outside of North America and the communist countries. This is in all likelihood the apex of the system of oligopolistic control over the oil sector. Already in 1957 the share is reduced to 92 per cent; in 1970 it reaches 68.4 per cent, with a decline which signals increasing competitive pressure from 'independent' producers and which opens the way to the 1973 oil crisis.

Competitive pressures, both internal and external, are always present in oligopolistic sectors; rules of behaviour (cartel agreements, public regulations, the profitability of collusion) and barriers to entry (economies of scale, fear of retaliation from unused capacity in low-cost oilfields) restrain but do not eliminate competition. This can assume the form of 'crawling competition' in the fight for marginal market shares, especially through the semi-concealed use of price differentials for specific kinds of crude, or the form of an all-out price war. For more than 40 years, the 'majors' succeeded in avoiding the latter, destructive form of competition; but they could not avoid a slow erosion of their power, especially after the cartel agreements had to be officially abandoned.

THE RISE AND DECLINE OF OPEC

A gradual erosion of the market power of major oil companies takes place in the 1950s and 1960s. New producing countries, such as Lybia and Egypt and above all the Soviet Union, favour the development of new oil companies: the 'independents' in the US, and state companies such as the Italian ENI. Due to increasing competitive pressures, both oil prices and the royalties of established exporting countries gradually decline. As a reaction to this, OPEC

(Organization of Petroleum Exporting Countries) is created on 14 September 1960, in Baghdad. Gradually OPEC acquires bargaining power, exploiting the fight for market shares between the old 'majors' and the new 'independents'. OPEC is also favoured by Malthusian alarmism on the impending exhaustion of oil reserves (as in the influential Club of Rome report, Meadows *et al.*, 1972), which creates in major consuming countries a cultural and political climate acquiescent – if not favourable – to oil price increases.[13]

The 1973 oil crisis is sparked by two events. Firstly, the fourth Arab–Israeli war, begun on 6 October 1973, leads to an embargo on Arab oil exports towards a number of OECD countries. Second, there is a drastic change in US strategy, at the time the first among both consuming and producing countries. On 18 April 1973, the US abolish the quota system for oil imports. Apart from reducing the pressure on relatively declining US oil reserves, this move aims at improving the international competitiveness of US manufactures, hit among other things by higher energy costs due to the use of national crude sources, relatively more costly than Middle East ones.[14] In the three years following the liberalization of US oil imports, the fall in US crude production is three times the cuts in exports from Arab countries due to the embargo. Between 1973 and 1979, while European imports diminish by more than 130 million tons per year and Japanese imports by 12 million tons, US imports more than double, increasing by 177 million tons per year.

All this increases OPEC's bargaining power, already favoured by some characteristics of oil, such as the easiness for producing countries to hold stocks (simply leaving oil in the fields) and the low price elasticity of oil products, at least in the short period. Thus the interplay of strategic policy choices of major producing and consuming countries, and the evolution in the structure of market power, opens a new stage of development for the oil sector: between 1973 and 1974 crude oil prices increase from 3 to about 12–14 dollars per barrel. A second oil crisis, with strong price increases, takes place between 1979 and 1980, spurred by demand pressure for refined products (a shortage of gasoline in California) and by the fears of supply cuts due to the Islamic revolution in Iran. In the meantime Arab countries nationalize the production consortia formerly controlled by the 'majors'; the state companies of the main exporting countries soon reach the top ranks among international oil companies.

However, since 1981 oil prices change course, with a 'step-by-step' decline: periods of oligopolistic control of prices on the side of major producers are followed by short but eventful periods of competitive outbursts, in which prices fall. OPEC lacks an internal coordination mechanism similar to the one of the Middle East consortia connecting in an interrelated web the major oil companies. OPEC is in fact a set of countries with diverging socioeconomic, cultural and political conditions, and different long-term perspectives of crude availability. Thus, after more or less prolonged periods in which tensions within OPEC are kept at bay, competition manifests itself in conflicts on production quotas, in the disguised use of price differentials for different kinds of crude in the fight for increased market shares, and in mini-price wars. The growth of petrochemical industries in some of the major producing countries exerts a competitive pressure on prices at the other extreme of the oil industry, at the level of refined products.[15]

While after the Second World War the sustained expansion of world oil consumption and international oil markets represented an element contributing some competitive pressure on major multinational companies,[16] following the 1973–74 and 1979–80 crises an increased competitive pressure within the group of the oil exporting countries stems from the process of dynamic substitution of oil as an energy source induced by its increased prices. 'Dynamic substitution' is a bias in the direction of the continuous process of technological change, induced by a change in the relative prices of inputs (cf. Sylos Labini, 1992, pp. 140–59); it is different from traditional neoclassical static substitution in one important aspect at least, its irreversibility: when after a period of price increases there is a phase of price decline, the energy savings brought about by the process of dynamic substitution in the first period are not lost in the second phase. For instance, the new gasoline-saving engines for cars that reached the market a few years after the first oil crisis have not been abandoned in favour of the previous ones as oil prices went back in real terms to their previous levels. Energy prices in real terms show a higher correlation with (lagged) income elasticities of energy consumption than with average energy inputs per unit of output.

A relatively short but harsh price war explodes in 1986, in the so-called 'oil countercrisis'. Up to that moment Saudi Arabia accepts a role of swing producer, absorbing the variations in world oil demand and the increases in supply from outside OPEC by reducing her own production, while other OPEC countries are able to maintain more or less stable production levels. As a consequence of this strategy, Saudi Arabia's quota shrinks. With a sudden change in strategy, in 1986 Saudi Arabia stops defending prices, and more than doubles her production in the very short time-span of a few months.[17] It becomes then clear to other major exporting countries that the costs of defending the new price level – about 50 per cent lower than the pre-countercrisis one – have to be more equally distributed.

An important effect of the countercrisis is the abandonment of the pricing mechanism based on an official price for a reference crude (Arabian light fob Ras Tanura). Saudi Arabia first substitutes it with the so-called 'netback pricing', whereby crude prices are derived from the market prices of refined products. As a result of the volatility of refined product market prices, this means shifting to a cargo-by-cargo pricing within long-term deals. At this point, referring to spot market prices appears as a simplification compared to the complexities of netback pricing formulas; thus the habit is soon established for long-term oil deals to link crude prices to the prices prevailing in a few spot markets. The system had already been adopted for North Sea oil; spot and futures markets operate on the model of stock exchanges, with standard contracts (as those for Brent crude in the London stock exchange and West Texas intermediate in the US) limited to standard characteristics for quantity and quality as well as for delivery arrangements.[18]

The new mechanism has an appearance of objectivity and efficiency, substituting administered (posted) prices with 'competitive' prices determined in a continuously operating stock exchange ready to register the changing evaluations of agents on the factors affecting supply and demand conditions. However, while the value of paper deals in such markets experiences a dramatic increase, with total yearly volumes now well over the total value of international yearly crude flows, the actual volume of physical deliveries contracted for in spot markets is but a small share of total production and consumption.[19] Thus the new mechanism introduces in a market previously based on long-term deals and a stable structure of production and commercial flows all the characteristics of globalized financial markets, such as instability and self-supporting price cycles driven by self-fulfilling expectations and very short term speculation. All this takes place, however, in a situation still characterized by a significant market power held by a few major oil companies and a few producing countries. The latter ones retain large margins of unused productive capacity – a typical characteristic of oligopolistic markets – as the 1991 crisis of the Gulf War showed, when the abrupt disappearance of Iraqi and Kuwaiti production was soon counterbalanced by increased production elsewhere, with prices experiencing a noticeable but not dramatic and above all not lasting increase.

THE STABILIZATION OF OIL PRICES

The story of the oil sector has thus been marked by changes in the relative power of the three groups of participants. We first have a nearly absolute dominance of major oil companies. This is followed by a gradual decrease in their power and an increasing power on the side of exporting countries and their international organization, OPEC. The latest stage is characterized by an increase in competition among producers and a decline in the power of OPEC, though crude oil prices remain much higher than production costs. In the meantime, quite inadvertently, the role of consuming countries grows, with an increasing share of the value of oil product sales absorbed by consuming countries' governments through taxes, in response both to budgetary needs and to the growing favour for ecological policies based on 'carbon taxes'. In this stage volatile crude oil prices are determined, as we have seen above, in what are mainly financial markets dominated by speculative activity.

The volatility of oil prices, hence, does not reflect the establishment of a fully competitive market for crude oil. It is rather the result of a pricing mechanism accepted *faute de mieux* by the main agents in the oil sectors, after the collapse of previous pricing arrangements. While it is difficult to foresee how the situation will evolve in the future,[20] it is clear that price instability in such a basic commodity is a serious problem for the world economy.

As is well known,[21] oscillations in the prices of primary commodities generate alternately inflation and stagnation: inflation, since increases in primary commodity prices are translated, through mark-up mechanisms, into price increases of manufactured goods, generally produced under oligopolistic conditions; stagnation, since the decreases in primary commodities prices imply a loss of income for producing (generally developing) countries, and hence a reduction in their demand for manufactured goods.[22] Disequilibria in trade balances also favour stagnation, because of the asymmetry in the pressure for adjustment (deficit countries are under greater pressure to adopt retrenchment policies than surplus countries to adopt expansionary policies). Furthermore, instability in an important sector of the world economy such as the oil trade increases uncertainty, creating an atmosphere less favourable to investments, especially those with a long recoupment period.

Stabilization policies based on the use of buffer stocks have been tried for other primary commodities, with contrasting results of noticeable successes and important failures.[23] The latter ones are generally connected to the setting of unrealistically high prices. These can be defended for some time, but tensions cumulate and in the long period the stabilization policy has to be abandoned. Thus it is clear that any policy of this kind has to take into account the fundamentals of the sector, including not only prevailing technologies and necessary production costs but also the dominant market form and its foreseeable evolution. This means, in our case, taking into account the downward pressures on crude oil prices which are likely to prevail in the medium term at least, accompanied by a progressive reduction in the share of oil in the overall energy sector. All these elements enhance the political difficulty of organizing a successful stabilization policy in the case of oil. However, there are also favourable elements. Noticeably, in a trilateral oligopoly stabilization does not require a general coordination of all agents operating in the sector. A coordination of major agents on each of the three sides should be sufficient, provided that their strategies keep into account the existence of, and the competitive pressures stemming from, the multitude of smaller agents. Account must also be taken of competition from potential entrants, and above all – if the policy is to be a long-period one – from other energy sources. Such a coordination could leave the door open to the play of market forces, since it should concern not so much the stabilization of market shares but the 'rules of the game', namely the energy policies adopted by consuming and producing countries and the pricing rules. The International Energy Association could provide the initial forum for such a stabilization policy; this, of course, would require the abandonment, on this side, of any remnant of the Hotelling-type culture.

SUMMARY AND CONCLUSIONS

If marginalist economics is interpreted, as Robbins (1932) suggested, as dealing with the allocation of scarce resources, then the issue of exhaustible natural resources should naturally represent the preferred field for the application of marginalist analysis. Rigorous tools, such as the Hotelling theorem and its elaborations, have in fact been developed for dealing with exhaustible natural resources. However, the leading example of an exhaustible natural resource, namely oil, represents a clear case where other approaches – specifically, the classical Keynesian one, stressing the role of uncertainty and market forms – appear better suited to the interpretation of historical events and as a guide to policy choices.

After briefly discussing the counterposition between the marginalist (scarcity) and the classical Keynesian (reproducibility) approaches, the 'trilateral oligopoly' interpretation of the international oil market has been summarily illustrated. According to it, there are three groups of agents to be considered – oil companies, oil exporting countries, consuming countries – each including many individual agents, but with a few major strategic leaders. The market structure depends on institutional and technological elements affecting the power structure within the sector, especially the pressure of internal and external competition (degree of collusion, size of barriers to entry). The interplay of these factors is better considered through an analysis of the evolution over time of the market structure.

The main stages through which the international oil market underwent over time have thus been considered. First, in the stage up to the early 1970s, dominated by a few vertically integrated oil companies, the market structure is mainly determined by four institutional pillars – the prorationing system and oil import quotas within the US, and two cartel agreements among major oil companies for operation outside the US – and by economies of scale and other technical and economic factors favouring major vertically integrated firms. The second stage is the golden period of OPEC, from the early 1970s until the 'countershock' of 1985–86; here the relevant factors are the unequal geographical distribution of giant low-cost fields, the low cost of inventories for 'oil kept in the ground', and the elements favouring or hindering the collusion between OPEC countries (diverging socioeconomic, cultural and political conditions, and different long-term perspectives of crude availability). Thirdly, the present stage of highly volatile oil prices, determined on relatively small spot markets, is characterized by increased competitive pressure within the group of exporting countries and within the group of multinational oil companies, and by a greater role of consuming countries with their policies concerning taxation of oil products. Finally, since the instability of the oil market is a source of world-wide upheaval, the possibility of stabilization policies is discussed.

The ideologies of scarcity and *laissez-faire* create dangerous illusions on the working of the oil sector. Recognition of the existence of market power, of a changing market structure, of the relevance of strategic choices on the side of the main agents are prerequisite for a rational debate on policy choices; such choices have a decisive influence on the vicissitudes of the world economy.

NOTES

1. This chapter is part of a research project on 'I mercati delle fonti di energia', financed by MURST.
2. At a less sophisticated level, marginalist applied analyses of oil and oil product markets often utilize supply–demand comparisons for determining prices, especially in short or middle period forecasts. Here of course supply and demand schedules refer to production and consumption flows; thus the applied economist avoids the need to consider unreliable estimates of the stock of ultimately available oil, as it would be necessary to do within the Hotelling framework. However, in oligopolistic sectors these exercises are a wrong application of static marginalist analysis, since supply cannot be considered independent from demand. This is a crucial point, since a basic prerequisite of the theory is not satisfied in reality, and is especially true in the oil sector, because of the easiness of adapting production flows. A decrease in demand (or in its rate of growth) may even push exporting countries to 'stick together'; in general, the degree of collusion among exporting countries appears to be mainly influenced by political elements, and to be largely independent from demand. Moreover, consumption eventually responds to oil product prices, and these are affected in a crucial way by the energy tax policies of consuming countries. Finally, a static analysis in terms of supply and demand obscures the main effect of high oil prices, acting through a dynamic process of technological change (on which see below, 'The Rise and Decline of OPEC').
3. See for example Adelman (1976, 1979): 'What lies ahead in the late twenty-first century, nobody knows, but a shortage of oil reserves is less to be feared than a shortage of drinkable water or breathable air.' Cf. also Adelman 1972 (p. 253); 1995 (pp. 11–13).
4. Cf. Roncaglia (1985, pp. 27–8).
5. 'Marginal' high-cost fields cannot constitute the reference for the evaluation of production costs, since their supply could easily be substituted by supply from lower-cost underexploited giant oilfields in the Middle East and elsewhere. This means that the

causal sequence of Ricardian rent theory does not hold. According to the latter, an increase in the demand for corn cannot be satisfied by high-fertility land, and hence requires lower-fertility lands to be put into cultivation, which necessitates price increases. In the case of oil, demand can be satisfied by a higher degree of utilization of high-fertility fields: it is because production on these fields is restrained and the price is high, that high-cost fields can be profitably exploited.

For estimates of costs in the main oil provinces, see Adelman (1995).

6. Roncaglia (1985, p. 7); let me recall that the book was first published in Italian in 1983, and written in 1981–2. A few articles – including the forecast of irregular price decreases with periods of oligopolistic competition alternating with periods of oligopolistic collusion – were also published at the time in the political monthly magazine *Mondoperaio* and in the newspaper *Il Messaggero*.

7. A few dissenters foresaw a price collapse down to production costs in Middle East oilfields, i.e. to well below 3 dollars per barrel due to competition. Among them, Milton Friedman (*Newsweek*, 4 March 1974): 'Even if [OPEC countries] cut their output to zero, they could not for long keep the world price of crude at 10 dollars a barrel. Well before that point the cartel would collapse.' What escaped the generality of marginalist economists was the likelihood of a middle course: neither natural monopoly and scarcity, nor competition, but oligopoly, with high but not insurmountable barriers to entry, changing over time with the evolution of the market structure.

8. For a more detailed account the reader is referred to Roncaglia (1995).

9. We are thus reminded that antitrust policy is a most important factor among those determining market structure and its evolution.

10. For an interpretation of the oil market at the time along these lines, see Frankel (1946).

11. See Federal Trade Commission (1952) and Blair (1976). Adelman (1972, 1975) downplays – nearly ignores – the role of these two cartel agreements in his interpretation of the oil market; in his opinion sufficient competition prevails among oil companies, while the huge (and volatile) differences between crude oil prices and costs are attributed to OPEC's successes (and failures) in monopolistic price setting. In developing this interpretation Adelman appears to ignore the crucial relevance, both in the real world and in theory, of market forms intermediate between competition and monopoly; his faulty recourse to increasing marginal cost (with justifications which could apply to the individual firm in the short run or to the whole industry in the long run, but not to the individual firm in the long run, as the marginalist theory of competition would require – see Roncaglia (1985, pp. 31–4) is decisive in this respect. Adelman thus appears to repeat the same mistakes of the Marshallian tradition definitively criticized by Sraffa (1925, 1926).

12. On the role of vertical integration, see Penrose (1968). Vertical integration favours oligopolistic control, since the elements of market power characterizing one stage of the oil sector (for instance, economies of scale in transport) reinforce the elements present in other stages (such as the control of huge low-cost fields in production); moreover, vertical integration by itself adds market power, through increased political leverage, economies of scale in financing, tax savings through transfer pricing.

13. Of course, behind the cultural climate created by fears of scarcity there are, in determining US policy choices, important economic interests, such as those of US oil producers. See Adelman (1995) for an account of the 'high price climate' in the United States. Davidson (1963, p. 106) recalls that the percentage depletion deduction from taxable income available in the US 'gives many integrated refiners a vested interest in higher oil prices'; a powerful element operating in the same direction is the so-called 'golden gimmick' introduced in 1950, allowing international companies to offset tax liabilities in the US with royalty payments to producing countries (cf. Roncaglia, 1985, p. 166).

14. Nixon's 15 August 1971 unilateral declaration of inconvertibility of dollars in gold, which marks the end of the Bretton Woods international monetary system, reflects among other things this decline in competitivity.

15. This aspect was stressed in the Preface to the Italian edition of my book in 1983 (pp. 9–10), where I argued against the proposed transformation of ENI into a mainly petrochemical company, with huge investments on the acquisition and upgrading of Italian-based

petrochemical plants. A rebalancing of the vertically integrated structure was rather required, in my view, with the main investment efforts centred in research and development of new crude sources in new oil provinces.

16. In the oligopoly theory developed by Sylos Labini (1962), the greater is the size of the market (measured in terms of optimal plant size) and the higher the rate of growth of the market, the smaller are, *ceteris paribus,* the barriers to entry and the oligopolistic extra-profit margin.

17. Cf. Askari, 1991; Adelman, 1995, chapter 7. Using Sylos Labini's (1962) analysis of oligopolistic price wars, it was quite easy to diagnose such a situation (as I did at the time in a few articles published in the daily *Il Messaggero*). For Saudi Arabia, with costs at (or lower than) 1 dollar per barrel, it was better to sell 10 mb/d (million barrels a day) at a price as low as 10 dollars per barrel (with 90 million dollars rent per day) than 3 mb/d at 30 dollars per barrel (with a rent of 87 million dollars per day).

18. On spot and futures oil markets, cf. Roeber (1993).

19. Recall also that spot markets refer to well-defined types of crude, representing a small share of production and consumption. West Texas intermediate is not shipped, and hence not traded internationally.

20. Though it is likely that downward pressures on prices will continue, following competition from the far ends of the hydrocarbons spectrum, namely natural gas on the one side and tar sands (Venezuela's Orinoco Belt) on the other side: see Roncaglia (1996).

21. See particularly Sylos Labini (1984, chapter 6).

22. Manufactured goods prices are less flexible downward, as Sylos Labini's (1984, chapter 7) analysis of oligopolistic markets shows.

23. For a survey, cf. Sabbatini (1989a). For the Keynesian background to such policies, cf. Sabbatini (1989b).

REFERENCES

Adelman, M.A. (1972), *The World Petroleum Market*, Baltimore: Resource for the Future, Johns Hopkins University Press.

Adelman, M.A. (1976), 'The World Oil Cartel', *Quarterly Review of Economics and Business*, **16**, 7–18.

Adelman, M.A. (1979), 'Reply to Harkin', *Challenge*, **22**, 70–1.

Adelman, M.A. (1995), *The Genie out of the Bottle*, Cambridge, Mass.: MIT Press.

Askari, H. (1991), 'Saudi Arabia's Oil Policy: Its Motivations and Impacts', in *After the Oil Price Collapse*, edited by W.L. Kohl, Baltimore: Johns Hopkins University Press, pp. 28–42.

Blair, J.M. (1976), *The Control of Oil*, New York: Pantheon Books.

Dasgupta, P.S. and Heal, G.M. (1979), *Economic Theory and Exhaustible Resources*, Cambridge: Cambridge University Press.

Davidson, P. (1963), 'Public Policy Problems of the Domestic Crude Oil Industry', *American Economic Review*, **53**, 85–108.

Davidson, P. (1978), 'Natural Resources', in *A Guide to Post-Keynesian Economics*, edited by A.S. Eichner, White Plains (NY): ME Sharpe, 151–64.

Davidson, P. (1979a), 'What is the Energy Crisis', *Challenge*, July–August, 41–6.

Davidson, P. (1979b), 'Reply to Harkin', *Challenge*, November–December, 71–2.

Eichner, A.S. (1976), *The Megacorp & Oligopoly*, Cambridge: Cambridge University Press.

Federal Trade Commission (1952), *The International Petroleum Cartel*, Staff Report, Washington.

Frankel, P.H. (1946), *Essentials of Petroleum*, London: Frank Cass.

Hotelling, H. (1931), 'The Economics of Exhaustible Resources', *Journal of Political Economy*, **39**, 137–75.

Meadows, D.H., Meadows, D.L., Randers, J. and Beherens, W.W., III (1972), *The Limits to Growth*, London: New American Library.

Penrose, E. (1968), *The Large International Firm in Developing Countries*, London: Allen and Unwin.

Robbins L. (1932), *The Nature and Significance of Economic Science*, London: Macmillan.

Roeber, J. (1993), *The Evolution of Oil Markets: Trading Instruments and Their Role in Oil Price Formation*, London: Royal Institute of International Affairs.

Roncaglia, A. (1985), *The International Oil Market*, London: Macmillan (Italian edn, *L'economia del petrolio*, Roma-Bari: Laterza, 1983).

Roncaglia, A. (1995), *I mercati petroliferi internazionali e la crisi petrolifera*, mimeo (to be published in *Enciclopedia del XX secolo*, Roma: Istituto della Enciclopedia Italiana) .

Roncaglia, A. (1996), 'Russia and International Oil and Gas Markets', mimeo.

Sabbatini, R. (1989a), 'La stabilizzazione dei prezzi delle materie prime attraverso l'utilizzo di scorte cuscinetto', degree dissertation, Faculty of Statistics, University of Rome 'La Sapienza'.

Sabbatini, R. (1989b), 'Il progetto di Keynes di stabilizzazione dei prezzi delle materie prime', *Quaderni di storia dell'economia politica*, **7**, 55–73.

Sraffa, P. (1925), 'Sulle relazioni fra costo e quantità prodotta', *Annali di economia*, **2**, 277–328.

Sraffa, P. (1926), 'The Laws of Return Under Competitive Conditions', *Economic Journal*, **36**, 535–50.

Streifel, S.S. (1995), *Review and Outlook for the World Oil Market*, World Bank Discussion Paper 301, Washington.

Sylos Labini, P. (1962), *Oligopoly and Technical Progress*, Cambridge, Mass.: Harvard University Press (Italian edn, *Oligopolio e progresso tecnico*, Milano: Giuffrè, 1956).

Sylos Labini, P. (1984), *The Forces of Economic Growth and Decline*, Cambridge, Mass.: MIT Press.

Sylos Labini, P. (1992), *Elementi di dinamica economica*, Roma-Bari: Laterza.

11. Financial liberalization: Myth or reality?

Philip Arestis and Panicos Demetriades

INTRODUCTION

Paul Davidson has played a leading role in the fight against the 'tyranny of the markets'. This chapter is dedicated to his untiring efforts to demonstrate the futility of 'market liberalization' by concentrating in an area where renewed interest has resurfaced, this being financial markets. More precisely, the focus of this contribution will be on the setting of financial prices by central banks, especially in developing countries, a fairly common practice in the 1950s and 1960s, which was challenged by Goldsmith (1969) in the late 1960s, and by McKinnon (1973) and Shaw (1973) in the early 1970s. They ascribed the poor performance of investment and growth in developing countries to interest rate ceilings, high reserve requirements and quantitative restrictions in the credit allocation mechanism. These restrictions were sources of 'financial repression', the main symptoms of which were low savings, credit rationing and low investment.

Goldsmith (1969) argued that the main transmission channel of financial repression was the effect on the efficiency of capital. McKinnon (1973) and Shaw (1973) stressed two other channels: first, financial repression affects how efficiently savings are allocated to investment; and second, through its effect on the return to savings, it also affects the equilibrium level of savings and investment. In this framework, therefore, investment suffers not only in quantity but also in quality terms because bankers do not ration the available funds according to the marginal productivity of investment projects but according to their own discretion. Under these conditions the financial sector is likely to stagnate. The low return on bank deposits encourages savers to hold their savings in the form of unproductive assets such as land rather than potentially productive bank deposits. Similarly, high reserve requirements restrict the supply of bank lending even further while directed credit programmes distort the allocation of credit since political priorities are, in general, not determined by the marginal productivity of different types of capital.

The policy implications of this analysis are quite straightforward: remove interest rate ceilings, reduce reserve requirements and abolish directed credit programmes. In short, liberalize financial markets and let the free market determine the allocation of credit. With the real rate of interest adjusting to its equilibrium level low yielding investment projects would be eliminated, so that the overall efficiency of investment would be enhanced. Also, as the real rate of interest increases, saving and the total real supply of credit increase, which induces a higher volume of investment. Economic growth would, therefore, be stimulated not only through the increased investment but also due to an increase in the average productivity of capital. Moreover, the effects of lower reserve requirements reinforce the effects of higher saving on the supply of bank lending, while the abolition of directed credit programmes would lead to an even more efficient allocation of credit, thereby stimulating further the average productivity of capital.

Even though the financial liberalization thesis encountered increasing scepticism over the years, it nevertheless had a relatively early impact on development policy through the work of the IMF and the World Bank who, perhaps in their traditional role as promoters of free market conditions, were keen to encourage financial liberalization policies in developing countries as part of more general reforms or stabilization programmes. The experience following the implementation of financial liberalization reforms did not justify the theoretical premises. There occurred a revision of the main tenets of the thesis. Two types were initiated. The first was concerned with what has come to be labelled as 'the sequencing of financial liberalization' (for example, Edwards, 1989; McKinnon, 1991), and the second called attention to the broader macroeconomic environment within which financial reforms were to be undertaken (Sachs, 1988). These *post hoc* theoretical revisions were thought of as sufficient to defend the original thesis of a disappointing empirical record.

Results broadly similar to financial liberalization are also evident in the literature on endogenous growth. In such models financial development can affect growth not only by raising the saving rate but also by raising the amount of saving funnelled to investment and/or raising the social marginal productivity of capital.[1] With few exceptions (for example, Easterly, 1993) the endogenous growth literature views government intervention in the financial system as distortionary and predicts that it has a negative effect on the equilibrium growth rate. Increasing taxes on financial intermediaries is seen as equivalent to taxes on innovative activity, which lowers the equilibrium growth rate.

New growth theory suggests that there can be self-sustaining growth without exogenous technical progress. Thus, financial intermediation can be shown to have not only level effects but also growth effects. Utilizing an AK production technology, the steady-state growth rate can be shown to be (Pagano, 1993):

$$g = A\Phi s - \delta$$

where g = growth rate, A = social marginal productivity of capital, Φ = proportion of saving funnelled to investment, s = private saving rate, and δ = depreciation. Financial development can affect growth through:

1. raising A through collecting information to evaluate alternative investment projects and through inducing individuals to invest in riskier but more productive technologies by providing risk sharing. Banks are seen as accepting highly liquid deposits and investing them in illiquid and productive projects; stock markets by allowing portfolio diversification reduce rate-of-return risk. These two considerations clearly imply willingness to invest in less liquid and more productive projects. Thus setting up a stock market raises the productivity of investment and the growth rate;
2. increases in Φ (by, for example, reducing reserve requirements);
3. through affecting s, which can be done through financial liberalization, which increases the amount of savings and the quality of investment.

In more general terms, financial markets enable agents to share both endowment risks (such as health hazards) and rate-of-return risk (such as that due to the volatility of stock returns) through diversification. They channel funds from people who save to those who dissave in the form of consumer credit and mortgage loans. If the loan supply falls short of demand, some households are liquidity-constrained, their consumption is limited by current resources and savings increase. There is, however, an important difference between the financial liberalization and the endogenous growth theses (Singh, 1997). The endogenous growth theory proponents argue for deliberate and fast development of stock markets, especially in developing countries. By contrast, the financial liberalization advocates view stock market development as either unimportant or at best as a slow evolutionary process, thereby ignoring this aspect completely in their analysis (Fry, 1997, for example).

We wish to argue in this chapter that there are a number of issues in these arguments which are critical in the development of the financial liberalization thesis; and that these propositions are not problem-free. They are, in fact, so problematic that they leave the thesis without serious theoretical and empirical foundations.

PROBLEMS WITH FINANCIAL LIBERALIZATION

This section deals at some length with the financial liberalization thesis, in an attempt to draw conclusions on both its theoretical and empirical importance. They can be summarised briefly:

1. free banking leads to stability of the financial system;
2. financial liberalization enhances economic growth;
3. relationship between savings and investment;
4. absence of serious distributional effects;
5. no role for stock markets and speculation;
6. empirical evidence.

We proceed now to discuss these critical issues at some length.

FREE BANKING LEADS TO STABILITY OF THE FINANCIAL SYSTEM

In the limit, as there would be no possibility of government bailouts in free banking, any hint of imprudence would cause customers to shift to competitors. Consequently, the market discipline would be stronger the larger the number of independent note issuers. The underlying assumption of the thesis is that market forces do produce stability in the banking and financial systems, as they do in other sections of the economy. Rigidities and instabilities, therefore, emanate from interference with the normal working of the 'market'.

Experience with Free Banking

The proponents refer to a number of examples to demonstrate the advantages of free banking, and thus provide strong support for it. We refer to three cases which have been most frequently discussed.[2]

USA
During the period 1837 to 1863, in 18 States (including New York), there was free banking. However, there were problems, bankruptcies and the issue of 'too much money' being the most serious ones. Friedman's argument, in his *A Program for Monetary Stability*, is relevant here. This suggests that, as under free banking competition, money would be issued until marginal revenue is equal to marginal cost, and with the latter being zero, over-issue of

private money is inevitable. Fiduciary currency is likely to degenerate into a commodity standard.

Scotland

During the years 1695 to 1845 Scotland experienced a period of free banking. There was no central bank, and Scottish commercial banks issued their own banknotes backed by their own holdings of gold specie and were not under any legal supervision. Nor were there any restrictions on entry to the banking industry and almost no legal regulations. Allegedly it was a far more stable banking system than that enjoyed by England at the time, where there was government intervention. But the Scottish system depended upon the English Banks whenever problems arose. Indeed, and as Dow (1996) observes, the experience of Scottish commercial banks during that period could not be isolated from the presence of the Bank of England. Furthermore, even in that era of Scottish free banking the system evolved its own form of central banking. The two 'old banks', the Bank of Scotland and the Royal Bank of Scotland, performed that function. They:

> set up a note exchange and an exchange equalisation system, accepted the notes of other banks to curtail runs (most notably in the case of the Ayr Bank), disciplined banks whose credit creation was judged excessive (by refusing access to clearing) and made representations to Westminster on behalf of the banking system as a whole. The other banks in turn held their reserves with the old banks, which adopted an authoritative role, based on market power. (Dow, 1996, p. 704)

Canada

Over the period 1820 to 1935 Canada experienced allegedly free banking. However, the main characteristic of this period was that the main two banks, the Bank of Upper Canada and the Bank of Montreal were not as 'free' as it is alleged. They were actually owned to a significant extent by politicians of Upper Canada and Lower Canada respectively (Dow, 1996).

Clearly, then, even in the most frequently discussed cases of free banking, the system may either have worked because of support emanating from outside the system itself, or it was simply accompanied by serious problems. There are further serious theoretical drawbacks which spring from two aspects ignored by the proponents of free banking, these being *asymmetric information* and *uncertainty* which we now proceed to discuss.

Asymmetric Information

This drawback originates from the new Keynesian perspective of asymmetric information (see, for example, Stiglitz and Weiss, 1981). Asymmetric information leads to two type of problems: *adverse selection* and *moral hazard*.

Adverse selection refers to cases when selection is likely to produce adverse results. In the market for loans, for example, the problem refers to borrowers who may not be able to repay their loans. For example, they use the loans for excessively risky investments, but lenders do not know about them due to lack of information. The problem with adverse selection is particularly acute when interest rates are on an upward trend. In such cases, 'sensible' borrowers who are not prepared to take excessive risks reduce their demand for loans, unlike the 'high' risk borrowers who do not reduce their demand for loans. Thus, the probability of borrowers who are likely to default increases substantially. In a free banking system, adverse selection implies that banks, in view of incomplete information, cannot distinguish between 'reliable' and 'unreliable' customers. Adverse selection may ensue in which case even the 'reliable' customers undertake high risks to be able to compete with 'unreliable' ones.

Moral hazard describes situations where the borrower acts 'immorally', that is in a way that is not in the best interest of the lender who possesses incomplete information. For example, depositors due to incomplete information cannot observe the high risks banks may undertake, which may encourage unscrupulous behaviour. In a free banking system moral hazard allows banks with small initial capital to accumulate excessive deposits due to lack of information on the part of lenders (depositors). It opens up the possibility of higher risk loans than what the depositors would accept if they had full information. The soundness of the banking system suffers as a result, threatening the process of financial intermediation.

The market might solve this problem, though, through the creation of 'professional clubs' which impose a professional code of behaviour on their members. Although the solution of 'professional clubs' might cure some of the problems associated with free banking, it creates a different problem nonetheless: from one market failure, asymmetric information, to another, that is the oligopoly situation of the 'professional club' which behaves as a cartel. In addition, the lender of last resort would remain an unresolved issue because it is unlikely *one* bank or the cartel would be able to perform this function.

Uncertainty

Given the very special economic role of money and the intrinsic uncertainty associated with it, financial *laissez-faire*, if ever implemented, would at best give way to its own form of central banking. Uncertainty is unquantifiable risk and in order for the economic process to proceed in spite of uncertainty, society adopts conventions, supported crucially by the state, to create elements of stability to aid decision-making. The legal system enables the establishment of contracts, while the provision of outside money and bank regulation, as well as supervision, supports the evolution of a banking system which produces money as an asset to hold in times of particular uncertainty (see Davidson, 1978; Dow, 1996, for further details on all these propositions). Money is integral to the economic process, just as the state is to the evolution of private sector institutions and conventions. In this role, the state provides an important support which is to inspire confidence in money's capacity to retain value. It is this confidence that underpins the roles of money as means of payment and store of value, as well as unit of account and thus as a denominator of contracts. Free banking is, therefore, unworkable in practice. It is also unstable, and as such it needs central banks to regulate it. Indeed, and as Dow (1996) argues, we need, not deregulation, but *better* regulation.

FINANCIAL LIBERALIZATION AND ECONOMIC DEVELOPMENT

In demonstrating that a positive relationship exists between financial liberalization and economic development, the thesis under scrutiny ignores a number of aspects which are of significant importance. These we discuss next beginning with hedge effects and curb markets.

Hedge Effects and Curb Markets

This critique emanates from the structuralist theory (Taylor, 1983; Van Wijnbergen, 1983). It suggests that higher interest rates from financial liberalization might leave unchanged or, indeed, decrease the total supply of funds. This is due to hedge effects which may not materialize in which case the total supply of funds may not be affected, or to curb effects which may reduce it. Hedge effects are due to substitution of hedge assets, gold and land are the most obvious examples, for bank deposits brought about by higher interest rates. Neostructuralist theorists maintain that *risk-averse* investors may not choose to substitute hedge assets for bank deposits. Consequently, financial liberalization would fail to stimulate an increase in savings. Curb effects emanate from the possibility that increased deposits may very well come from the curb markets where there are no reserve requirements. As in the official markets there are reserve requirements, it follows that financial liberalization may produce a lower volume of loans than without it. Furthermore, to the extent that the assumptions adopted by the structuralist theory, especially of mark-up pricing, increased interest rates and higher exchange rates, are validated, there is the real danger that financial liberalization may lead to slower level of economic activity. All in all, structuralist theory predicts *stagflationary* outcomes as a result of financial liberalization. However, it should be readily conceded that both the hedge and curb effects have not been unambiguously empirically validated (Ghate, 1992).

Lack of Perfect Competition and Asymmetric Information

The McKinnon and Shaw type of models are based on the unrealistic assumption of perfect competition, which is particularly arbitrary in the case of Less Developed Countries (LDCs). Given that banking sectors are undoubtedly rather oligopolistic, the result of financial liberalization could very well be the monopoly result whereby a decrease in loans and an increase in the real interest rate may ensue (Demetriades and Luintel, 1996a). Moreover, the possibility of inadequate regulation over banking practices may lead to undue risk-taking, especially in the presence of deposit insurance. Under such circumstances the banks benefit from an unfair bet against the government: if the projects they have financed do well they make a lot of profit, if they do badly they rely on the government to rescue them. Such a situation has been termed 'upward financial repression'.

Differential Speeds of Adjustment and Competition of Instruments

Differential speeds of adjustment are now thought of as possible causes of serious problems to attempts at financial liberalization (McKinnon, 1991). There are different speeds of adjustment in the financial and goods markets, whereby the latter are sluggish. Thus, financial markets could not be reformed in the same manner and in the same instance as other markets without creating awkward difficulties. Recognition of these problems has led the proponents of the financial liberalization thesis to suggest the desirability of *sequencing* in financial reforms. Successful reform of the real sector came to be seen as a prerequisite to financial reform. Thus, financial repression would have to be maintained during the first stage of economic liberalization.

Furthermore, there is the possibility that different aspects of reform programmes may work at cross-purposes, disrupting the real sector in the process. This is precisely what Sachs (1988) labelled as 'competition of instruments'. Such conflict can occur when abrupt increases in interest rates cause the exchange rate to appreciate rapidly thus damaging the real sector. Sequencing becomes important again. It is thus suggested that liberalization of the 'foreign' markets should take place after liberalization of domestic financial markets. In this context, proponents suggest caution in 'sequencing' in the sense of gradual financial liberalization emphasizing the achievement of macroeconomic stability and adequate bank supervision as preconditions for successful financial reform. It is also argued by the proponents that the authorities should move more aggressively on financial reform in good times and more slowly when borrowers' net worth is reduced by negative shocks, such as recessions and losses due to terms of trade (see, also, World Bank, 1989). In a recent study, Caprio, Atiyas and Hanson (1994), have reviewed the financial reforms in a number of primarily developing countries with the experience of six countries studied at some depth and length. They conclude that managing the reform process rather than adopting a *laissez-faire* stance is important, and that sequencing along with the initial conditions in finance and macroeconomic stability are critical elements in implementing successfully financial reforms.

Despite all these modifications, however, there is absolutely no question of the fundamental premise of the financial liberalization thesis being abandoned. No amount of revision has changed the objective of the thesis which is concerned with developing the *optimal* path to financial liberalization, free from any political, that is state, intervention. Sequencing does not salvage the financial liberalization thesis for the simple reason that it depends on the assumption that financial markets clear in a Walrasian manner while the goods markets do not. But in the presence of asymmetric information, financial markets too are marred by imperfections. But even where the 'correct' sequencing took place (that is, Chile), where trade liberalization had taken place before financial liberalization, not much success can be reported (Lal, 1987). The opposite is also true, namely that in those cases, like Uruguay, where the 'reverse' sequencing took place, financial liberalization before trade liberalization, the experience was very much the same as in Chile (Grabel, 1995).

Public Finance Aspects and Low Interest Rates for Development

The public finance aspects of 'financial liberalization' are important, and can produce serious destabilizing effects. 'Financial repression' by keeping interest rates at a low level, enables governments to borrow cheaply, which has beneficial effects on the level of public debt as a result – and also enables the government to stabilize the economy through the normal Keynesian mechanism. Thus, financial liberalization by producing higher interest rates, is likely to be accompanied by destabilizing consequences for the macroeconomy. In addition, the thesis ignores the advantages of using low interest rates and thus credit selection for development purposes.

RELATIONSHIP BETWEEN SAVINGS AND INVESTMENT

In the McKinnon–Shaw model, of course, savings take place before investment. But savings can only fund investment, that is it can only facilitate the
finance of investment. Savings cannot *finance* capital accumulation; this is
done by the banking sector which provides loans for investment without
necessitating increases in the volume of deposits. With a credit-creating
financial system, it is banks, and not savers, which finance investment. Consequently, it is finance, and not saving, along with the entrepreneurial long-
term expectations, which are the prerequisites to capital accumulation. Savings,
nonetheless, has a different, and important, role to play which is to achieve
and maintain the financial stability of the growing economy (Studart, 1995).

A second problem with the McKinnon–Shaw model is the assumption that
deposits create loans. In modern banking systems, including most LDCs,
loans create deposits not the other way round. The liquidity preference of the
banks is very important in this context as well as the ability of the banking
sector to innovate, a good example in this sense is liability management. A
more important determinant of investment is profit expectations and the level
and pace of aggregate demand, both affected adversely by higher real interest
rates. A further relevant consideration is the impact of high real interest rates
on the exchange rate, in the case of open economies. In these economies high
real interest rates following financial liberalization can cause appreciation of
the exchange rate. This can hit adversely domestic production of tradeable
goods and expected profitability, and thus reduce investment (not increase the
volume of investment as predicted by the financial liberalization thesis).

INTEREST-RATE CHANGES AND DISTRIBUTION OF INCOME

The financial liberalization thesis does not pay much attention to distributional effects of changes in interest rates. As a result, the contributions initiated on this issue have been rather small, both theoretical and quantitative.
Fry (1995) surveys the limited work that has been conducted on this issue, to
conclude that 'financial repression and the ensuing credit rationing worsen
income distribution and increase industrial concentration' (p. 205). Consequently, financial liberalization and the ensuing freeing of credit markets
improves income distribution and decreases industrial concentration, due to
widened access to finance and decreased degree of credit market segmentation.
This benefits small firms because it avoids subsidizing priority sectors which
leads to market segmentation, an obvious characteristic of the financial repression case, which hits them harshly.

There are, however, more important and significant effects which are ignored by the financial liberalization thesis. We turn to these effects next.

Pricing: Demand-determined and Cost-determined Sectors

We begin with pricing in the two important sectors of a modern economy (Kalecki, 1971). There is the competitive sector, essentially agriculture and raw materials. In this sector prices are determined by supply and demand as in the neoclassical tradition. This is a 'demand-determined' price sector. The other sector which is the dominant one, is the 'cost-determined' price sector, manufacturing and services, where prices are set at some stable mark-up over average variable costs. Prices are thus administered on the basis of some expected normal rate of capacity utilization through a mark-up process over normal average variable costs, sufficient to cover fixed costs, dividends and the internal finance of planned investment expenditures. So that the mark-up is chosen to produce a level of retained profits, after depreciation, interest, and dividend payments, sufficient to provide for the required internal finance as dictated by planned investment expenditure. The price leaders effectively set the market price as just described, in order to yield their target-profits. The rest follow the price leaders and they may have higher or lower average costs and so lower or higher mark-ups and net profits. Firms are, therefore, price-setters and quantity-takers. Firms set their prices and then proceed to produce the output they expect to be forthcoming. In the case of developing countries these types of firms are mostly multinational companies or firms controlled tightly by them.

Interest is a cost and must be passed on if firms are to achieve their profit targets to finance their investment plans. The bigger the size of the firm, the easier it is for it to pass on the increase in interest rates. It follows that increases in interest rates hit the small-sized firms particularly hard. The latter suffer in the same way the 'demand-determined' price firms do. Interest rate changes in the case of demand-determined price firms are absorbed by them in the short run. In the long-run interest rate changes may be expected to be passed on in prices if the profit rate is to remain unchanged.

Savings: 'Small' and 'Big' Firms

There is a further important redistributional effect which we may discuss by also referring to the distinction between 'cost-determined' and 'demand-determined' price sectors. An important difference in this respect is that the 'demand-determined' price firms, the small firms such as farming and small retailing, save very little. Any funds which they save are deposited with the commercial banking sector to be lent to other firms subsequently. Small firms, therefore, are very sensitive to interest rate changes. 'Cost-determined' price firms, that is big firms, by contrast, possess a preponderant amount of savings. They prefer to have too much rather than too little savings, which gives them independence from lenders and it enables them to substitute capital for labour, if need be. It is internally created funds which are utilized for investment purposes, so that these firms are insulated from capital markets. It follows that high interest rates hit the 'small' firms rather harshly, but leave the 'big' firms fairly unscathed. The weak, therefore, are victimized. An undesirable distributional effect is thus created which promotes sectoral inequalities. It also retards socially desirable sectors, as for example the case with the housing sector which has a high propensity to borrow.

Household and Government Sectors

The extent to which the household sector is affected by interest rate changes depends crucially on the size of their debt/asset ratio. The higher this ratio, the more adversely the household sector will be affected from an increase in the rate of interest. The wealthy receive a large proportion of their income from interest payments but they can also maintain a higher debt/asset ratio too. Similar redistributional effects of increases in interest rates apply in the case of governments. But there is another problem with the government sector. To the extent that their debt/asset ratio incorporates a substantial proportion in foreign debt, global increases in interest rates can have serious redistributional effects across countries. The recent Third World debt crisis clarifies this case very vividly.

This analysis clearly corroborates Keynes's (1973) argument that increases in interest rates enhance the degree of income inequality substantially. This inequality suggests that monetary policy that aims to sustain high levels of interest rates entails a certain degree of moral responsibility about it. We have argued this for the case of developing economies where in addition to the redistributional issues there is also, in many cases, the awkward problem of external debt. For higher interest rates at a global level are accompanied by an increase in third world debt which implies redistributional effects across countries. The importance of the ethical issues which arise from this analysis cannot be exaggerated. It is also for this reason that we would support interest rate policies which aim at *a stable and permanently low level of interest rates.*

THE ROLE OF STOCK MARKETS AND SPECULATION

These are two interrelated aspects which have received scant attention from the financial liberalization proponents. We begin with the role of stock markets.

Stock Markets

There has been an enormous growth of stock markets over the last ten to fifteen years (Arestis and Demetriades, 1977; Singh, 1997). Not only have stock markets played a significant role in domestic financial liberalization, but they have also played an important role in external financial liberalization due essentially to external inflows, especially in LDCs where foreign portfolio flows, as opposed to bank financing, have been dominant. Eatwell (1996) refers to estimates of the total stock of all financial assets traded in global markets produced by the McKinsey Global Institute. According to these calculations, they rose from $5000 billion in 1980 to $35 000 billion in 1992 and they are expected to reach $83 000 billion (about three times the OECD GDP) by the year 2000. These substantial increases prompted Eatwell (op. cit.) to argue that the extraordinary growth of international capital flows 'is the product of the most important systematic transformation of the world economy since the establishment of the new world order at the end of World War II' (p. 1). Despite these developments, financial liberalization supporters have paid very little attention to stock market development. Essentially, the reason for this neglect is the belief that there is very little flow of funds from the household to the business sector via the stock market (Fry, 1997).

Well-developed stock markets may be able to offer different kinds of financial services than banking systems and may, therefore, provide a different kind of impetus to investment and growth than the development of the banking system. Specifically, increased stock market capitalization, measured either by the ratio of the value of listed shares to GDP or by the number of listed companies, may improve an economy's ability to mobilize capital and diversify risk, on the reasonable assumption that market size is positively correlated with capital mobilization and risk diversification. Liquidity is another important indicator of stock market development in that it may be inversely related to transactions costs, which impede the efficient functioning of stock markets. Liquidity may be measured by total value of shares traded relative to either GDP or total market capitalization. The total value traded ratio measures the organized trading of stocks and shares as a proportion of GDP and is expected to reflect liquidity positively at the macro-level. This ratio complements the market capitalization ratio because the size of a market may be substantial, but trading may be on a small scale. The ratio of total value of shares traded over market capitalization, known as the turnover ratio, may be a good indicator of low transaction costs (high turnover can be an indicator of low transaction costs). This ratio, too, complements market capitalization. A small but active market will have small market capitalization but high turnover ratio. It also complements total value of shares traded over GDP which captures trading as compared with the size of the economy, whereas the turnover ratio measures trading relative to the size of the stock market. A small and liquid market will have a high turnover ratio, but a small total value traded over GDP. Internationally integrated stock markets by facilitating risk sharing, affect saving decisions and the allocation of capital; other aspects of stock market performance may be captured by the presence or absence of excess volatility of market returns, excessive concentration (high concentration affects adversely the liquidity of the market) and asset pricing efficiency, that is whether markets price risk efficiently (the more integrated and the more efficiently markets price risk, the more developed they are thought to be). Measures of the latter are inversely related to the degree of risk mis-pricing between domestic and world capital market stocks and may, therefore, indicate the degree of integration of national stock markets into world capital markets.

Atje and Jovanovic (1993), Levine (1996) and Levine and Zavros (1996), provide empirical evidence of a strong, and positive, relationship between stock market developments and economic growth. They argue that stock markets may affect growth through liquidity, which makes investment less risky. Companies enjoy permanent access to capital through liquid equity issues. These considerations lead to the proposition that 'stock market development explains future economic growth' (Levine, 1996, p. 8).[3]

Speculation

Financial liberalization induces two types of speculative pressures: expectations-induced and competition-coerced, both of which contribute to the increased presence of short-term, high-risk speculative transactions in the economy and to the increased vulnerability to financial crises. The first emanate from expectations-induced pressures to pursue speculative transactions in view of the euphoria created by financial liberalization. Given the proliferation of speculative opportunities, this euphoria rewards those speculators who have short-time horizons and punish the investors with a long term view (Keynes, 1936, chapter 12; see Arestis and Demetriades, 1996b, for evidence supportive of these arguments).

The competition-coerced type of pressures emanate from the pressures on non-financial corporations who may feel compelled to enter the financial markets in view of higher returns, induced by financial liberalization, by borrowing to finance short-term financial speculation. A critical manifestation of this possibility is increasing borrowing to finance short-term financial speculation. Lenders in their turn may feel compelled to provide this type of finance, essentially because of fear of loss of market share (Minsky, 1986). An undesirable implication of these types of pressures is that economies are forced to bear a greater degree of 'ambient' risk and thus uncertainty with financial liberalization than without it (Grabel, 1995). This may very well lead to a reduced volume of real-sector investment (Federer, 1993), while exerting upward pressures on interest rates in view of the higher risk.

The types of speculation just referred to are particularly acute in the case of stock markets. The related developments that have taken place recently and discussed earlier, enhance the importance of speculation in the stock market. These stock market developments represent a source of macroeconomic instability in that stock market financial assets are highly liquid and volatile, thus making the financial system more fragile rather than less fragile (Arestis and Demetriades, 1996b). Consequently, encouraging short-termism at the cost of long-term growth. Financial liberalization, therefore, is less likely to enhance the long-term growth prospects, especially of developing countries. Additionally, dependence on the external inflows which have produced the stock market expansion, particularly in developing countries, erodes policy autonomy and forces monetary authorities to maintain high interest rates to sustain investor confidence and greed.

There is also the argument that external financial liberalization may lead to a reduction in the rate of return as a result of increased capital flows which reduces the domestic saving rate. Domestic institutions may face so much competition from foreign institutions, which may cause excessive pressure on domestic institutions and eventually lead to their bankruptcy.

EMPIRICAL EVIDENCE

We refer to two types of evidence. The first is the experience of countries which went through financial liberalization and the second is based on econometric evidence.

Experience with Individual Economies

Colombia, Uruguay and Venezuela in the early 1970s, Malaysia in the late 1970s, Argentine, Brazil, Chile and Mexico in the mid to late 1970s, Turkey, Israel, the Philippines and Indonesia in the early 1980s, all implemented financial reforms. Their experience was catastrophic, in that interest rates exceeded 20 per cent, a number of 'bad' debts and waves of bank failures and other bankruptcies ensued, extreme asset volatility and the whole financial system reached a near collapse stage. As a result the real sectors of the affected economies entered severe and prolonged recessions. On the whole, financial liberalization in these, and other, countries had a destabilizing effect on the economy and was abandoned. It is instructive to note at this stage that even the successful East Asian 'tiger' economies have not escaped the consequences of financial liberalization. The enormous private sector capital flows which took place in the recent past, are thought to have led to a potentially unstable financial situation.[4] Already there are fears that, at least in Indonesia and certainly in Thailand, investor confidence has taken a turn for the worst and there are real fears that demand in construction, property and finance sectors is shrinking (see the reference in footnote 4).

What was thought to have happened in these economies is that financial liberalization typically unleashed a massive demand for credit by households and firms that was not offset by a comparable increase in the saving rate. Loan rates rose as households demanded more credit to finance purchases of consumer durables, and firms plunged into speculative investment in the knowledge that government bailouts would prevent bank failures. In terms of bank behaviour, banks increased deposit and lending rates to compensate for losses attributable to loan defaults. High real interest rates completely failed to increase savings or boost investment – these actually fell as a proportion of GNP over the period. The only type of savings that *did* increase was foreign savings, that is external debt. This, however, made the 'liberalized' economies more vulnerable to oscillations in the international economy, increasing the debt/asset ratio and thus service obligations and promoting the debt crises experienced in the recent past. Financial liberalization thus managed to displace domestic for international markets. Long-term productive investment never materialized either. Instead, short-term speculative activities flourished whereby firms adopted risky financial strategies, thereby causing banking crises and economic collapse.

The experience of South Korea over the period since 1965 is both relevant and interesting. In the 1960s 'financial liberalization' meant higher real interest rates and higher deposits. The increase in deposits, however, emanated from the 'curb' markets. It is also argued that it was government intervention in the allocation of credit, especially to industry and to promote exports, which helped growth in this economy. The World Bank (1993) contended that 'Our judgement is that in a few economies, mainly in North East Asia, government interventions resulted in higher and more equal growth than otherwise would have occurred' (p. 6). In the same study, however, 'financial repression' affects financial development negatively. By contrast, in the study by Demetriades and Luintel (1996b) it is shown that 'financial repression' in this country exerts a direct positive long-run influence on the development of the South Korean financial system. They also provide evidence that supports the endogenous growth proposition that causality runs from financial development to the level of output. These results suggest that it could very well be that South Korea is a good example of a country where better regulation, not less, produced the desirable effect.

Econometric Evidence

We examine two types of evidence. The first refers to the elasticity of the savings and investment relationships which are, of course, at the heart of the thesis. The real interest rate elasticity of the savings relationship is either insignificant or when significant, it is rather small. The investment relationship with respect to the real rate of interest is also questionable. It is shown in this case that the effect of higher domestic interest rates on the cost of capital outweighs the effect of an enhanced supply of investible funds on investment, so that interest rate liberalization has, on balance, a negative effect on investment (for a comprehensive review of the literature, see Fry, 1995).

The second type of evidence we refer to is a more important and significant step in terms of the empirical evidence of the financial liberalization thesis. This is the attempt by King and Levine (1993a, b) to tackle the issue of the strength and causation of the relationship between finance and economic development. It is more 'aggregate' and more recent but also refers to the need for further work. The difficulty of establishing the direction of causality between financial development and economic growth was first identified by Patrick (1966) and further developed by McKinnon (1988) who actually questioned the direction of causation. The causality between financial development and economic growth is, therefore, a controversial issue which could be resolved potentially by resorting to empirical evidence. The recent study by King and Levine (1993a), makes the point that Schumpeter (1959) may very well have been 'right' in that the banker is 'the ephor of the exchange economy' (p. 74), with the distinct implication that financial intermediaries promote economic development. Using data for a number of countries, covering the period 1960 to 1989, they find that 'higher levels of financial development are significantly and robustly correlated with faster current and future rates of economic growth, physical capital accumulation and economic efficiency improvements' (pp. 717–18). From these results the authors conclude that the link between growth and financial development is not just a contemporaneous correlation and that 'finance seems importantly to lead economic growth' (op. cit., p. 730).

We have demonstrated elsewhere (Arestis and Demetriades, 1996a) that the results of King and Levine (1993a), which are obtained from cross-section country studies, are not able to address the issue of causality satisfactorily. We produce two types of evidence in this context. The first is to show that King and Levine's (op. cit.) causal interpretation is based on a fragile statistical basis. Specifically, we show that once the contemporaneous correlation between the main financial indicator and economic growth has been accounted for, there is no longer any evidence to suggest that financial development helps predict future growth. The second type of evidence demonstrates that cross section data sets cannot address the question of causality in a satisfactory way. To perform such a task, time series data and a time series approach are required. We proceed by proposing a taxonomy based on different institutional characteristics and financial policies. Using data for 12 representative countries and cointegration techniques, we show that there are systematic differences in causality patterns across countries.

It is clear from this excursion in the literature that no convincing evidence has been provided in support of the propositions of the financial liberalization hypothesis. On the contrary, the available evidence can be interpreted as indicating that the theoretical propositions of the thesis are at best weak.

SUMMARY AND CONCLUSIONS

We have considered in this chapter the theoretical premise that has come to be known as the financial liberalization thesis. We have identified a number of theoretical propositions, which we have examined closely. We concluded that these critical issues of the thesis are marred by serious difficulties. We looked at the available evidence and found that it is not of much help to the thesis either. We may, therefore, end this chapter with the overall conclusion, one that Paul Davidson would not dissent from, which suggests that the financial liberalization thesis is 'based on an ideological commitment to an idealised conception of markets that is grounded neither in fact nor in economic theory' (Stiglitz, 1994, p. 20).

NOTES

1. In traditional growth theory financial intermediation is related to the level of the capital stock per worker or to the level of productivity, but not to the respective growth rates which were ascribed to exogenous technical progress.
2. We may also mention in passing the incident of a classic case of banking panic and crisis in Rome in the year AD 33. At that time the Romans debated intensely the possibility of putting a hitherto liberal banking under government control.
3. The studies of Levine and Zervos (1995, 1996) and of Atje and Jovanovic (1993) differ in two respects. First, Levine and Zervos (op. cit.) use indexes of stock market development just as Atje and Jovanovic (op. cit.) do, but unlike the latter, their indexes combine a number of characteristics. Unlike Atje and Jovanovic (op. cit.), Levine and Zervos (op. cit.)

control for initial conditions and other relevant factors that may influence economic growth. See, also, Arestis and Demetriades (1996b) for a critique and further empirical evidence.

4. See the *Guardian*, 16 October, 1996 under the title 'East Asian Tigers are Endangered'. It is interesting to cite a few figures for one or two of these countries. For example, in Thailand, between 1983 and 1993 a 20-fold increase in market capitalization took place, which made them larger than the average-sized European stockmarkets. In Taiwan the market capitalization to GDP ratio rose from 11 per cent to 74 per cent over the period 1981 to 1991 and in Thailand from 3.8% to 55.8% (Singh, 1997).

REFERENCES

Arestis, P. and Demetriades, O.P. (1996a), 'Finance and Growth: Institutional Considerations and Causality', presented at the *Royal Economic Society Annual Conference,* Swansea University, 1–4 April 1996.

Arestis, P. and Demetriades, O.P. (1996b), 'Financial Development and Economic Growth: The Role of Stock Markets', *mimeo,* University of East London and University of Keele.

Arestis, P. and Demetriades, O.P. (1997), 'Financial Development and Economic Growth: Assessing the Evidence', *Economic Journal,* May, 783–99.

Atje, R. and Jovanovic, B. (1993), 'Stocks Markets and Development', *European Economic Review,* **37** (2/3), April, 634–40.

Caprio, G. Jr, Atiyas, I. and Hanson, J.A. (eds) (1994), *Financial Reform: Theory and Experience,* Cambridge: Cambridge University Press.

Davidson, P. (1978), *Money and the Real World,* 2nd edn, London: Macmillan.

Demetriades, O.P. and Luintel, B.K. (1996a), 'Financial Development, Economic Growth and Banking Sector Controls: Evidence from India', *Economic Journal,* **106** (435), March, 359–74.

Demetriades, O.P. and Luintel, B.K. (1996b), '"Financial Repression" in the South Korean Miracle', *Working Paper,* No. 96/13, October, Department of Economics, University of Keele.

Dow, C.S. (1996), 'Why the Banking System Should be Regulated', *Economic Journal,* **106** (436), May, 698–707.

Easterly, W.R. (1993), 'How Much Do Distortions Affect Growth?', *Journal of Monetary Economics,* **32** (2), November, 187–212.

Eatwell, J. (1996), 'International Capital Liberalisation: An Evaluation', *UNDP Report,* SSA, No. 96-049.

Edwards, S. (1989), 'On the Sequencing of Structural Reforms', *Working Paper,* No. 70, OECD Department of Economics and Statistics.

Federer, P. (1993), 'The Impact of Uncertainty on Aggregate Investment Spending', *Journal of Money, Credit and Banking,* **25** (1), 30–45.

Fry, M.J. (1995), *Money, Interest and Banking in Economic Development,* London: Johns Hopkins University Press.

Fry, M.J. (1997), 'In Favour of Financial Liberalisation', *Economic Journal,* May, 754–70.

Ghate, P. (1992), 'Interaction Between the Formal and Informal Financial Sectors', *World Development,* **20** (6), 859–72.

Goldsmith, R.W. (1969), *Financial Structure and Development,* New Haven, Conn.: Yale University Press.

Grabel, I. (1995), 'Speculation-Led Economic Development: A Post-Keynesian Interpretation of Financial Liberalization Programs', *International Review of Applied Economics*, **9** (2), 127–49.

Kalecki, M. (1971), 'Costs and Prices', in *Selected Essays on the Dynamics of the Capitalist Economy, 1933–1970*, chapter 5, edited by M. Kalecki, Cambridge: Cambridge University Press.

Keynes, J.M. (1936), *The General Theory of Employment, Interest and Money*, London: Macmillan.

Keynes, J.M. (1973), *The General Theory and After, Collected Writings*, **XIV**, London: Macmillan.

King, R.G. and Levine, R. (1993a), 'Finance and Growth: Schumpeter Might Be Right', *Quarterly Journal of Economics*, **VIII**, 717–37.

King, R.G. and Levine, R. (1993b), 'Finance, Entrepreneurship and Growth: Theory and Evidence', *Journal of Monetary Economics*, **32** (3), December, 513–42.

Lal, D. (1987), 'The Political Economy of Economic Liberalization', *World Bank Economic Review*, **1** (2), 273–99.

Levine, R. (1996), 'Stock Markets: A Spur to Economic Growth', *Finance and Development*, **33** (1), April, 7–10.

Levine, R. and Zervos, S. (1995), 'Policy, Stock Market Development and Long-Run Growth: Part I', *mimeo, World Bank*. Presented at a World Bank conference on *Stock Markets, Corporate Finance and Economic Growth*, 16–17 February.

Levine, R. and Zervos, S. (1996), 'Stock Market Development and Long-Run Growth', *World Bank Economic Review*, **10** (2), May, 323–39.

McKinnon, R.I. (1973), *Money and Capital in Economic Development*, Washington D.C.: Brookings Institution.

McKinnon, R.I. (1988), 'Financial Liberalization in Retrospect: Interest Rate Policies in LDCs' in *The State of Development Economics*, edited by G. Ranis and T.P. Schultz, Oxford: Basil Blackwell.

McKinnon, R. (1991), *The Order of Economic Liberalization: Financial Control in the Transition to a Market Economy*, Baltimore: Johns Hopkins University Press.

Minsky, H.P. (1986), *Stabilizing an Unstable Economy*, New Haven, Conn.: Yale University Press.

Pagano, M. (1993), 'Financial Markets and Growth: An Overview', *European Economic Review*, **37** (2–3), April, 613–22.

Patrick, H. (1966), 'Financial Development and Economic Growth in Underdeveloped Countries', *Economic Development and Cultural Change*, **14**, 174–89.

Sachs, J. (1988), 'Conditionality, Debt Relief and the Developing Countries' Debt Crisis' in *Developing Country Debt and Economic Performance*, edited by J. Sachs, Chicago: University of Chicago Press.

Schumpeter, J.A. (1959), *The Theory of Economic Development*, Cambridge, Mass.: Harvard University Press.

Shaw, E.S. (1973), *Financial Deepening in Economic Development*, New York: Oxford University Press.

Singh, A. (1997), 'Stock Markets, Financial Liberalisation and Economic Development', *Economic Journal*, May, 771–82.

Stiglitz, J.E. (1994), 'The Role of the State in Financial Markets' in *Proceedings of the World Bank Annual Conference on Development Economics*, edited by M. Bruno and B. Pleskovic, Washington D.C.: World Bank, 19–52.

Stiglitz, J.E. and Weiss, A. (1981), 'Credit Rationing in Markets with Imperfect Information', *American Economic Review*, **71** (3), June, 393–410.

Studart, R. (1995), *Investment Finance in Economic Development*, London: Routledge.

Taylor, L. (1983), *Structuralist Macroeconomics: Applicable Models for the Third World*, New York: Basic Books.

Van Wijnbergen, S. (1983), 'Interest Rate Management in LDCs', *Journal of Monetary Economics*, **12**, 433–52.

World Bank (1989), *World Development Report*, Oxford: Oxford University Press.

World Bank (1993), *The East Asian Miracle*, Oxford: Oxford University Press.

Paul Davidson: A bibliography

BOOKS

Theories of Aggregate Income Distribution, New Brunswick: Rutgers University Press, 1960.

Aggregate Supply and Demand Analysis (with E. Smolensky), New York: Harper and Row, 1964.

The Demand and Supply of Outdoor Recreation (with C.J. Cicchetti and J.J. Seneca), Bureau of Economics Research, Rutgers University, reprinted by Bureau of Outdoor Recreation, US Department of Interior, 1969.

Money and the Real World, 2nd edn, London: Macmillan, 1978; New York: Halsted Press, John Wiley, 1978; Japanese edition, 1980.

Milton Friedman's Monetary Theory: A Debate with His Critics (with M. Friedman, J. Tobin, D. Patinkin, K. Brunner, A. Meltzer), Chicago: University of Chicago Press, 1974; Japanese edition, 1978.

International Money and the Real World, London: Macmillan; New York: Halsted Press, John Wiley, 1982.

International Money and the Real World, revised edition, London: Macmillan; New York: St Martin's Press, 1992.

Economics for a Civilized Society (with G. Davidson), London: Macmillan; New York: W.W. Norton, 1988.

The Struggle Over the Keynesian Heritage (a script for an audiotape narrated by Louis Rukeyser), Knowledge Products, 1989.

Macroeconomic Problems and Policies of Income Distribution: Functional, Personal, International (co-edited with J.A. Kregel), Aldershot, Hants: Edward Elgar, 1989.

Money and Employment: The Collected Writings of Paul Davidson, Volume 1, edited by Louise Davidson, London: Macmillan, 1990; New York: New York University Press, 1991.

Inflation, Open Economics and Resources, The Collected Writings of Paul Davidson, Volume 2, edited by Louise Davidson, London: Macmillan, 1991; New York: New York University Press, 1991.

Controversies in Post Keynesian Economics, Aldershot, Hants: Edward Elgar, 1991.

Economic Problems of the 1990s: Europe, the Developing Countries and the United States (co-edited with J.A. Kregel), Aldershot, Hants: Edward Elgar, 1991.

Can the Free Market Pick Winners? Editor and author of 'Introduction', Armonk, N.Y.: M.E. Sharpe, 1993.

Post Keynesian Macroeconomic Theory: A Foundation for Successful Economic Policies in the Twenty-First Century, Aldershot, Hants: Edward Elgar, 1994.

Employment, Growth and Finance: Economic Reality and Economic Growth (co-edited with J.A. Kregel), Aldershot, Hants: Edward Elgar, 1994.

ARTICLES

'A Clarification of the Ricardian Rent Share', *Canadian Journal of Economics and Political Science*, May 1959.

'Increasing Employment, Diminishing Returns, Relative Shares and Ricardo', *Canadian Journal of Economics and Political Science*, February 1960.

'Rolph on the Aggregate Effects of a General Excise Tax', *Southern Economic Journal*, July 1960.

'Wells on Excise Tax Incidence in an Imperfectly Competitive Economy', *Public Finance*, 1961.

'More on the Aggregate Supply Function', *Economic Journal*, June 1962.

'Employment and Income Multipliers and the Price Level', *American Economic Review*, September 1962.

'Public Policy Problems of the Domestic Crude Oil Industry', *American Economic Review*, March 1963; reprinted in *Economics of Natural and Environmental Resources*, edited by V.L. Smith, New York: Gordon and Breach, 1977.

'Public Policy Problems of The Domestic Crude Oil Industry: A Rejoinder', *American Economic Review*, March 1964.

'Modigliani on the Interaction of Real and Monetary Phenomena' (with E. Smolensky), *Review of Economics and Statistics*, November 1964.

'Keynes's Finance Motive', *Oxford Economic Papers*, March 1965; reprinted in Japanese in *Reappraisal of Keynesian Economics*, edited by Toyo Keizai Shinpo Sha.

'The Social Value of Water Recreational Facilities Resulting from an Improvement in Water Quality in an Estuary: The Delaware – A Case Study' (with F.G. Adams and J.J. Seneca), in *Water Research*, edited by A.V. Kneese and S.C. Smith, Baltimore, Md: Johns Hopkins University Press, 1966.

'The Importance of the Demand for Finance', *Oxford Economic Papers*, July 1967.

'A Keynesian View of Patinkin's Theory of Employment', *Economic Journal*, September 1967; reprinted in *Disequilibrio, Inflación y Desempleo*, edited by Vicens-Vives, Madrid, 1978; reprinted in *The Keynesian Heritage*, edited by G.K. Shaw, Cheltenham, Glos.: Edward Elgar, forthcoming.

'An Exploratory Study to Identify and Measure the Benefits Derived from the Scenic Enhancement of Federal-Aid Highways', *Highway Research Record*, no. 182, 1967.

'The Valuation of Public Goods' in *Social Sciences and the Environment*, edited by M.G. Garnsey and J. Hibbs, Boulder: University of Colorado Press, 1968; reprinted in *Economics of the Environment*, edited by R. Dorfman and N.S. Dorfman, New York: W. W. Norton, 1972.

'Money, Portfolio Balance, Capital Accumulation, and Economic Growth', *Econometrica*, April 1968; reprinted in *Post Keynesian Theory of Growth and Distribution*, edited by C. Panico and N. Salvadori, Aldershot, Hants: Edward Elgar, 1993.

'The Demand and Supply of Securities and Economic Growth and Its Implications for the Kaldor–Pasinetti vs. Samuelson–Modigliani Controversy', *American Economic Review*, May 1968; reprinted in *Post Keynesian Theory of Growth and Distribution*, edited by C. Panico and N. Salvadori, Aldershot, Hants: Edward Elgar, 1993.

'An Analysis of Recreation Use of TVA Lakes' (with J.J. Seneca and F.G. Adams), *Land Economics*, November 1968.

'The Role of Monetary Policy in Overall Economic Policy', *Compendium on Monetary Policy Guidelines and Federal Structure*, US Congress, December 1968.

'A Keynesian View of Patinkin's Theory of Employment: Comment', *Economic Journal*, March 1969.

'A Keynesian View of the Relationship Between Accumulation, Money and the Money Wage Rate', *Economic Journal*, June 1969.

'The Economic Benefits Accruing from the Scenic Enhancement of Highways' (with J. Tomer and A. Waldman), *Highway Research Record*, no. 285, 1969.

'The Depletion Allowance Revisited', *Natural Resources Journal*, January 1970; reprinted in *Towards a National Petroleum Policy*, edited by A. Utton, Albuquerque, NM: University of New Mexico Press, 1970.

'Discussion Paper' in *Money in Britain 1959–69*, edited by D.R. Croome and H. G. Johnson, Oxford: Oxford University Press, 1970.

'Money and the Real World', *The Economic Journal*, March 1972.

'A Keynesian View of Friedman's Theoretical Framework for Monetary Analysis', *Journal of Political Economy*, September/October 1972.

'Income Distribution, Inequality, and the Double Bluff', *The Annals*, September 1973; reprinted in *Mercurio*, April 1974.

'Money as Cause and Effect' (with S. Weintraub), *The Economic Journal*, December 1973; reprinted in *Keynes, Keynesians and Monetarists*, edited by S. Weintraub, Philadelphia: University of Pennsylvania Press, 1978; reprinted in *The Money Supply in the Economic Process*, edited by M. Musella and C. Panico, Aldershot, Hants: Edward Elgar, 1995.

'Market Disequilibrium Adjustments: Marshall Revisited', *Economic Inquiry*, June 1974.

'Oil: Its Time Allocation and Project Independence' (with L.H. Falk and H. Lee), *Brookings Papers on Economic Activity*, 1974:2.

'The Relations of Economic Rent and Price Incentives to Oil and Gas Supplies' (with L.H. Falk and H. Lee) in *Studies in Energy Tax Policy*, edited by G. M. Brannon, Cambridge, Mass.: Ballinger Publishing, 1975.

'Disequilibrium Market Adjustment: A Rejoinder', *Economic Inquiry*, April 1977.

'Post-Keynesian Monetary Theory and Inflation' in *Modern Economic Thought*, edited by S. Weintraub, Philadelphia: University of Pennsylvania Press, 1977.

'The Case for Divestiture', *Chemical Engineering Process 73*, 1977.

'A Discussion of Leijonhufvud's Social Consequences of Inflation' in *Microfoundations of Macroeconomics*, edited by G. Harcourt, Cambridge: Cambridge University Press, 1977.

'Divestiture and the Economics of Energy Supplies' in *R&D in Energy: Implications of Petroleum Industry Reorganization*, edited by D.J. Teece, Stanford, Calif.: Institute for Energy Studies, 1977.

'The Carter Energy Proposal', *Challenge*, September/October 1977.

'Money and General Equilibrium', *Économie Appliquée, 4–77*, 1977.

'Why Money Matters: Some Lessons of the Past Half Century of Monetary Theory', *Journal of Post Keynesian Economics,* **1**, Fall 1978; reprinted in *Keynes: La Macroeconomía del Desequilibrio*, edited by C.F. Obregon Diaz, Mexico City: Editorial Trillas, 1983.

'The United States Internal Revenue Service: The Fourteenth Member of OPEC?', *Journal of Post Keynesian Economics*, **1**, Winter 1979.

'Post Keynesian Approach to the Theory of Natural Resources', *Challenge*, March/April 1979; reprinted in *A Guide to Post-Keynesian Economics*, edited by A.S. Eichner, Armonk, N.Y.: M.E. Sharpe, 1979.

'Monetary Policy, Regulation and International Adjustments' (with Marc A. Miles), *Économies et Sociétés*, no. 1, 1979.

'Is Monetary Collapse in the Eighties in the Cards?', *Nebraska Journal of Economics and Business*, **18**, Spring 1979.

'Oil Conservation: Theory vs. Policy', *Journal of Post Keynesian Economics*, **2**, Fall, 1979.

'What is the Energy Crisis?', *Challenge*, July/August 1979.

'Keynes Paradigm: A Theoretical Framework for Monetary Analysis' (with J. A. Kregel), in *Growth, Property and Profits*, edited by E.J. Nell, Cambridge: Cambridge University Press, 1980.

'Money as a Factor of Production: A Reply', *Journal of Post Keynesian Economics*, **2**, Winter 1979–80.

'The Dual Faceted Nature of the Keynesian Revolution: The Role of Money and Money Wages in Determining Unemployment and Production Flow Prices', *Journal of Post Keynesian Economics*, **2**, Spring 1980.

'On Bronfenbrenner and Mainstream Views of the Essential Properties of Money: A Rejoinder', *Journal of Post Keynesian Economics*, **2**, Spring 1980.

'Keynes's Theory of Employment, Expectations and Indexing', *Revista de Economía Latinoamericana*, no. 57/58.

'Causality in Economics: A Review Article', *Journal of Post Keynesian Economics*, **2**, Summer 1980.

'Post Keynesian Economics: Solving the Crisis in Economic Theory', *Public Interest*, special issue 1980; reprinted in *The Crisis in Economic Theory*, edited by D. Bell and I. Kristol, New York: Basic Books, 1981.

'Is There a Shortage of Savings in the United States? The Role of Financial Institutions, Monetary and Fiscal Policy in Capital Accumulation During Periods of Stagflation' in *Special Study on Economic Change, Vol. 4 Stagflation: The Causes, Effects and Solutions*, Washington, D.C.: Joint Economic Committee, 1980.

'Can VAT Resolve the Shortage of Savings (SOS) Distress?', *Journal of Post Keynesian Economics*, **4**, Fall 1981.

'Alfred Marshall is Alive and Well in Post Keynesian Economics', *IHS Journal*, Journal of the Institute for Advanced Studies, Vienna, **5**, 1981.

'A Critical Analysis of the Monetarist–Rational Expectations Supply Side (Incentive) Economics Approach to Accumulation During a Period of Inflationary Expectations', *Kredit und Kapital*, 1981.

'Expectations and Economic Decision Making', *Compendium on Expectations in Economics*, Joint Economic Committee, US Congress, 1981.

'Post Keynesian Economics' in *Encyclopedia of Economics*, edited by D. Greenwald, New York: McGraw-Hill, 1982.

'Rational Expectations: A Fallacious Foundation for Studying Crucial Decision-Making Processes', *Journal of Post Keynesian Economics*, **5**, Winter 1982–83.

'Monetarism and Reagonomics' in *Reagonomics in the Stagflation Economy*, edited by S. Weintraub and M. Goodstein, Philadelphia: University of Pennsylvania Press, 1983.

'The Dubious Labor Market Analysis in Meltzer's Restatement of Keynes's Theory', *Journal of Economic Literature*, **21**, March 1983; reprinted in *John Maynard Keynes*, **1**, edited by M. Blaug, Aldershot, Hants: Edward Elgar, 1991.

'International Money and International Economic Development', *Proceedings of the Conference on Distribution, Effective Demand and Economic Development at Villa Manin, Italy, 1981*, London: Macmillan, 1983.

'The Marginal Product Curve Is Not The Demand Curve For Labor and Lucas' Labor Supply Function Is Not the Supply Curve for Labor', *Journal of Post Keynesian Economics*, **6**, Fall 1983.

'An Appraisal of Weintraub's', *Eastern Economic Journal*, **9**, 1983.

'Reviving Keynes's Revolution', *Journal of Post Keynesian Economics*, **6**, 1984; reprinted in *John Maynard Keynes*, **1**, edited by M. Blaug, Aldershot, Hants: Edward Elgar, 1991.

'Why Deficits Hardly Matter', *The New Leader*, August 1984.

'The Conventional Wisdom on Deficits Is Wrong', *Challenge*, November/December 1984.

'Incomes Policy as a Social Institution' in *Macroeconomic Conflict and Social Institutions*, edited by S. Maital and I. Lipnowski, Cambridge, Mass.: Ballinger Publishing, 1985.

'Policies For Prices And Incomes', *Keynes Today: Theories and Politics*, edited by A. Barrere, Paris: Economica, 1985; reprinted in *Money, Credit and Prices in a Keynesian Perspective*, edited by A. Barrere, London: Macmillan, 1988.

'Financial Markets and Williamson's Theory of Governance: Efficiency vs. Concentration vs. Power' (with Greg S. Davidson), *Quarterly Review of Economics and Business*, 1984.

'Liquidity and Not Increasing Returns Is The Ultimate Source of Unemployment Equilibrium', *Journal of Post Keynesian Economics*, **7**, 1985.

'Can Effective Demand and the Movement Towards Income Equality Be Maintained in the Face of Robotics?', *Journal of Post Keynesian Economics*, **7**, 1985.

'Sidney Weintraub – An Economist of the Real World', *Journal of Post Keynesian Economics*, **7**, 1985.

'Can We Afford To Balance The Budget?', *The New Leader*, January 1986.

'A Post Keynesian View of Theories and Causes of High Real Interest Rates', *Thames Papers in Political Economy*, Spring 1986: reprinted in *Post Keynesian Monetary Economics: New Approaches to Financial Modelling*, edited by P. Arestis, Aldershot, Hants: Edward Elgar, 1988.

'Finance, Funding, Savings, and Investment', *Journal of Post Keynesian Economics*, **9**, Fall 1986.

'The Simple Macroeconomics of a Nonergodic Monetary Economy vs. A Share Economy: Is Weizman's Macroeconomics Too Simple?', *Journal of Post Keynesian Economics*, **9**, Winter 1986–87.

'Aggregate Supply' in *The New Palgrave: A Dictionary of Economic Theory and Doctrine*, edited by J. Eatwell, M. Milgate and P. Newman, London: Macmillan, 1987.

'User Cost' in *The New Palgrave: A Dictionary of Economic Theory and Doctrine*, edited by J. Eatwell, M. Milgate and P. Newman, London: Macmillan, 1987.

'Financial Markets, Investment, and Employment' in *Barriers to Full Employment*, edited by E. Matzner, J.A. Kregel and S. Roncoglia, London: Macmillan, 1988; also German language edition *Arbeit Für Alle Ist Möglich*, Berlin: Edition Sigma, 1987.

'Sensible Expectations and the Long-Run Non-Neutrality of Money', *Journal of Post Keynesian Economics*, **10**, Fall 1987.

'Whose Debt Crisis is it Anyway?', *New Leader*, August 1987.

'A Modest Set of Proposals for Remedying The International Debt Problem', *Journal of Post Keynesian Economics*, **10**, Winter 1987–88; reprinted in *Research In International Business and Finance: The Modern International Environment*, edited by H.P. Gray, Connecticut: JAI Press, 1989; reprinted in *Ensayos de Economía*, **1**, 1990 (Columbia).

'Weitzman's Share Economy And The Aggregate Supply Function' in *Keynes and Public Policy After Fifty Years*, edited by O.E. Hamouda and J.N. Smithin, Aldershot, Hants: Edward Elgar, 1988.

'Endogenous Money, The Production Process, And Inflation Analysis', *Économie Appliquée*, **XLI**, no. 1, 1988; reprinted in *The Money Supply in the Economic Process: A Post Keynesian Perspective*, edited by Marco Musella and Carlo Panico, Cheltenham, Glos.: Edward Elgar, 1995.

'A Technical Definition of Uncertainty and the Long Run Non-Neutrality of Money', *Cambridge Journal of Economics*, September 1988.

'Achieving a Civilized Society', *Challenge*, September/October 1989; reprinted in *Economics 90/91*, edited by D. Cole, Guilford, Conn.: Dushkin Publishing, 1990.

'Keynes and Money' in *Keynes, Money and Monetarism*, edited by R. Hill, London: Macmillan, 1989.

'Prices and Income Policy: An Essay in Honor of Sidney Weintraub' in *Money, Credit, and Prices in Keynesian Perspective*, edited by A. Barrere, London: Macmillan, 1989.

'Patinkin's Interpretation of Keynes and the Keynesian Cross', *History of Political Economy*, **21**, 1989; reprinted in *John Maynard Keynes (1883–1946)*, Volume 2, edited by Mark Blaug, Aldershot, Hants: Edward Elgar, 1991.

'Only in America: Neither The Homeless Nor The Yachtless Are Economic Problems', *Journal of Post Keynesian Economics*, **12**, Fall 1989.

'The Economics of Ignorance Or Ignorance of Economics?', *Critical Review*, **3**, nos 3 & 4, Summer/Fall 1989.

'Shackle and Keynes vs. Rational Expectations Theory on the Role of Time, Liquidity, and Financial Markets' in *Unknowledge and Choice in Economics*, edited by S. Frowen, London: Macmillan, 1990.

'Liquidity Proposals for a New Bretton Woods Plan' in *Keynesian Economic Policies*, edited by A. Barrere, London: Macmillan, 1990.

'On Thirlwall's Law', *Revista de Economía Política*, **10**, October–December 1990.

'Is Probability Theory Relevant For Choice Under Uncertainty?: A Post Keynesian Perspective', *Journal of Economic Perspectives*, **5**, Winter 1991.

'A Post Keynesian Positive Contribution To "Theory"', *Journal of Post Keynesian Economics*, **13**, Winter 1990–91.

'What Kind of International Payments System Would Keynes Have Recommended for the Twenty-First Century?' in *Economic Problems of the 1990s: Europe, the Developing Countries and the United States*, edited by P. Davidson and J.A. Kregel, Aldershot, Hants: Edward Elgar, 1991.

'Money: Cause or Effect? Exogenous or Endogenous?' in *Nicholas Kaldor and Mainstream Economics*, edited by E.J. Nell and W. Semmler, London: Macmillan, 1992.

'How To Avoid Another Great Depression?', *The New Leader*, 10–24 February 1992.

'Eichner's Approach to Money and Macroeconomics' in *The Megacorp and Macrodynamics*, edited by W. Milberg, Armonk, N.Y.: M.E. Sharpe, 1992.

'Reforming The World's Money', *Journal of Post Keynesian Economics*, Winter 1992–93.

'It's Still The Economy Mr. President', *The New Leader*, 11 January 1993.

'Clinton's Economic Plan – Putting Caution First', *The Nation*, 1 March 1993.

'The Elephant and the Butterfly; or Hysteresis and Post Keynesian Economics', *Journal of Post Keynesian Economics*, 1993.

'Would Keynes Be a New Keynesian?', *Eastern Economic Journal*, October 1992.

'Asset Deflation and Financial Fragility' in *Money and Banking – Issues For The Twenty-First Century*, edited by P. Arestis, London: Macmillan, 1993.

'Post Keynesian Economics' in *The McGraw-Hill Encyclopedia of Economics*, edited by D. Greenwald, New York: McGraw-Hill, 1993.

'Monetary Theory and Policy In A Global Context With A Large International Debt' in *Monetary Theory and Monetary Policy: New Tracks For The 1990s*, edited by S.F. Frowen, London: Macmillan, 1993.

'Austrians and Post Keynesians on Economic Reality: A Response to the Critics', *Critical Review*, **7**, 1993.

'Tampering With The American Dream', *The New Leader*, April 11–25, 1994.

'Do Informational Frictions Justify Federal Credit Programs?: A Discussion of S.D. Williamson's Paper', *Journal of Money, Credit, and Banking*, 1994.

'The Asimakopulos View of Keynes's General Theory', in *Investment and Employment in Theory and Practice*, edited by G.C. Harcourt and A. Roncoglia, London: Macmillan, 1994.

'Uncertainty in Economics' in *Keynes, Knowledge and Uncertainty*, edited by Sheila Dow and John Hillard, Cheltenham: Edward Elgar, 1995.

'Reforming the World's International Payments System', in *Trade Policy and Global Growth*, edited by R. Blecker, New York: M.E. Sharpe, 1995.

'The Nature of Money', *Durell Journal of Money and Banking*, **8**, 1996.

'The Viability of Keynesian Demand Management In An Open Economy Context', *International Review of Applied Economics*, **10**, January 1996 Reprinted in *The Relevance of Keynesian Economic Policies Today*, edited by P. Arestis and M. Sawyer, London: Macmillan, 1997.

'What Are The Essential Characteristics of Post Keynesian Monetary Theory?' in *Money in Motion, Proceedings of a Conference on French-American Mon-*

etary Theory, edited by G. Deleplace, E.J. Nell, and D.B. Papadimitriou, London: Macmillan, 1996.

'Some misunderstanding on Uncertainty in Modern Classical Theory', in *Uncertainty in Economic Thought*, edited by Christian Schmidt, Cheltenham: Edward Elgar, 1996.

'In Defense of Post Keynesian Economics: A Response to Mongiovi' in *Interactions in Political Economy: Malvern After ten Years*, edited S. Pressman, London: Routledge, 1966.

'Reality and Economic Theory', *Journal of Post Keynesian Economics*, **17**, Summer 1996.

'Colondo As Evidencias Em Ordem', in *Keynes: Teoria Geral 60 Anos, Suplemento Ensaios Fee*, Fundacao de Economia e Estatistica, Puerto Alegre, 1996.

'What Revolution? The Legacy of Keynes', *Journal of Post Keynesian Economics*, **18**, Winter 1996–97.

'The General Theory in an Open Economy' in *A Second Edition of the General Theory*, edited by G.C. Harcourt and P. Riach, London: Macmillan, 1996.

'Did Keynes Reverse the Marshallian Speeds of Adjustment? Using Harcourt's Method to Resolve Theoretical Controversies and Gain Insight into the Real World' in *Capital Controversy, Post Keynesian Economics and the History of Economic Thought*, edited by P. Arestis, G. Palma, and M. Sawyer, Routledge: London, 1996.

'Are Grains of Sand in the Wheels of International Finance Sufficient to do the Job When Boulders Are Often Required', *Economic Journal*, **107**, May 1997.

Growth in Output and Employment in a Global Economy, edited by P. Davidson and J.A. Kregel, Edward Elgar: Cheltenham, 1997.

'Setting The Record Straight' in *New Keynesian Economics/Post Keynesian Alternatives*, edited by R. Rotheim, London: Routledge, 1997.

'Uncertainty in Economics' in *Encyclopedia for Statistical Sciences*, edited by S. Katz, C.B. Read, and D.L. Banks, New York: Wiley, 1997.

'Post Keynesian Employment Analysis and The Macroeconomics of OECD Employment', *The Economic Journal*, May 1998.

'Global Employment and Open Economy Macroeconomics' in *Foundations in International Economics: a Post Keynesian Perspective*, edited by J. Deprez and J. Harvey, Routledge: London, 1998.

'Stagflation' in *Routledge Encyclopedia of International Political Economy*, edited by R.J.B. Jones, Routledge: London, 1998.

'The General Theory of Employment With Open National Economies', *Journal of Economic and Social Policy*, forthcoming, 1998.

Index